T0295617

Debt Sustainability of Subnational Governments in India

Debt Sustainability of Subnational Governments in India

Lessons from International Debt Crises

HARI KRISHNA DWIVEDI

OXFORD
UNIVERSITY PRESS

Great Clarendon Street, Oxford, OX2 6DP,
United Kingdom

Oxford University Press is a department of the University of Oxford.
It furthers the University's objective of excellence in research, scholarship,
and education by publishing worldwide. Oxford is a registered trade mark of
Oxford University Press in the UK and in certain other countries

Published in the United States of America by Oxford University Press
198 Madison Avenue, New York, NY 10016, United States of America

British Library Cataloguing in Publication Data

Data available

Library of Congress Control Number: 2023947335

ISBN 978–0–19–890311–6

DOI: 10.1093/oso/9780198903116.001.0001

Foreword

Debt Sustainability of Subnational Governments in India: Lessons from International Debt Crises by Dr Hari Krishna Dwivedi is an important and timely contribution to this important subject. Macroeconomic management in the post-Covid world requires a fresh perspective and a fine balance between providing stimulus for revival and prudence in fiscal management. The book combines a fresh perspective and cautions policymakers on overindulgence. It combines conceptual clarity with international experience in the post-Covid world. Unlike the private sector, governments do not suffer bankruptcy due to poor fiscal misman-agement as there is some mechanism or other to bail them out. This is particularly true of subnational governments (SNGs). In this situation, government failure needs to be checked by creating systems and insti-tutions, and being cautious in macroeconomic management. This book helps in understanding macroeconomic management better.

The analytical clarity and lessons from international experiences in the book could provide sound advice and guidance to avoid the pitfalls of debt crisis. Creating the necessary checks and balances requires analysis of level of debt and its impact on macroeconomic stability. The recent experiences of debt crises in Sri Lanka throw light on the importance of policy stability and the dangers of resorting to international debt. The Latin American experiences too bring out the importance of austerity and avoidance of debt crisis. The lesson from Greece shows the contra-dictions when a system is a monetary union but not a fiscal union with SNGs hiding their fiscal problems under a monetary umbrella. It also shows the failure of the system to enforce the fiscal deficit limit imposed by the Maastricht Treaty. Dwivedi combines his analytical clarity and ad-ministrative experience with the lessons from the experiences of these countries to forewarn the dangers of indulging in profligacy and the need to avoid debt crisis.

The importance of studying the subject is best described in Feldstein's insightful analogy. He states:

Fiscal deficits are like obesity. You can see your weight rising on the scale and notice your clothing size is increasing, but there is no sense of urgency in dealing with the problem. That is so even though the long-term consequences of being overweight include an increased risk of sudden heart attack as well as various chronic conditions like diabetes. Like obesity, government deficits are the result of too much self-indulgent living as the government spends more than it collects in taxes.

(RBI, 2004)

The book is particularly important as it focuses on the problem at the subnational level. The incentive structure is such that the SNGs are less concerned about the problem, as the effects of excessive debt are not entirely borne by the SNG. The problem at the SNG level eventually spills over to the nation as the centre eventually has to bail out states, further softening the budget constraint. Although Musgrave–Oates's formulation of assignments shows that calibrating macroeconomic stability is effective predominantly at the central level, the impact of macro-economic policies spills over into subnational jurisdictions, due to which the SNGs would be less concerned about their own fiscal prudence.

Given the shortening time horizon of the political parties and the frequent electoral budget cycles, a variety of mechanisms are used by SNGs to overcome the controls on borrowing imposed in the Constitution (under article 293 on off-budget mechanisms). Borrowing through state enterprises outside the budget is one such mechanism to circumvent the borrowing controls, but eventually the liability falls on the state. Incurring significant losses in power utilities has been a perennial problem imposing significant committed liabilities on states. Keeping the contractors' bills pending not only adds to the costs of projects but also makes the budgeting system opaque. Despite recommendations by several Finance Commissions to move to an accrual accounting system, the cash accounting system continues to obfuscate the government budgeting system. The problem is not unique to SNGs as even the Union government has been indulging in practices creating huge off-budget liabilities casting doubts on the credibility of the budgets. But, ultimately, the responsibility for macroeconomic management predominantly lies with the centre.

The book not only cautions policymakers on impending crisis from such self-indulgent profligacy, it also offers some solutions to avert the crisis. These measures include augmenting tax and non-tax revenues by the states. Within tax revenues, states could look at increasing collections from Goods and Service Tax, excise, Motor Vehicle Tax, and stamp and registration. To increase non-tax revenues, states need to look at improving the design of user charges. Besides augmenting tax and non-tax revenues, the book also recommends increasing user charges, reducing subsidies, improving the performance of state-level public enterprises, better expenditure management, and improved financial management of local bodies including enhancing property taxes. This is an important contribution in a much under-researched area and is a must-read for all those concerned with the future of the country, and more particularly for policymakers, besides students and teachers of Indian public finance.

M. Govinda Rao
Member, Fourteenth Finance Commission (FC)
Former Director, National Institute of Public Finance and Policy

Preface

The crisis in Sri Lanka arising out of the country's failure to repay its debt has taken the world by surprise. Scenes of rioting, looting of shops for basic necessities, fuel shortages, and ransacking of the presidential palace, have caught the imagination of even the common man. While people are shocked and confused over what went wrong so quickly in Sri Lanka to trigger the sudden collapse of the government, policymakers across the world have tried to bring attention to the criticality of managing public finances for the financial and political stability of the country. To them, this financial crisis arising out of bad debt management is not the first and will not be the last. Many countries in the past, notably among them, Greece and the Latin American countries, have witnessed similar situations both at national and subnational levels. Many other countries are currently facing a similar situation. The financial crises in these countries have lessons for all of us.

Globally, government debt has increased from 70 per cent of GDP in 2000 to a record 99 per cent of GDP in 2021. The ratio has increased at a higher rate in developed economies compared to emerging and developing economies. While the debt-to-GDP ratio for developed economies rose from about 70 per cent in 2007 to 120 per cent in 2021, for emerging and developing economies, this ratio has risen at a marginally lower rate from about 40 per cent in 2007 to 67 per cent in 2021 (Gaspar et al., 2021). The debt-to-GDP ratio across both developed and developing countries was already at elevated levels after the 2008 global financial crisis much before the outbreak of the Covid-19 pandemic. However, the recent economic shocks from the pandemic and Russia's invasion of Ukraine have further intensified the risk of debt increasing to unprecedented levels.

In addition to the rising debt levels, inflation across countries is also rising, due to which borrowing costs of governments may increase, making it difficult for countries with weaker fundamentals to service their debt. In March 2022, the World Bank warned that over the next twelve months more than a dozen developing economies may not be able to service their debt. In April 2022, IMF Managing Director Kristalina Georgieva raised a similar warning stating that about 60 per cent of low-income countries were in or near 'debt distress'. In the last six years, the number of countries in the category of 'high risk of debt distress' or 'debt distress' has increased by about 60 per cent (Chabert et al., 2022).

Given the rise in the number of countries finding it difficult to service their debt, the concept of debt sustainability has again taken centre stage in policy debate. Federal countries with high degrees of subnational autonomy face another challenge. In such countries, apart from the finances of the federal government, debt sustainability of subnational governments (SNGs) becomes even more important for multiple reasons. First, in decentralized countries, SNGs play a major role in spending and borrowing decisions. For instance, in India, SNGs are responsible for around 60 per cent of the combined expenditure of the centre and states. Second, major sources of revenue are skewed in favour of the centre and also SNGs have limited freedom to raise borrowing through internal and external sources. Finally, SNGs, being in more direct contact with the people, are under immense pressure to provide quality social and economic infrastructure, and compete with other states in overall development. If SNGs as a whole perform poorly in terms of debt sustainability, this adversely impacts the macroeconomic stability of the country.

In a recent working paper published by the Reserve Bank of India (RBI), Misra et al compared India's subnational debt with the BRICS countries. The paper observed that India's subnational debt-to-GDP ratio was 24.8 per cent which was the highest followed by China (2018). With the pandemic-induced revenue shortfalls and subsequent slowdown in the economy, the debt of SNGs in India has soared to unprecedented levels. As per the RBI state finances data for the fiscal year 2021, the combined SNG debt in India has increased from 26.3 per cent of GDP in 2019–20 to 31.1 per cent in 2020–21, which is far off the target of 20 per cent for the financial year 2023 as per the FRBM Review Committee recommendations (2017). Hence, the focus of the book is on the debt sustainability of SNGs in India.

To examine the debt sustainability of SNGs, existing approaches to measuring debt sustainability are studied and gaps are identified. On the basis of the gaps identified, an alternative approach is discussed to assess the debt sustainability of SNGs. Although the debt of the SNGs in India is sustainable as per the alternative approach, there are emerging risks which may lead to debt soaring to unsustainable levels. The book examines such risks and highlights some of the corrective measures SNGs in India can leverage to avert the looming debt crisis. Along with SNGs, local bodies play a crucial role in the economic growth of the country. However, due to a paucity of funds, they are unable to contribute to the overall development of the country in a larger way. Therefore, the book also highlights the need to strengthen the finances of the local bodies in India.

Acknowledgement

Writing a book is never a solitary endeavour. It's a journey shaped by the support, guidance, and encouragement of numerous individuals who generously contributed their time, expertise, and unwavering belief in the project.

I would like to express my deepest gratitude to my wife, Smt. Nidhi Dwivedi whose unwavering support and encouragement allowed me to focus on my office work and devote time for this book. Her belief in this project never wavered, providing the strength needed to see it through to completion.

I am lucky to have by my side, my daughters, Anukriti and Soumya who make me proud every day and gave me the fuel to sustain through the countless hours devoted to this endeavour.

Blessings of my parents have always been with me in abundance in any venture that I have undertaken. This debut has not been an exception.

I would like to extend my sincere thanks to Dr. M. Govinda Rao, Dr. Pinaki Chakraborty and Dr. Hiranya Mukhopadhyay for their invaluable comments and suggestions on the book.

I would like to thank my colleagues with whom I would discuss and regurgitate my ideas with, particularly, Dr. Sudip Kumar Sinha, whom I have worked closely with for more than a decade.

I am indebted to Mr. Kartik Agarwal and Mr. Joseph Rohan Thomas, both graduates from the Delhi School of Economics (DSE), for their support in bringing academic rigour in the book. Their suggestions and feedback have helped in refining the ideas presented in this book.

Special thanks goes out to my friends, Dr. Achin Chakraborty and Dr. Indrani Chakraborty of the Institute of Development Studies Kolkata for their invaluable suggestions and technical support. Their expertise and dedication have been a constant source of inspiration.

My appreciation extends to the entire team at Oxford University Press, whose expertise and dedication transformed this manuscript into a reality. Their professionalism and commitment to excellence have been invaluable.

Lastly, I am grateful to all those whose names might not appear here but whose influence and support have left an indelible mark on this book.

Thank you all for being a part of this journey.

Contents

Figures

Tables

Abbreviations

ADB	Asian Development Bank
ADF	augmented Dickey–Fuller
ADJ	adjusted
AIIB	Asian Infrastructure Investment Bank
AOMB	additional open market borrowing
AP	Andhra Pradesh
ARDL	autoregressive distributed lag
ARV	annual rental value
BBR	budget balance rules
BE	budget estimate
BPL	below poverty line
BRICS	Brazil, Russia, India, China, and South Africa
BWSSB	Bangalore Water Supply and Sewerage Board
CAG	Comptroller and Auditor General [of India]
CAGR	compound annual growth rate
CBDT	Central Board of Direct Taxes
CENVAT	central value added tax
CFI	Consolidated Fund of India
CMB	cash management bills
CO	capital outlay
CPEC	China–Pakistan Economic Corridor
CPI	Consumer Price Index
CSO	Central Statistics Office
CSS	centrally sponsored schemes
CV	capital value
DBT	direct benefit transfer
DCRF	debt consolidation and relief facility
DEVEX	development expenditure
DFID	Department for International Development
DISCOM	distribution companies
DMO	debt management office
DOLS	dynamic ordinary least squares
DR	debt rules
DSS	debt swapping scheme
DWSHH	drinking water, sanitation, hygiene, and housing
EAP	externally aided projects

ECB	European Central Bank
EMC	Expenditure Management Commission
ER	expenditure rules
EU	European Union
FC	Finance Commission
FE	fixed effects
FIR	first information report
FMFL	foreign made foreign liquor
FMOLS	fully modified ordinary least squares
FPS	fiscal policy strategy
FRBM[A]	Fiscal Responsibility and Budget Management [Act]
FRL	fiscal responsibility legislation
FY	financial year
GCS	general category states
GDP	gross domestic product
GDR	general debt relief
GFD	gross fiscal deficit
GIS	geographic information system
GoI	Government of India
GRF	guarantee redemption fund
G-SAP	Government Security Acquisition Programme
GSDP	gross state domestic product
G SEC	government security
GST	goods and services tax
GTR	gross tax revenue
GVA	gross value added
HP	Hodrick–Prescott
IBC	intertemporal budget constraint
ICBC	Industrial and Commercial Bank of China
ICR	investible grade rating
IGFT	intergovernment fiscal transfer
IGST	integrated goods and services tax
IMF	International Monetary Fund
IOCL	Indian Oil Corporation Ltd
IPS	Im, Pesaran, and Shin
JICA	Japan International Cooperation Agency
JSERC	Jharkhand State Electricity Regulatory Commission
KfW	Kreditanstalt für Wiederaufbau
LLC	Levin, Lin, and Chu
LM	Lagrange multiplier
LR	long run
MIS	management information system
MMT	modern monetary theory

MoF	Ministry of Finance
MOSPI	Ministry of Statistics and Programme Implementation
MPL	municipal premier league
MRP	maximum retail price
MSME	micro, small, and medium enterprises
MTEF	medium-term expenditure framework
MTFF	medium-term fiscal framework
MTFP	medium-term fiscal plan
NABARD	National Bank for Agriculture and Rural Development
NIPFP	National Institute of Public Finance and Policy
NITI	National Institute for Transforming India
NMAM	*National Municipal Accounts Manual*
NPRD	non-plan revenue deficit
NSC	non-special category states
NSSF	national small saving fund
NSSO	National Sample Survey Office
OBC	other backward classes
OD	overdraft
OECD	Organisation for Economic Co-operation and Development
OLS	ordinary least squares
OTR	own tax revenue
OTS	one time settlement
PAN	permanent account number
PB	primary balance
PD	primary deficit
PFM	public financial management
PFMS	Public Finance Management System
POL	Petroleum, Oils and Lubricants
PP	process performance
PRB	primary revenue balance
PS	primary surplus
PSU	public sector undertaking
PV	present value
PVBC	present value budget constraint
QR	[code] quick response [code]
RBI	Reserve Bank of India
RC	registration certificate
RE	revised estimates
RECO	revenue expenditure to capital outlay
RR	revenue receipts
SC	scheduled caste
SCS	special category states

SDL	state development loans
SEBI	Securities and Exchange Board of India
SFC	state Finance Commission
SGST	state goods and service tax
SMAM	*State Municipal Account Manual*
SMS	short message service
SNG	subnational government
SOR	state's own revenue
SOTR	state's own tax revenue
SR	short run
SSL	small savings loan
ST	scheduled tribe
TE	total expenditure
UAV	unit area value
UDAY	Ujjwal Discom Assurance Yojana
ULB	urban local bodies
UNEP	United Nations Environment Programme
UP	Uttar Pradesh
US	United States
UT	Union Territories
VAT	value added tax
VECM	vector error correction mechanism
VIF	variance inflation factor
VMC	Vadodara Municipal Corporation
WB	West Bengal
WMA	ways and means advances

1

An Introduction to Public Debt

1.1 Context

The recent debt crisis in Sri Lanka and earlier crises in other countries at the national and subnational levels, notably among them, Brazil, Argentina, and Mexico, have underscored the importance and criticality of debt management for the sound financial health of the country. Firstly, it is worthwhile to understand the concept of public debt, its necessity and importance in a country's economic development, and secondly, how much debt a country can sustain without endangering its financial stability and future growth.

1.2 What Is Public Debt?

Public debt is basically a subset of the broader concept of debt. As such for the sake of clarity it is important to understand the concept of debt in general before we discuss public debt. Debt is simply the amount of money one has borrowed in the past, with an obligation to repay the borrowed amount with an additional amount as interest to compensate the lender for parting with his or her money for the agreed duration. The concept of borrowing or debt is not novel. At some point in life, many of us will borrow money from someone for a specific purpose or for an unforeseen event with a promise to pay it back. When you borrow money, you usually have to pay back an additional amount on top of the sum borrowed, which is called interest. Interest is the cost associated with borrowing. Now the question arises why someone would take a loan and pay additional interest. People borrow for many reasons. This includes making payment fully or partly for college fees, buying a house or a car or a household good, working capital for running an enterprise, capital

Debt Sustainability of Subnational Governments in India. Hari Krishna Dwivedi, Oxford University Press.
© Hari Krishna Dwivedi 2024. DOI: 10.1093/oso/9780198903116.003.0001

for setting up a commercial or an industrial unit. for which one does not have sufficient money at present to pay .

While borrowing is seen to be increasingly important to meet the needs of households and businesses, it is also seen that many individuals find themselves in a situation where debt has spiralled out of control, and they are unable to pay it back. Defaulting on a loan repayment can have severe consequences and, therefore, while debt can be beneficial in many aspects, a certain caution and wisdom needs to be applied when incurring debt.

In a manner similar to households and businesses, governments also have to borrow. Governments borrow when its revenues are less than its expenditure requirements. Government revenues is the money it receives from tax, non-tax, and other sources, and the expenditure responsibilities typically include spending on national security, development and welfare programmes, creation of social and economic infrastructure and for running the affairs of the government. In addition, governments also spend a large part of their revenue on subsidies like food, petroleum, fertilizer etc. to keep the prices of these essential products low so that people can afford them. Out of the total expenditure (TE) of the government, a large part is committed expenditure for the government's day-to-day functioning. This includes interest payments (IPs) on loans taken by the government, expenditure on salaries, wages, and pensions of government functionaries. The gap between the revenue and expenditure of the government is usually made up through borrowing. The accumulated borrowing over the years is the government debt or public debt. While the debt accumulates due to borrowing, the governments keep servicing the debts through periodic payment of principal and interest.

The governments borrow from both internal as well as external sources. Borrowing from internal or domestic sources is known as internal debt, whereas borrowings from external or foreign sources is the external debt. In India, internal debt of the government includes borrowing from the domestic market, loans from financial institutions, securities against the National Small Savings Fund (NSSF), compensation and other bonds. On the other hand, external debt comprises loans taken by the government from foreign countries or international funding institutions. For example, loans of Government of India (GoI) or subnational governments (SNGs) from any foreign country or from an international funding institution such as the World Bank, Asian Development Bank (ADB), BRICS Bank.

Public debt, depending upon the term of loan, can be further classified as short-term, medium-term, or long-term. Debt which is incurred for a period of less than one year is known as short-term debt. The interest rate on such short-term debt is low. This includes Ways and Means (WMA) advances, Treasury bills (T-bills), and cash management bills (CMB). On the other hand, long-term debt comes with a maturity period of at least ten years. This borrowing is usually taken to carry out medium- to long-term infrastructure projects or development programmes. The rate of interest on these loans is higher than short-term loans. Loans with maturity period between one and ten years are usually known as medium-term loans. Generally medium term loans have a maturity of three to five years.

It is usually seen across the world that the revenue collected by the government primarily takes care of the expenditure in the revenue account, that is, expenditure required to maintain and run the government. This expenditure is also known as committed expenditure as governments do not have much leeway in reducing it. It is a function of past policies followed by successive governments. So, generally the government borrows to meet expenditure required for the creation of new assets, which are capital in nature, for example, construction of roads, railways, irrigation projects, power generation projects. This is also termed as discretionary spending by governments as the quantum of funds to be set aside for capital expenditure is at the discretion of the government . It is a function of the fiscal headroom available with the government after meeting its committed and other expenditure, which includes, interest payments on existing loans, expenditure on salaries, wages and pensions, expenditure on other essential for running the government and ongoing welfare and development schemes.

Economists belonging to diverse schools of thought believe that growth is primarily driven by capital expenditure. Increase in capital expenditure positively impacts economic growth through the multiplier effect. This principle holds true even more for developing countries where the organized private sector does not have a significant presence and is not fully developed. In these countries, it primarily falls on governments to channel funds into creating infrastructure and capital assets to promote private investment. In other words, nations borrow to facilitate investment for economic growth and job creation.

The golden rule of fiscal policy, as defined by Musgrave, states that governments should borrow only to invest and not to finance their current spending.[1] This principle is from the point of view of maintaining intergenerational equity, that is, the future generations who would have to repay the debt should be able to reap the benefits of the present borrowing. While undertaking current spending through borrowing benefits the present generation and pushes the burden of bearing the cost of borrowing to the next generation, capital investment benefits the future generation as it leads to higher capital formation and economic growth.

Although borrowing should be used to finance capital spending, it has been observed that more often governments borrow primarily for financing their revenue expenditure, that is, current expenditure. This happens when the pace of growth of revenue expenditure surpasses revenue collection either due to poor collection of taxes or fall in central transfers or both. This is what happened in 2021, when the world experienced the Covid-19 pandemic. While the revenues of governments across the world shrank due to reduced economic activity resulting from pandemic-induced lockdown, the revenue expenditure on welfare schemes increased significantly to help vulnerable populations affected by the pandemic. The resulting increased mismatch in revenue collection and revenue expenditure forced governments to finance their revenue expenditure from additional borrowing.

There is another reason why governments resort to excessive borrowing. Alesina and Tabellini (1990) observe that borrowing becomes excessive when the government feels that it is unlikely to be re-elected. When there is disagreement among alternating policymakers and uncertainty about who will be elected in the future, the current government does not fully internalize the cost of leaving debt to its successors. As a result, the equilibrium stock of public debt tends to be larger than is socially optimal (Alesina & Tabellini, 1990). The equilibrium level of public debt tends to be larger when there is a larger degree of polarization between

---

[1] https://www.indianeconomy.net/splclassroom/what-is-golden-rule-in-fiscal-policy/

alternating governments and when it is more likely that the current government will not be reappointed.

It is interesting to note that higher debt (in absolute terms or relative to GDP) by a government does not simply imply that the government is likely to default on debt. This is because the likelihood of default largely depends upon a country's debt-servicing capacity and the stability of its political systems. Countries with low likelihood of default can continue to borrow at lower rates of interest even when they have large amounts of outstanding debt. For example, countries such as the USA or Japan have one of the highest debts in the world, that is, 133 per cent and 257 per cent of their GDPs respectively, but, still, they are managing their finances without risk of default. The debt tolerance of a country is determined by its fiscal performance, debt structure, macroeconomic stability, financial sector development, trade openness, political stability, and institutional strength, among others. It can, therefore, safely be stated that although all countries borrow for economic development, only a few have faced financial crisis where they had accumulated debt to an unsustainable level beyond their capacity to service the debt.

We now examine various views on public debt: whether it is good for the economy, acting as a force multiplier for economic growth, or whether its accumulation is fraught with dangerous consequences for the economy.

1.3 Is Public Debt Good or Bad for the Economy?

Interestingly, there is no unanimity among economists on the effect of debt on the fiscal state of the economy. Their views on debt are quite different from one another.

David Hume, generally considered as a pre-classical theorist, in 1752 argued that having public debt results in serious social and political consequences. He considered, national debt is a slowly metastasizing cancer at the core of society. If it isn't cut out completely, it will eventually consume the host body. "It must, indeed, be one of these two events; either the nation must destroy public credit, or public credit will destroy the nation" (Hume, 1758). Similar views were echoed by another famous classical economist Adam Smith, who considered public debt as predominantly unfavourable. In his words, 'the progress of the enormous debts which at present oppress, and will in the long-run probably ruin, all the great nations of Europe, has been pretty uniform' (Adam Smith, 1776: pg 753). Smith's theory demanded the liberation of public revenue (tax) from debt servicing. As taxes are increased to finance debt, it will become a burden on society which will impact private investment and hence economic growth. It was Smith who explored the idea of a sinking fund to ease the budget from the burden of interest payments. According to Smith, the sinking fund should be financed from government taxes.

David Ricardo, another classical economist, proposed a theory in the early nineteenth century called the 'Ricardian equivalence', according to which government spending financed by a rise in debt did not have any impact on the economy since it does not impact aggregate demand. The main assumption being that consumers are rational and hence, a rise in expenditure by government would be accompanied by a decline in consumer spending as consumers expect tax increase in future to finance the debt. The rising debt will also result in the crowding out of private spending by public borrowing which will keep the demand at the same level. However, the basic assumption underlying this proposition is that consumers are rational. This is a bold assumption, as, in reality, consumers may not be rational. They may not expect a tax rise in the future and may not increase their savings and continue spending thereby increasing aggregate demand.

Paul Krugman (2011), a famous American economist, criticized Ricardo's equivalence theory. According to Krugman, if consumers have perfect foresight, live forever, have perfect access to capital markets, etc., then they will take into account the burden of future taxes that will be levied upon them for funding additional government spending. Suppose government introduces a new programme that will cost US$100bn a year forever, then taxes must equivalently go up by the present value of US$100bn forever. Given the assumptions mentioned earlier, consumers would reduce their consumption by US$100bn every year to offset this tax burden, wiping out any expansionary effect of the government spending.

But suppose that the increase in government spending is temporary, not permanent—that it will increase spending by US$100bn per year for only one or two years, not forever. This clearly implies a lower future tax burden than US$100bn a year forever, and therefore implies a fall in consumer spending of less than US$100bn per year. So, the spending programme *is* expansionary in this case, *even if* you have full Ricardian equivalence (Krugman 2011).

So, classical economists considered indebtedness as transfer of resources from productive uses to non-productive uses, which affects the accumulation of revenue-generating assets and in the long run negatively impacts economic growth and development.

Contrary to the view of classical economists, the Keynesian view considers public indebtedness favourably, as public expenditure in excess of revenues can boost overall demand if growth suffers because of weak effective demand. It essentially advocates government action to boost demand through higher spending.

Keynesian economics was developed during the Great Depression of 1930 and was in stark contrast to the aggregate supply focused classical economics. J. M. Keynes, a British economist, argued in his book, *The General Theory of Employment, Interest and Money* (1936), that during economic depression there was no certainty that goods produced by individuals and effective demand for goods would match. During depression, high unemployment can be anticipated especially when an economy contracts. He believed that during depression full employment equilibrium of an economy could not be maintained by itself and advocated government intervention to increase demand. Government spending can raise aggregate demand which increases economic activity leading to reduced unemployment and deflation.

Later, Abba Lerner (1943), a Russian-born economist, during the Second World War developed a functional finance theory advocating government intervention in the economy. The main argument of the functional finance theory is that the government should focus not on the budgetary impact of its fiscal policy but on the outcome of its fiscal policies. Lerner presented three guidelines to drive the fiscal policies of the government. First, the government is obligated to always maintain a reasonable level of demand. It must raise expenditure or lower taxes if there is too little spending and a high unemployment rate and reduce its own spending or raise taxes to combat inflation if there is excessive expenditure. Second, the government must maintain a rate of interest that stimulates the maximum amount of investment. The government should borrow money when it wants to raise the rate of interest and lend money or pay off its debt when it wants to decrease the rate of interest. Finally, according to the third principle, if government requires money to implement the first two principles, then it should print it.

Around 1958, James Buchanan published his alternative public debt theory in *Public Principles of Public Debt*. He outlined three claims that significantly contrast with the core Keynesian principles. Buchanan's first argument is that public debt passes the burden onto future generations. In other words, the debt financed through lowering of taxes for current taxpayers is offset by higher taxes paid by future taxpayers to amortize the debt. This is contrary to the Keynesian argument that borrowing does not burden future generations and the cost of the borrowing is borne by the present generation because the resources obtained through borrowing are put to good use for future generations.

Buchanan's second argument is that the analogy between private debt and public debt is fundamentally correct. When the government borrows from the domestic market, it issues a bond to the lender. The lender in the process of purchasing the bond reduces another asset, for example, cash or private bonds, and swaps it with the government bond. This process leaves the net worth of the lender unchanged. This means that the individual balance sheet is not affected by public debt creation implying that private debt and internal public debt are the same and there is no difference between the two. This is based on the assumption that the interest rate on government securities is the same as the rate of return on private investments.

The third point made by Buchanan was that internal and external debt are not fundamentally different. The difference between the internal and external debt should happen only if the rate of interest between internal and external borrowing is different. If the two rates are equal, then the question of whether to borrow from external or internal sources should not arise. Suppose we take the case where the interest rates on internal and external borrowing are equal. If an internal loan is taken, then it means the domestic private investment would reduce by the same amount. The reduction in domestic private investment will further reduce future income from such investment. On the other hand, if an external loan is taken, then it would not result in a reduction in domestic private investment. In this case, the future income would be higher by exactly the amount required to service the external loan. In these two cases, net income after tax payments and interest receipts will be the same. Going by the same argument, if the interest rate on internal loan is higher than the external loan, then the economy would be better off borrowing externally. Similarly, if the interest rate on internal loan is lower than external loan, then the economy would be better off borrowing internally, keeping the assumptions regarding return on domestic private investment unchanged.

And, lastly, the modern monetary theory (MMT), a term coined by Bill Mitchell, an Australian economist, argues that since countries moved away from the days of the gold standard, governments can borrow and spend as required without any burden of increased taxes in the future as long as the government issues and controls its own currency. In other words, the government will never have to default on its debt. The liabilities arising out of the borrowed funds can be repaid by the government printing currency. The only concern is inflation, which can rise because of expansionary government spending. The rise in inflation can be curbed by increasing taxes. The proponents of MMT argue that there need not be any prescribed limit for spending, that is, governments can spend without any upper cap (risk-free government spending). It is interesting to note that MMT builds on Lerner's theory of functional finance which removes debt limits on government borrowing. However, one major difference between MMT and functional finance theory is that the former rejects monetary policy's relevance to inflation. MMT policy has not found favour with the majority of economists because of its oversimplification of key issues. For instance, increasing borrowing to finance spending will ultimately lead to a rise in interest payments which will eat up increasing portions of revenues at a certain point, after which the government may no longer be in a position to borrow any further.

Thus, there has been no unanimity among economists either on 'analytical grounds or on the basis of empirical results that financing government spending by incurring debt is good or bad or neutral' (Rangarajan & Srivastava, 2005). However, the conventional view on economic effects of public indebtedness, is a combination of classical and Keynesian arguments wherein the effect of public debt on economic growth is different over the short term, medium term, and the long term.

It is now widely held that Keynesian economics is generally useful in short-term when the economy is in recession and higher public spending stimulates demand and investment which can bring the economy out of recession. However, in the long run, having higher public debt leads to the crowding out of private investment due to increasing interest rates thereby negatively affecting investments and growth of the economy. Hence, in the long run, the classical view will hold good.

In addition to the short-term and long-term effects of high public debt, there are other effects of public debt. First, it could lead to a deadweight loss of taxation on account of the taxes that would need to be imposed to finance the repayment of debt. Second, it can lead to inflationary pressure if the government finances the debt using seigniorage income, which is the difference between the value of money and the cost of printing the money. Third, it could also result in a loss of confidence in the global financial markets about the country's ability to repay debt which may limit its ability to borrow in its own currency, an effect known as original sin (Eichengreen et al., 2007).

It is observed that the size of the debt is increasing rapidly across countries. In 2020, global government debt reached close to 100 per cent of GDP for the first time in history. In 2010, the figure was a little more than 75 per cent (IMF Global Debt Monitor, 2022). Government debt levels have increased across almost all countries. This ten-year period witnessed government debt increase by 26.4 per cent in advanced economies, 27.1 per cent in emerging market economies, and 20 per cent in low-income developing countries. Moreover, the recent spike due to the pandemic has forced countries to follow liberal fiscal and monetary policies to boost their economies. This in turn has fuelled inflation which will further increase the requirements of debt servicing. The inflationary pressures have been made worse due to the supply constraint resulting from the geopolitical situation in Eastern Europe.

The World Bank has recently stated that there is a risk of a global debt crisis after warning of the biggest accumulation of debt over the past five decades. While the impact of public debt is yet to be conclusively established, the need to assess whether government debt is sustainable is increasingly important in order to ascertain whether government could be faced with a situation of insolvency. A government turning insolvent would have catastrophic consequences for the living standards of its citizen

1.4 Conclusion

Recent debt crises in some countries have again brought to the fore the discussion on public debt and management of public finances. The crises in these countries have had catastrophic consequences for their people and their economy. Does this mean that borrowing by governments is always bad? The views on debt have evolved from being considered as a cancer at the core of society to being regarded as the way to steer an economy out of a crisis.

Despite the naysayers, debt has become an integral part of public finances with governments running large deficits year after year. How much debt a government can take depends crucially on the macroeconomic health and the political stability of the country. We have seen that countries such as the United States or Japan have very high levels of debt, yet are considered by the financial market as having low chances of default. However, countries with a much lower level of debt have found themselves in a crisis situation, which has paralysed their economies. Therefore, the likelihood of default depends on a country's ability to repay, which depends on macroeconomic and fiscal parameters.

In the next chapter, we will examine the debt crises in other countries both at the national and subnational levels, and the reasons behind them. Countries that are currently witnessing spikes in their debt levels could learn from those countries who have already endured debt crises, so that they might avoid them.

2

International Debt Crises

What Went Wrong?

2.1 Context

The debt crisis in some countries has resulted in political and economic upheaval, impacting people's lives. It will be interesting to examine what went wrong in these countries. Did they follow similar fiscal policies which led to financial disaster? Or were there unique factors operating in these countries that caused the crisis? The answers to these questions are also relevant when we study debt crises at the subnational level as ultimately the factors that determine the fiscal policies at the centre and the state are fairly similar, such as the political economy, market forces, and other social factors. Both the levels of the government have to respond to the demands from different sections of society and at the same time ensure that their creditworthiness remains at a good level. Now, when we look at the question of how countries slipped into debt crisis, we find that the common feature which comes out in these countries is that the debt crisis arose not because of their high debt-to-GDP ratio but low tax collection as a percentage of their GDP which constrained them to service their debt. Generally, the low tax collection was a result of either faulty tax policy driven mainly by populism, inherent inefficiencies in the tax administration, some extraneous factors, or a combination of these factors. Moreover, despite poor tax collection, these countries indulged in excessive borrowing at high interest rates to finance their deficits and service their payment liabilities. Also, the borrowing was majorly utilized for economically unviable projects which did not generate significant future returns. As a result, excessive borrowing was not adequately matched with commensurate growth in revenues. These countries were all trapped in a vicious debt cycle wherein more and more debt was created to service

Debt Sustainability of Subnational Governments in India. Hari Krishna Dwivedi, Oxford University Press.
© Hari Krishna Dwivedi 2024. DOI: 10.1093/oso/9780198903116.003.0002

the existing debt. These crises have been discussed in reverse chronological order starting with the most recent crisis.

2.2 Debt Crises in India's Neighbourhood

Sri Lanka has defaulted on its debt repayment, and Pakistan is on the brink of default saved only by bailouts. The crises in these countries have been simmering for decades and have similar origins. The Covid-19 pandemic merely triggered the crises in these countries. Inefficiencies in the taxation system coupled with tax cuts had forced these countries to depend on excessive borrowing to finance their expenditure. Moreover, borrowing was largely from foreign sources at high-interest rates and such costly borrowing was mainly utilized for economically unviable projects. With increasing debt-servicing costs due to high interest borrowing coupled with low revenues, these countries found it difficult to service their current debt levels. Let us now discuss in further detail the origin of the crises in these countries.

2.2.1 Sri Lankan debt crisis (2022)

The crisis that unfolded in Sri Lanka in 2022 had been brewing for a while due to ill-designed policies and actions of the government such as the

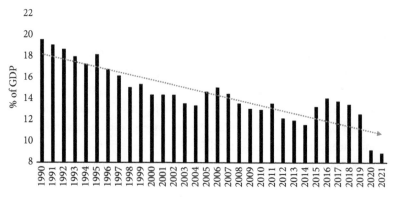

Figure 2.1 Longer-term trend of declining revenues
Source: IMF (2022d)

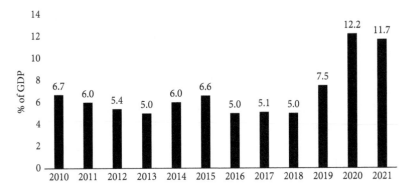

Figure 2.2 Rising general government fiscal deficit pre-Covid
Source: IMF (2022b)

mismanagement of government finances and ill-timed tax cuts (Figure 2.1). The global pandemic only exacerbated the debt crisis.

There were a number of reasons which led to the crisis. Revenues have been declining since 1990s. The government revenues as a percentage of GDP declined from 19.6 in 1990 to 8.9 in 2021(see Figure 2.1). The fall in revenue-to-GDP ratio was due to lack of expansion of tax base and large number of tax concessions and reliefs provided by the government. Post 2019, deep tax cuts were announced by the government to fulfil its election promises. The VAT rate was brought down from 15 per cent to 8 per cent and seven different taxes were abolished. Due to abolishment of key taxes, the tax base of the country significantly reduced by 5 lakh tax-payers each in 2020 and 2021. Even before the tax cuts, the country had a low tax-to-GDP ratio and with these tax cuts, the revenues fell further. With the disruptions following pandemic in 2020, the lowering of direct tax rates did not augment private investment in the country. Instead, it led to a reduction in tax-to-GDP ratio by 33 per cent, from 12.6 per cent in 2019–20 to 8.9 per cent in 2020–21. In order to make up for the drastic fall in revenues, the government resorted to higher borrowing which led to the fiscal deficit soaring to more than 12 per cent of GDP in 2020–21[1](see Figure 2.2).

---

[1] https://www.treasury.gov.lk/api/file/546a705a-2fc2-4a9f-a78b-b686693c3aab

Another fallout of the pandemic was a significant fall in revenues from tourism which is a major source of foreign exchange earning. This had a very debilitating effect on the already stressed financial position of the country. Coupled with this, the government policy of imposing a ban on importing chemical fertilizers to prevent foreign currency shortages created a crisis in the farm sector. Both the production and exports of farm products were very adversely affected. The economy of the country, which is highly dependent on agriculture and tourism, took a bad hit.

Due to shrinking revenues, heavy borrowing and implementation of faulty policies by the government, the public debt rose from 86.8 per cent at the end of 2019 to 107.2 per cent of GDP in 2021(see Figure 2.3). In addition to the high levels of debt, the composition of the debt is what made the condition even more precarious. The high levels of external debt and substantial contingent liabilities, owing to the stock of state-owned enterprises which were now largely exposed to the currency fluctuations and rising oil prices, posed a massive threat to the fiscal condition of the country (see Figure 2.3).

The government's contingent liabilities have also continued to increase at a rapid pace in the last 15 years. The government kept revising the targets for outstanding guarantees (as per Fiscal Management (Responsibility) Act 2003) thereby circumventing the objective of the Act. In the last 15 years, the guaranteed limit was revised four times from 4.5 per cent of GDP in 2006 to 15 per cent of GDP in 2021. In 2020, the

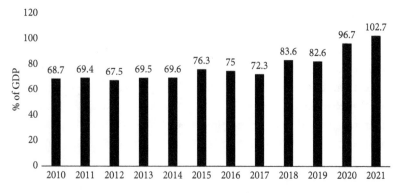

Figure 2.3 Rising general government debt-GDP ratio
Source: IMF (2022a)

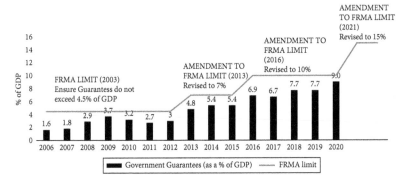

Figure 2.4 Government guarantee (as a % of GDP)(Responsibility) Act consistently revised upwards in Sri Lanka
Source: PublicFinance.lk (2021)

outstanding guarantees of the government as a percentage of GDP stood at 9 which is a threefold increase from 3 per cent in just eight years (see Figure 2.4).

The rating agencies significantly downgraded the credit rating of the government. Many foreign agencies were reluctant to lend to Sri Lanka. Instead of devising a plan to raise revenues to reduce its dependence on borrowing, the government continued to borrow for investment in capital projects such as the southern international port of Hambantota, the Mattala airport, and the four-lane Chinese-built expressway from Colombo to Hambantota. Not only did the loans from China come with high interest, the completion of such infrastructure projects was also unsatisfactory. While the scarce domestic resources had already been drained, most of the new assets turned out to be white elephants.

Currently, multiple international organizations and countries have extended help through lines of credit and financial assistance. The World Bank has provided Sri Lanka with US$600m as aid. India has committed more than US$3bn to Sri Lanka through loans, credit lines and credit swaps. The International Monetary Fund (IMF) in its Article IV Consultation Assessment has advised that certain structural reforms be undertaken to correct the situation in the country. The suggestions include revenue augmentation measures including strengthening VAT and income tax, through increase in rates and broadening of tax base. It has also suggested inflation targeting through tightening of monetary policy which was loosened to counter the impact of Covid. In addition, it has recommended careful sequencing to transition to a flexible market-determined exchange rate.

2.2.2 Pakistan debt crisis (2022)

In January 2021, Malaysian authorities seized a Pakistan International Airlines Boeing 777 plane, with passengers on board, for not paying leasing fees worth US$15m (PTI, 2021). This was an awkward incident, as the carrier in question was the Pakistani national airlines and many experts predicted that more such payment defaults by the Pakistani government and government-owned entities would follow, if concrete measures were not put in place. In the three years from 2018, the country's debt-to-GDP ratio rose from 64 per cent to a whopping 74 per cent.

A large part of the country's tax revenues goes in servicing its debt despite decline in the tax-to-GDP ratio. The tax-to-GDP ratio of the country has shown a stagnation over the years. It has slightly declined from 10.8% in FY18 to 9.4% in FY21 (see Figure 2.5).

This is particularly of concern as the tax-to-GDP ratio of the country was 9.3 per cent in 2020, which is much lower than the Asia and Pacific average of 19.1 per cent (by more than eight percentage points) and significantly lower than the OECD average of 33.5 per cent (by more than 23.5 percentage points) (OECD, 2022). Low tax-to-GDP ratio of the government is on account of several tax exemptions, multiple rate structures,

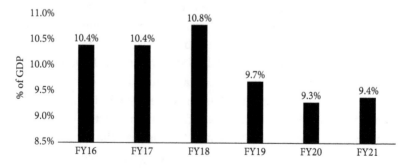

Figure 2.5 Tax-to-GDP ratio of Pakistan
Source: Finance Division, Government of Pakistan (2022)

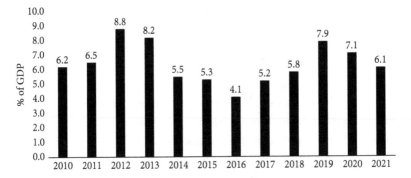

Figure 2.6 Rising general government fiscal deficit prior to the pandemic
Source: Finance Division, Government of Pakistan (2023)

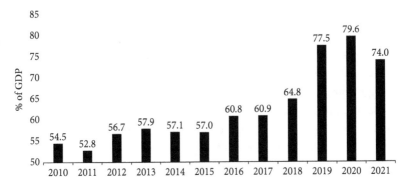

Figure 2.7 Rising general government debt-to-GDP ratio
Source: IMF (2022a)

and a fragmented tax administration system. The country has failed to implement reforms for strengthening its tax administration system. Less than 1 per cent of the population is under the ambit of income tax (which includes personal and corporate income tax). On the other hand, high subsidies, large interest payments, and off-budget expenditure led to consistently high fiscal deficits. Fiscal deficit which was over 5.2 per cent in 2017 increased to about 7.9 per cent in 2019–20. The fiscal deficit is estimated to be as high as 6.1 in 2021 (RE) (see Figures 2.6 and 2.7).

Moreover, much of the borrowing was undertaken at high-interest rates. This borrowing was utilized for non-developmental and economically unviable projects. This added to the already worsening debt position of the country (see Figure 2.7). China is Pakistan's largest bilateral creditor. Most notably, Pakistan has also borrowed money from Chinese commercial banks like Bank of China, and China Development Bank. The interest rates on loans from Chinese banks are about 2 to 3 per cent higher than the long-term interest rates of ADB and World Bank. The high-interest loans from China have further increased the debt burden of the country. A large part of the borrowing from China is for the China–Pakistan Economic Corridor (CPEC) project which increased Pakistan's debt by US$47bn in 2014. The value of the CPEC loan increased further to US$64bn due to a depreciation of Pakistan's currency over the years (Choudhury, 2022).

Therefore, mismanagement of government funds, excessive borrowing from external sources, and financing of unviable infrastructure projects through long-term debt instruments have all contributed to a situation where the country is at very high risk of default. In 2018, IMF suggested several reforms for the country, such as reduction in deficits, strengthening of social safety net for poor households, improving banking and tax legislation, eliminating electricity subsidies, and reducing foreign exchange market intervention by the federal bank. However, the country could not fulfil any of these objectives (Razdan, 2022). The country's only hope of coming out of the high debt situation is to broaden its tax base and rein in wasteful civil and military government spending.

2.3 European Debt Crises

The European debt crises in the 2010s affected many countries in Europe such as Greece, Portugal, Ireland, Spain, and Cyprus. Many of these countries lacked strong macroeconomic fundamentals, but were able to acquire cheap debt as a result of being in the same monetary union. These countries found themselves unable to service their debt by the 2010s. As a member state, they had no control over monetary policy. They were not able to devalue their currency to make their economies competitive in the longer run. This lack of control over the monetary policy and the moral hazard created by the common pool problem is similar to what is faced by subnational governments (SNGs) in most countries. An understanding of the European debt crises can therefore add value to the discussion on subnational debt.

2.3.1 Greek debt crisis (2010)

The Greek debt crisis occurred in 2010, with its debt-to-GDP ratio rising from 22.7 per cent in 1980 to 147.5 per cent in 2010. The crisis has had severe economic, political, and social impact. What is more disheartening is that, even after more than a decade of debt crisis, the economy has not fully recovered and is still struggling with low levels of growth, high levels of unemployment, and social distress. Unemployment in Greece continues to be almost 17 per cent. Between the 2008 global financial crisis and 2017, the proportion of the Greece population living in severe deprivation has doubled. The debt-to-GDP ratio instead of showing correction has further worsened from 147.5 per cent in 2010 to 211.9 per cent in 2020 (see Figure 2.8).

Let us see how the crisis started in Greece. When the euro was introduced in 1999, as the common currency for EU (European Union) member states, Greece could not adopt the currency because it failed to meet the fiscal criteria set by Maastricht. The criteria required less than 1.5 per cent inflation, a budget deficit less than 3 per cent, and a debt-to-GDP ratio below 60 per cent. Surprisingly, Greece later adopted the euro currency by misrepresenting its finances even when its budget deficit was significantly higher than 3 per cent and debt-to-GDP ratio greater than 100 per cent. Countries with high debt and deficit levels generally have higher interest rates. But this was not the case with Greece. There was insufficient risk assessment due to vested interests which led

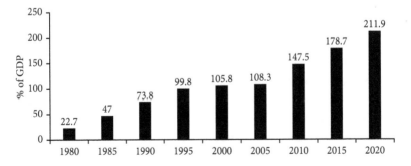

Figure 2.8 Rising general government debt-to-GDP ratio of Greece
Source: IMF (2022a)

to declining interest rates. Greece's entry to the eurozone allowed it to access low-cost borrowing despite years of deficit. This further led to excessive borrowing. Over and above this, the additional borrowing was largely utilized for public wage increases, social spending, etc. and not for the creation of long-term revenue-generating capital assets. For instance, Greece borrowed close to US$11.6 bn in 2004 to host the Olympics. This debt build-up and its utilization did not lead to higher economic growth. On the contrary, it worsened Greece's fiscal situation.

During the same period, with the burst of the real-estate bubble in the USA in 2008, there was a worldwide banking crisis. The global banking crisis and credit crunch led to rising borrowing costs and a drying up of financing. This was the final blow to the financial stability of Greece, and it plunged into bankruptcy. The year 2009 was the first time that there were talks about bailouts, and the troika—the European Commission, the European Central Bank, and the IMF—came to the rescue of Greece. However, they had to balance the pressure of ensuring that the crisis did not prove to be contagious to other banks which owned much of Greece's debt, along with ascertaining that the austerity measures did not further strangulate the economy.

Different relief packages have been extended by the troika over the years. In 2010, the IMF and EU agreed to bail out Greece with €110bn. A second EU–IMF bailout was declared in 2012 worth €130bn (Council on Foreign Relations, 2022). The year 2015 brought in the third bailout from the EU for €86bn, with the final bailout in 2018.

The debt crisis had a massive impact on the whole country. While bailouts were extended, the austerity measures which were mandated with it caused social and political unrest. From 2010 onwards, successive governments in Greece introduced austerity measures, through a memorandum of understanding with the troika. These measures required reduction in budget on health, education, and social services, reductions in salaries and wages for government employees, reductions in pension payments, and higher retirement age, cutting down public sector personnel through reduced hiring, laying off of personnel on limited-term contracts, higher taxation, higher public transport and electricity prices, and a large-scale privatization programme. Other measures to improve the competitiveness of the economy included decreasing the minimum wage and other labour law reforms to increase labour market flexibility.

Therefore, what comes out is that the Greek debt crisis was mainly caused by excessive government spending over the years, poor fiscal management, and slowdown in economic growth.

2.3.2 Portuguese debt crisis (2010)

Post-2008 global financial crisis, Portugal encountered a crisis mirroring the Greek debt crisis. The origins of the financial crisis in Portugal could be traced back to its decision to join the eurozone. Portugal's economy grew rapidly between 1995 and 2001 in anticipation of joining the eurozone, which would reduce inflation risks as well as exchange rate risks (Blanchard, 2007; Blanchard & Portugal, 2017). Due to this, consumers and businesses invested more and spent more (Blanchard & Portugal, 2017; Lourtie, 2012). This resulted in historically low rates of interest with real interest rates close to nil. When combined with an expansionary discretionary fiscal policy, easy lending led to a decline in private savings and a rise in consumption and investment which produced rapid economic development and low unemployment. However, the investment was mainly in domestically supplied uncompetitive industries, like telecommunications, energy, and healthcare, while increasing spending was mostly focused on current expenses (Gaspar, 2012).

The current account deficits widened as nominal wages outpaced gains in labour productivity and the country's competitiveness decreased. Between 2007–08 and 2010–11, debt as a percentage of GDP also skyrocketed (see Figure 2.9). At the same time, the economy was also under stress due to heightened competition from growing markets and countries in Central and Eastern Europe, particularly in its two main export industries, textiles and footwear. The current account deficit persisted, but this time it was accompanied by a gradual rise in the country's unemployment rate (Gurnani, 2016).

This average export growth above the EU-15 between 2006 and 2010 was more than offset by increased energy costs and a weakening income account. The current account deficits continued to be significant. Additionally, Portugal, even after a decade of sluggish growth, rose at an annual rate of barely 1 per cent between 1999 and 2010. Along with this, during this period, the unemployment rate rose from 5.5 per

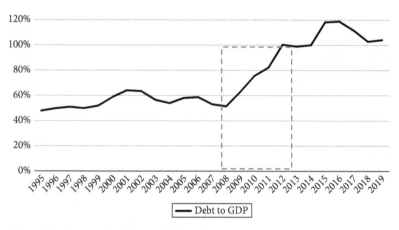

Figure 2.9 Portugal's debt-to-GDP ratio
Sources: World Bank (2022c), EuroStat (2022)

cent to 8.7 per cent. The public expenditure growth grew to partially offset a decline in private consumption growth, as a result the deficit rose to 3 per cent of GDP (Blanchard & Portugal, 2017). In 2007, the debt-to-GDP ratio rose to 68.4 per cent while the current account balance was around −10 per cent. Several factors, including a fall in remittances, rising competition from the Central and Eastern European nations that joined the EU during that time, and a fall in competitiveness due to increase in labour costs (a 4.3 per cent increase above the euro average), were seen as contributing to this economic situation (Blanchard & Portugal, 2017).

Markets were not convinced that Portugal would be able to implement budget austerity during the subsequent years. The government bond yields in the secondary market did not improve. The conservative policies and economic weaknesses were added to by rising interest rates on its national debt. The last blow happened towards the end of March and early April of 2011, when both Standard & Poor's and Fitch downgraded Portugal's ratings (from A+ to BBB−). Yields increased dramatically, making borrowing unaffordable. Only a few days later, the government was compelled to seek help from the international lenders.

On 16 May 2011, the lender groups eventually agreed to a bailout package of US$116bn. Portugal was obliged as part of the programme to enact austerity measures and carry out a number of structural changes in order to lower the government's budget deficit and encourage economic development.

But as was previously observed in the case of Greece, the nation as a whole has been significantly impacted by the growth of debt. Bailouts were continued but the accompanying austerity measures led to social unrest and political turmoil. Portugal has been implementing austerity measures since 2010 with excellent outcomes. However, public debt is still quite high—it was the third highest in the euro region in 2022 at nearly 120 per cent of GDP, and it is unlikely to drop below 100 per cent before 2025 (Lipton, 2019).

Having examined the reasons for debt crises at the national level, let us now turn our focus to analyse debt crises at the subnational level. Over the last three decades, several countries have experienced debt crises at the subnational level. Some of these countries—mainly the Latin American ones (i.e. Brazil, Argentina, Mexico)—have not only witnessed subnational debt crises but have seen multiple episodes of it, one after another. These three countries in Latin America are among the most fiscally decentralized countries in the world, with SNGs enjoying substantial level of fiscal autonomy. The crisis in these countries hold important lessons for SNGs of other countries which have a highly decentralized fiscal structure. Let us discuss these in detail to understand what exactly happened in these countries and what led to their debt crises.

2.4 Latin American Subnational Debt Crises (1980s–1990s)

Several countries in Latin America experienced subnational debt crises , most notably Brazil, Argentina, and Mexico. These countries have a long history of being federal nation with a significant degree of decentralization in their governance structure. The federal governments in these countries used different instruments to control the borrowing of SNGs, but these turned out to be less effective in preventing SNG debt crises. Federal governments in these countries had to bail out the SNGs multiple times for a variety of reasons. The nature of debt crises of SNGs in these countries and how they have managed to come out of the crises are discussed in the subsequent subsections.

2.4.1   Subnational debt crises in Brazil (1980s–1990s)

Brazil has been a federal country from 1891. However, with the adoption of the 1988 Constitution after twenty-one years of military rule, there was a significant increase in decentralization by giving more authority and resources to the SNGs. During the period from 1988 to 1998, Brazil encountered three significant debt crises at the subnational level, that is, in 1989, 1993, and 1997. The 1997 crisis was the severest of the three crises. The federal government was forced to bail out many provinces.

A decade before the crises, from 1970s and 1980s, saw SNGs borrowing heavily from international organizations, commercial banks (domestic and foreign), and the federal government. The states borrowed excessively, encouraged by the policy of the federal government in 1966 to issue fresh loans to repay earlier loans. Cumulatively, the SNGs accounted for around 42 per cent of the total public sector debt, making them the largest debtors in the country. Although, there were attempts by the federal government to bring the SNGs' debt under control, particularly, by entering into agreements with them, however, these were not successful as the states knew that the federal government would bail them out in case of a crisis. The adoption of the 1988 Constitution also increased the expenditure responsibilities of SNGs. Brazil during this period was faced with high inflation and a macroeconomic crisis. This forced the central government to implement a stabilization plan to bring inflation under control. However, the plan had an adverse effect on the economy. While the revenue of states suffered, they also found it difficult to control their real expenditure. They resorted to more and more borrowing which raised their debts to uncontrollable levels. The federal government had to finally give the state government a debt relief of around R$10.5bn in 1989, first of the three debt crises.

Post 1989 and in the early 1990s, Brazil implemented a macroeconomic stabilization programme to control hyperinflation. This reduced economic activity and lowered SNGs' revenue collection. The early 1990s then saw the stabilization plan failing, inflation rising again, and even some debt renegotiations of state with federal government could not succeed. This left the states with no option but to borrow more. Due to the increased borrowing, SNG debt as a percentage of GDP increased from 7.5 per cent in 1991 to 9.3 per cent in 1993. As the states' fiscal health deteriorated, many of the state bonds lost value and became unmarket-able. Many of the banks which were state-owned ended up with these unmarketable state bonds in their portfolio. The central government introduced bond swap programmes and also bailed out SNGs by refinancing R$39.4bn of state debt (excluding bonds) in 1993.

The third debt crisis that the SNGs faced in Brazil has its origins in the stabilization plan that the federal government introduced in 1994 called the Plano Real. As Brazil suffered from hyperinflation, a series of contractionary monetary and fiscal policies were put in place. Along with these, a new currency called the Real was introduced. These steps were together referred to as Plano Real. Although, hyperinflation was successfully brought under control through contractionary policies of the government, the states expenditure responsibilities increased in real terms. Coupled with a rise in real expenditure, contractionary policies of the government caused a slowdown in the economy resulting in a decline in revenues. The combined effect of these two led to SNG's debt to GDP rise from 9.2 per cent in 1993 to 10.7 per cent in 1996. Moreover, the interest rates were increased to control borrowing. As the interest rates became much higher than the rate at which the debt was contracted, capitalized interest on state debt that was not renegotiated at the end of 1994 caused an explosive increase in outstanding debt contracted (Vulovic, 2011) (see Figure 2.10). This resulted in a debt crisis in the SNGs in 1997.

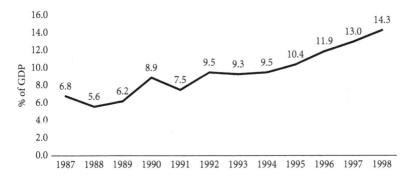

Figure 2.10 Rise in debt stock of SNGs (Brazil)

Note: data for 1999 and 2000 not available.

Sources: Vulovic (2011)

Following the 1980s and 1990s debt crises in Brazil, and several bail-outs from the federal government, the Fiscal Responsibility Law (FRL) was introduced in 2000 to instil fiscal discipline. The law defined a general framework for fiscal planning, execution, and reporting (Medas et al., 2019). The FRL mandated the debt ceilings for the states at 200 per cent of net current revenues and for municipalities at 120 per cent of net current revenues. As per the FRL, the federal government would deduct the fiscal transfers to the states to the extent of the states' debt with the federal government. There was a limit placed on SNG debt, and new borrowing was not allowed until debt above the stipulated limit was repaid. There were also penalties for non-compliance with the FRL (Bevilaqua, 2002).

The imposition of stronger controls through the implementation of FRL and robust economic growth resulted in a decline in debt of the SNGs in Brazil (Medas et al., 2019). From 2001 to 2013, the SNG debt of Brazil reduced by approximately 10 per cent of GDP (see Figure 2.11). However, after 2013, the SNG debt again started to rise due to poor economic conditions and an array of controls that were undermined by loopholes or bad incentives that discourage enforcement (Rodden & Eskeland, 2003) (see Figure 2.11).

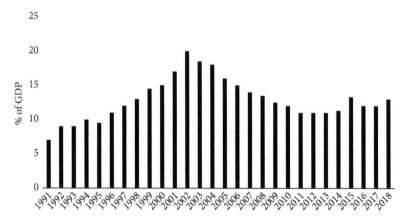

Figure 2.11   Brazil: Subnational Debt-to-GDP ratio (1991-2018)
Source: Medas et al. (2019)

2.4.2 Subnational debt crises in Argentina (1980s–2000s)

Argentina has a long history of debt crises with the government seeking IMF emergency assistance as many as twenty-two times. While there are many reasons for these crises, the role of subnational debt and the subnational credit market is quite significant. Argentinian system was marked by loose federal government structure, high deficit financing, and significant government ownership of banks (Freire & Petersen, 2004).

In the late 1970s and early 1980s, following the oil shocks, Argentina engaged in extensive borrowing. A significant part of the borrowing by SNGs (provincial governments) was from their own provincial banks. The central government banks had to repeatedly lend to the provincial banks to prevent their collapse. Large borrowing resulted in the public debt reaching 60 per cent of the GDP by the end of 1988. However, this practice was made difficult with the introduction of reforms in 1991 called the Convertibility Plan. The convertibility plan pegged the exchange rate of the Argentine peso to the US dollar, which eliminated the possibility of inflationary financing of the government deficit.

Under the Convertibility Plan, the central government also restructured its existing debt with the provincial authorities. The value of the outstanding debt owed to the central government by SNGs was subject to dispute, especially because the 1989 hyperinflation distorted its real value. So, the federal government and the provincial government sat down to find an acceptable value for the outstanding debt of the provinces. As an outcome of the negotiation between the federal and the provincial government, the provincial governments' debt to federal government were to be written off (Dillinger & Webb, 1999).

In 1990s, many SNGs were bailed out by the federal government due to very high debt levels which the SNGs found difficult to service. Moreover, now the federal government introduced controls that prohibited provincial banks from lending to SNGs (provincial governments). Nevertheless, the results of these measures were not as promising as anticipated, since the SNGs continued borrowing from banks with intergovernmental fiscal transfers as guarantee. The central government could not control this behaviour of the SNGs due to the significant autonomy they had under the Constitution.

The SNGs were allowed to regulate their own borrowing under the Constitution. This meant that different SNGs had different mechanism for control on borrowing. Most SNGs (provinces) only required permission from the provincial authority for new borrowing. Foreign borrowing, however, required approval from the Ministry of Economy. Further, provinces were not allowed to borrow for financing current expenditure. However, the implementation of these controls was not adequate and there was always an expectation that the subnational entities would be bailed out by the central government in case of a risk of default by the SNGs.

Several reforms were introduced in the early 1990s, such as preventing rolling over of existing debts from the provincial banks. From 1993, federal agencies were barred from paying a creditor on behalf of a province. Further, if intergovernmental transfers were used as collateral for provincial borrowing, the federal government would deduct any debt service from future transfers.

In 1994, Argentina faced a slowdown in its economy, due to the contagious effect of the Mexican tequila crisis which affected economies of several Latin American countries. The GDP (real) fell by 4 per cent and provincial revenues declined by around 8 per cent in 1995. When faced with the prospect of not receiving budgetary support from the federal government due to economic slowdown, provinces had to go for additional borrowing. This resulted in a drastic increase in the provincial debt to US$17.2bn or 6.3 per cent of GDP by mid-1996 (see Figure 2.12 & 2.13). Also, the reforms that were introduced in the early 1990s resulted in significantly lower intergovernmental transfers to SNGs because SNGs were using the transfers as a guarantee. The federal government deducted debt servicing from the transfers to the SNGs. As a result, some SNGs received as low as one-third of the amount that they used to receive.

In 1999, the Fiscal Solvency Law, which was aimed at significantly reducing government spending and controlling rising debt repayments was passed at the federal level. Later, provinces also passed their fiscal solvency rules. By 2001, fourteen out of twenty-three of the provinces introduced their own fiscal solvency rules. However, the compliance of the provinces with the fiscal rules remained limited. Hard budget constraints were complied with by only six provinces, expenditure limits by only six provinces, and debt-servicing rules by only ten out of sixteen provinces which had adopted these rules (see Figure 2.12). So, the adoption of Solvency Rule did not result in any substantial improvement in the debt position of the SNGs (see Figure 2.13).

The years 2001 and 2002 were marked by debt and currency crisis which again slowed down the economy. The SNGs were again forced to rely on borrowing to meet their expenditure requirements. However, the years immediately after the crisis saw the economy rebounding, creating a window of opportunity for reforms. The new Fiscal Responsibility Law was passed in 2004 which retained many of the measures of the 1999 law. The new law also set numerical expenditure limits and a 15 per cent limit of subnational debt service to its current revenues. In addition, the Federal Council of Fiscal Responsibility was also created to enforce the compliance of the new law .

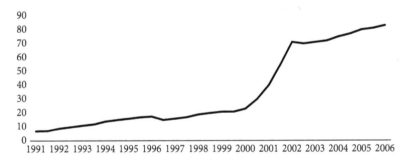

Figure 2.12 Provinces' debt (in billion pesos)
Source: Vulovic (2011)

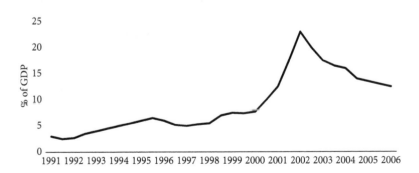

Figure 2.13 Provinces' debt in Argentina (% of GDP)
Source: for 1991–99: Rezk (2000); for 2000–06 Secretaria de Haicienda.

By 2010, almost all the provincial debt was restructured by the national government. The bailout reduced present value of debt by 53 per cent. The Argentine crisis highlighted the significance of implementing strong controls over SNG borrowing.

2.4.3 Subnational debt crisis in Mexico (1995)

In 1995, Mexico faced a similar situation in the aftermath of the tequila[2] crisis which led to credit expansion and a sharp increase in interest rates. The interest rates increased five-fold from 13.8 per cent to 74.8 per cent. This resulted in massive buildup of debt in SNGs. The accumulation of state debt rose by 62 per cent annually during 1988 to 1993 (Trillo et al., 2002). From 1993 to 1994, the debt grew by an additional 8 per cent in real terms mainly due to the increase in interest rates. By 1994, many states were highly indebted, the total debt representing 80 per cent of the total disposable income of the states. The States hardly had any income to service their debt obligations. Because of the centralization of the taxes, the states had limited capacity to raise additional revenues through taxes. With the interest rates soaring to 74.8 per cent in April 1995, the states debt continued to grow from Mex$27 mn in 1994 to Mex$71.6mn in 1998 (see Figure 2.14). The federal government had to provide a massive bailout of Mex$7bn in 1995 which continued till 1998, with a similar annual figure in real terms (Trillo et al., 2002). The bailout package reduced the debt of the SNGs to a large extent. However, this bailout in 1995 is one of the many bailouts which the Mexican national government was forced to give to SNGs from time to time. Such frequent bailouts created moral hazard problem by setting the expectation that the national government will bail out the SNGs even though they may follow irresponsible fiscal behaviour. In fact, central government bailouts in the past have largely contributed to the debt default by SNGs in Mexico (see Figure 2.14)

In exchange for the bailouts, the SNGs were asked to sign a letter of intent. The letter of intent required SNGs to commit to several fiscal control

---

[2] The Mexican debt crisis of 1994 is known as the tequila crisis in common parlance. The tequila crisis is also popularly known as the 'tequila effect'. It indicates the ripple effects that triggered economic crisis in Mexico and neighbouring countries in Latin America.

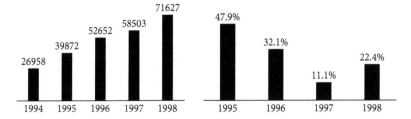

Figure 2.14 Debt stock of SNGs Total debt (Millions of Pesos), Growth rate (Mexico)

Source: Giugale, M., Trillo, F.H. and Oliveira, J.C. (2000)

measures. These measures included budget balancing (requiring the SNGs to reduce their current expenditure, increasing own revenues, and privatizing public sector enterprises), presenting financial statements in a uniform way, reducing debt ratios, and regulating debt limits/ceilings by introducing a law.

2.5   Conclusion

This chapter examined the reasons which led to debt crises in various countries both at national and subnational level. The recent experiences of debt crises in India's neighbourhood, that is, Sri Lanka and Pakistan, throw light on the importance of fiscal discipline. The Greek experience highlights the inherent contradictions of being in a monetary union without a fiscal union. SNGs often mask their fiscal issues within the monetary union. Portugal faced a debt crisis for similar reasons, exposing the system's inability to enforce the fiscal deficit limit set by the Maastricht Treaty. The discussion on debt crises at the national level was followed by a detailed discussion on SNG debt crises. The underlying factors for crises at the subnational level are more or less similar to those at the national level, such as poor fiscal management, limited controls on borrowing, erosion of revenue base, and borrowing at high interest rates. However, with regard to debt of SNGs, an additional issue is related to bailouts by the federal government which creates perverse incentives for them to borrow more. This is what happened in countries like Brazil, Argentina, and Mexico. Federal governments in these countries were forced to bail out the SNGs on many occasions, which not only affected the finances of the federal government but also encouraged the SNGs to borrow excessively from the market without worrying about insolvency.

3

Borrowing in a Decentralized Governance Structure

3.1 Context

In the previous chapter, we discussed debt crises in various countries both at the national and subnational levels. The crises at the subnational level naturally raise questions: why do subnational government (SNGs) borrow? What controls do federal or central government place on SNG borrowing? It is also essential to understand how central government policies affect state government debt and how excessive SNG debt poses risks to the central government's fiscal health.

3.2 Why Do SNGs Borrow?

In a decentralized governance structure, there is a federal or a central government at the national level and a state government (in case of India) or a subnational government (SNG) at the regional level. The revenue rights and expenditure responsibilities of SNGs vary greatly across countries. However, most SNGs have disproportionately higher expenditure responsibilities in comparison to their revenue rights. The gap in revenue necessary for discharging the expenditure responsibilities is usually corrected through transfer of resources, commonly termed as intergovernmental transfers, from the federal government to the SNGs. These intergovernmental transfers are sometimes not adequate to bridge this gap and the SNGs perforce have to borrow to meet their expenditure requirements. In addition, the capital expenditure that SNGs undertake also may be fully or partially funded through borrowing. It is interesting to note that by SNGs' borrowing, apart from being impacted by their

Debt Sustainability of Subnational Governments in India. Hari Krishna Dwivedi, Oxford University Press.

policies, are greatly influenced and determined by policies of the central government. We discuss these in the next section.

3.3 How Central Government Policies Affect SNG Debt

SNG borrowing is affected by the policies of central government as these impact the intergovernmental transfers and also alter the expenditure responsibilities of the SNGs.

Across the world, many central governments have in the past initiated debt consolidation plans that has also affected debt position of SNGs. The plans have cut down or, in some cases, frozen the transfers to the SNGs. Ireland reduced the transfers to SNGs by 15 per cent in 2009 and 18 per cent in 2010. France froze the transfers to SNGs from 2010 to 2013. Consolidation plans can also increase the expenditure responsibilities of the SNGs. Greece transferred many new responsibilities to the SNGs even though the transfers were not increased. In India, the rationalization of centrally sponsored schemes in 2016, increased the matching share of states in the schemes, putting pressure on state to provide additional resources for the continuation of the schemes. Further, the central government has introduced legislations such as the Right to Education Act (2009) and the National Food Security Act (2013) which increased the expenditure responsibilities of the SNGs. These consolidation plans which either reduce the transfers to the SNGs or increase the expenditure responsibilities of the SNGs create a situation where the SNGs have to resort to more borrowing to meet the increased resource requirements.

In most federal countries like India, the taxation powers are constitutionally delineated between the federal government and the SNGs. Some of the taxes fall under exclusive domain of the federal government and may be retained fully or shared with the SNGs. The federal government may follow policies which increases the central kitty at the cost of the share of taxes which is devolved to the SNGs. For instance, in India, the federal government has been imposing higher cess and surcharge (instead of tax increases) as constitutionally, it is not shared with the states.

Central government may also follow fiscal policies which can affect the inflation rate in the economy. For instance, an expansionary fiscal policy which stimulates aggregate demand may also cause inflation to rise beyond tolerance levels. In such a situation, the central bank may have to step in to control rising inflation by resorting to contractionary monetary policy. This may result in increases in interest rates which are likely to have a dual effect on SNG borrowing. First, this may reduce investment in the economy which may cause economic slow down (investment multiplier). A slowdown in the economy may result in a fall in the intergovernmental transfers from the centre due to a fall in central government revenues (buoyancy effect). Second, this may increase the debt-servicing cost for SNGs. Thus, a fall in total revenue (including transfers) coupled with increase in debt-servicing cost, may force SNGs to borrow excessively.

3.4 How Excessive SNG Borrowing Can Affect Central Government's Fiscal Position

Although borrowing is an important source of finance for SNGs, excessive or non-efficient levels of subnational borrowing can pose significant risks for central government. Some of these risks will now be discussed.

Rising risk premium on new borrowing: the cost of excessive and irresponsible borrowing by an SNG is borne not just by the SNG in question but has inter-jurisdictional externalities. The SNGs and federal government borrow mostly from the same market, and adverse market perception about one SNG can lead to higher yields on borrowing by other SNGs and the federal government.

Possibility of having to bail out SNGs: in the event of severe debt crisis at the SNG level, central government may have to agree to a bailout for the following reasons. First, national government is concerned about the welfare of the people in the specific province(s) experiencing financial difficulties. Second, by providing the bailout, it politically benefits the national government. Third, without a bailout, the rest of the country would be adversely affected as there will be questions raised about the creditworthiness of the federal government and other SNGs in the country.

Although a bailout is not guaranteed, some of the factors that increase the likelihood of a bailout are:

- **Population size of the subnational entity (too-big-to-fail hypothesis)**
  The larger the population of the subnational entity in question, the larger the impact of the debt crisis will be on the population within and outside the SNG in question.
- **Foreign or domestic creditor**
  Central government is more likely to bail out SNGs when the creditor in question is a foreign creditor, as a default by the SNG in the international capital markets can affect the country's creditworthiness globally. McKinnon (1997) argues that the Canadian federal government would be more likely to intervene in cases of major provincial default when compared to one in USA, as the provinces borrow heavily overseas in foreign currencies and because the contagion effect among foreign lenders could impair Canada's international credit standing.
- **Provision of key spending by SNG**
  Key spending includes education, social services, and health. When the SNG is responsible for more of these areas of key spending, there is a more serious effect on the life of the people of the SNG facing the debt crisis. This naturally puts greater pressure on central government to bail out the SNG in question.
- **Vertical imbalance of the SNG (too-weak-to-fail hypothesis)**
  Some states do not have the potential to raise internal resources and are dependent on transfers from central government. It is inevitable that central government will rescue such provinces when they are faced with financial distress. These states will find it difficult finding a way out of such crises through any meaningful reform of their own.
- **Political strength at the centre**
  Political pressure that SNGs can exert on central government is also linked to the likelihood of bailout by the central government.

Invoking explicit and implicit credit guarantees of central government extended to SNGs: In case of default by SNGs, the creditors who may have been issued guarantees by the central government may revoke such guarantees. This would result in significant liabilities for the central government.

In the case of loans that are on-lent by the central government to the SNGs, the liabilities of the SNG essentially would become the liability of the central government where the SNG cannot meet its debt servicing obligations.

Central government loans may have to be written off: The loans of central government to the SNGs may have to be written off or restructured in the case of a debt crisis in the SNG.

Central government transfers may have to be increased: There may be situations where SNG revenues decline drastically, expenditure skyrocket, or a combination of both, leading to a likelihood of default. In such a scenario, central government may have to increase either conditional or unconditional transfers or both.

Some examples of SNG debt affecting central government finances

There have been multiple occasions in the past where deterioration of SNG finances have affected the finances of the central government. Some of these are discussed below.

In Brazil, in 1997, the debt of subnational government was 40 per cent of the total debt . This affected the macroeconomic stabilization programme of the federal government (Cordes et al., 2014). The federal government was forced to provide a bailout package equivalent to 7 per cent of country's GDP which significantly affected the finances of the federal government.

In Mexico, between 1995 and 1998, after the tequila crisis, central government provided cash transfers which cost it an estimated 0.5 per cent of GDP (Cordes et al., 2014).

In Argentina, between 2001 and 2004, it is estimated that around US\$9.7bn (Cordes et al., 2014) to US\$12.1bn (Braun, 2006) was provided as a bailout package to SNGs by the federal government.

In India, during the second half of the 1990s and early 2000s, state finances deteriorated significantly. The state's debt rose to 32.8 per cent of GDP in 2003–04. The deterioration of state finances put severe pressure on central government finances. The combined deficit of the general government increased from 7.3 per cent of GDP in 1997–98 to about 9.3 per cent of GDP from 1998 to 2004 (Rangarajan & Prasad, 2013).

3.5 How Is Subnational Borrowing Controlled?

In the previous section, we examined how excessive borrowing by SNGs can affect the central government. In this section, we look at how SNG borrowing is regulated, as unregulated SNG borrowing can have serious consequences for the macroeconomic stability of the country. Regulation of SNG borrowing is particularly important for three reasons. The first is the common pool problem whereby the cost of fiscal indiscipline is not borne alone by the SNG in question, but travels across SNG boundaries. The second factor is that of a moral hazard that the SNGs face, when there is a history of bailouts by the central government. The third is the deficiency in the system of intergovernmental fiscal transfer (IGFT) in addressing large variations of capacity in SNGs' to provide public services. If the large variations go unaddressed, the SNGs with lower capacity may face pressure to run large deficits to meet the capacities of the better-equipped SNGs.

A study was undertaken for the period 1980–2008 to assess the effectiveness of subnational borrowing regulations on maintaining fiscal sustainability. It was observed that a well-designed regulation framework for SNG borrowing is very effective in preventing SNG insolvency (Vulovic, 2011).

Across the world, countries use a variety of methods to control SNG borrowing. We can categorize them as market discipline, cooperative control, rules-based control, administrative control, and prohibited borrowing.

Market discipline is the ability of the markets to prevent unsustainable borrowing through price mechanism. In other words, the market assesses the financial health of the borrowing entity and if it perceives that the fiscal health of the entity in question is poor, the loan is either refused or reduced and is given at a higher rate of interest. Sole reliance on market discipline may not always be ideal as market discipline works effectively only when certain conditions are fulfilled. These are: (1) capital markets must be free and open; (2) potential lenders must have available information about a borrower's outstanding debt and repayment capacity; (3) there should be no possibility of a bailout of lenders by the central government; (4) borrowers must have the ability to respond with adequate policies to the signals sent by the market (Lane, 1993).

Cooperative control refers to a system where indebtedness of SNGs is not dictated by central government but is arrived at through negotiation between the two tiers of government. Australia is a country that utilizes such an arrangement. Through a negotiated process, an agreement on the overall deficit targets and the guidelines for growth of main items of revenue and expenditure are arrived at. In Australia, the Loan Council enables this process. This system has the added advantage of providing more political accountability on the political establishment at the SNG level as they are party to the decision-making with respect to the borrowing limits of the state.

Rule-based approaches include having standing rules called fiscal rules on borrowing by the SNGs as stated in the constitution or in law. These fiscal rules can be broadly categorized into four groups, namely, budget balance rules (BBR), debt rules (DR), expenditure rules (ER), and revenue rules (RR). These rules are generally in the form of percentage ceilings or limits that aim to control public debt accumulation either directly or indirectly. BBR are also known as fiscal and revenue balance rules. BBR or fiscal balance rules place limits on the fiscal deficit to GDP ratio whereas revenue balance rules place limits on the revenue deficit to GDP ratio. Debt rules or DR place limits on government's debt-to-GDP ratio. The DR help the government to keep its borrowing under check and avoid unsustainable levels. ER place limits on government expenditure and are generally set in absolute or growth terms and sometimes as a percentage of GDP for a medium-term horizon. Lastly, the RR place ceilings or lower limits on revenues. The RR aim to enhance revenue collection or avoid high tax burden. The RR thus help government in reducing their dependency on borrowing to finance their expenditure by directly targeting government debt-to-GDP ratio.

Administrative control over subnational borrowing by central government may include placing limits on overall debt or annual borrowing of SNGs, review and authorization of individual borrowing operations, and centralization of borrowing (through on-lending).

Prohibited borrowing is the last and the most extreme control of SNG borrowing. Many countries place prohibition on overseas borrowing by SNGs. Some also place prohibition on domestic borrowing.

3.5.1   Country comparison: controls on SNG borrowing

In the following paragraphs, we examine how certain countries regulate borrowing by their SNGs.

To this end, most countries use a combination of the five methods discussed in the previous section. Very few countries use market discipline as the only method. Canada and previously Brazil were the countries using just market discipline as the instrument to keep SNG borrowing in check. Germany and Japan use some form of rules-based controls. Countries that employ administrative control on SNG borrowing include India, the United Kingdom, Argentina, Brazil, and Chile. Table 3.1 shows SNG borrowing controls in select countries.

There is no one single answer to which is the best form of controls for SNG borrowing. It depends on the country's existing fiscal architecture, maturity of financial markets, and level of political accountability at different levels of government. However, we observe that lately many countries are moving towards using administrative and rules-based controls as the dominant type of regulation. Sole reliance on market discipline as well as using the strictest form of regulation (i.e. prohibited borrowing) is not being favoured by countries, as shown in Figure 3.1.

3.6   Conclusion

The borrowing behaviour of SNGs is highly dependent on central government policies and actions. An improperly designed intergovernment fiscal transfer (IGFT) arrangement between central government and SNGs can cause the SNGs to borrow more than the optimal level. The central government may also increase the expenditure responsibilities of the SNGs without adequately increasing the revenue sources, or freeze the transfers as part of consolidation plans. These policies and actions result in a worsening of gap between the revenues and expenditure of the SNGs leaving them with no option other than to go for more borrowing.

Excessive SNG borrowing also entails risks for central government. Central government has to accept a higher interest rate on its borrowing as the effect of SNG debt default has inter-jurisdictional consequences. Central government may have to bail out an SNG to avoid default. This

Table 3.1 Country comparison of strictest (dominant) form of controls

Country	Market discipline		Cooperative control		Rules-based control		Administrative Control		Borrowing prohibited	
	Overseas	Domestic	Overseas	Domestic	Overseas	Domestic	Overseas	Domestic	Overseas	Domestic
Developed countries										
Australia			•	•						
Canada	•	•								
France	•	•								
Germany					•	•				
Japan								•	•	
Portugal	•	•								
United Kingdom							•	•		
United States					•	•				
Developing countries										
Argentina							•	•		
Brazil							•	•		
Chile							•	•		
China									•	•
India							•	•	•	
Mexico								•	•	

Source: IMF, Fiscal Federalism in Theory and Practice, 1997.

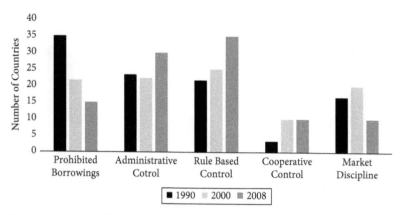

Figure 3.1 Controls on SNG borrowing-Dominant Control Mechanisms
Note: sample consists of 60 industrialized, developed, and transitioning countries.
Source: Martinez-Vazquez and Vulovic (2016).

causes a significant strain on central government finances. Another way in which central government may be affected is through invocation of any central government guarantees extended to SNGs.

Thus, the control of SNG borrowing is of crucial importance. The SNGs also face a moral hazard in their debt operations stemming from the common pool problem. There are various methods that the central government uses to control SNG debt. These include reliance on market discipline, cooperative controls, a rules-based approach, administrative control, and prohibited borrowing. More countries have moved towards using more administrative controls and a rules-based approach as the dominant method to control SNG borrowing.

In the next chapter, we look at the borrowing by SNGs in India—their sources, how the debt operations are conducted, and the various controls in India. We will also be looking at the Fiscal Responsibility and Budgetary Management Acts and rules in some detail and the various issues and challenges associated with them.

4

Subnational Government Borrowing in India

4.1 Context

In the previous chapter, the discussion centred around the fiscal controls across different countries on subnational government (SNG) borrowing. In this chapter, the focus is on understanding the debt operations in India at the subnational level and nature of fiscal controls at the subnational level. The efficacy of these controls to sufficiently prevent SNGs in India from becoming insolvent is also explained.

India follows a three-tier governance structure which comprises the union government, the state government, and the local government. The Constitution of India clearly demarcates the powers and responsibilities between the union government and the state government. Local governments were given constitutional recognition with the 73rd and 74th amendments to the Constitution. However, local governments have a relatively weak discretionary and decision-making power over revenues, expenditure, and debt management. Hence, our focus in this book is primarily on the sub-national state governments.

The subnational debt of all states is close to one-third of the national debt and 25 per cent of national GDP. This high debt highlights its importance in state governments' fiscal management and given its size, its importance for the fiscal stability of the country as a whole.

4.2 Why Do SNGs in India Borrow?

The state governments have disproportionate expenditure responsibilities when compared to their revenue rights. While the expenditure

Debt Sustainability of Subnational Governments in India. Hari Krishna Dwivedi, Oxford University Press.
© Hari Krishna Dwivedi 2024. DOI: 10.1093/oso/9780198903116.003.0004

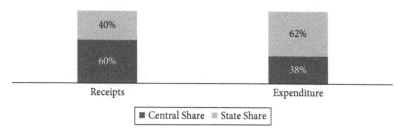

Figure 4.1 Share of receipts and expenditures by states and centre (2020–21)
Source: author's calculation based on data from RBI.

accounts for around 62 per cent of total government expenditure, their own revenue is only 40 per cent of total government revenues (Figure 4.1). The Constitution of India does recognize this imbalance, commonly referred to as vertical imbalance between the central government and states and provides for a mechanism of transfers from central government to state government. This mismatch in revenue-raising capacity and expenditure responsibilities is partly corrected through transfers from the central government and partly through borrowing by SNGs.

While it may be ideal for central government to cover the shortfall in revenue expenditure and revenue receipts of the states through transfers, it often is not the case. Hence, the states have to rely on borrowings not just for capital expenditure requirements but also for revenue expenditure requirements. As Ter-Minassian and Craig (1997) note, the growth of subnational public debt is frequently a symptom of an inappropriate design of intergovernmental fiscal relations in the country in question, involving, for example, large vertical or horizontal imbalances or a system of intergovernmental transfers lacking transparent criteria and conducive to ad hoc bargaining or *ex post* gap filling. This may indeed be the case in India. As Rao (2019), in his analysis of intergovernmental fiscal transfers, points out that the transfers based on the recommendations of the Finance Commission are unable to fully offset the revenue disabilities of certain states.

A temporary mismatch in cash position is another reason for borrowing by the state. At times, SNGs have to borrow due to lack of planning of expenditure that lead to temporary shortfall in the resources.

4.3 Sources of SNG Borrowing in India

Indian SNGs borrow from both internal and external sources. Internal sources include domestic market borrowing, loans from banks and financial institutions, special securities issued to the National Small Savings Fund (NSSF), loans from Centre and liabilities in public account (which includes small savings and provident funds, reserve funds, and deposits) (see Figure 4.2). Borrowing from small savings has been discontinued since 2016.

Borrowing from the market has been steadily increasing over the past decade and now constitutes about 80 to 90 per cent of the internal borrowing of SNGs in India. Market borrowing is government-raised market loans through the sale of government securities or bonds. State government securities are known as SDLs (state development loans). These SDLs are largely held by commercial banks, insurance companies, and mutual fund managers in the form of bonds. These SDLs (or bonds) are of different maturities ranging from five to generally ten, fifteen, or twenty years. Over the tenure of the SNGs, the state governments pay interest on them. This can be understood using a simple example of how the government pays interest on market borrowing. Suppose the government issues a bond worth ₹1,000 of a ten-year maturity, and the bond is purchased by an individual, bank, or mutual fund manager. The government is obligated to make interest payments to the bondholder half yearly or annually as the case may be, till the end of the loan term or at maturity. At closure of the loan term, the government has to pay back the entire principal to

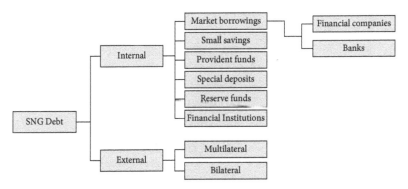

Figure 4.2 Sources of SNG borrowing

the bondholder as a bullet payment. Commercial banks, mutual fund companies, and insurance companies are the major bondholders of the government securities or SDLs.

Another source of SNG borrowing is loans from financial institutions like Life Insurance Corporation, General Insurance Corporation, National Bank for Agriculture and Rural Development (NABARD), State Bank of India, etc. SNGs also borrowed from NSSF until March 2016. NSSF was established within the Public Account of India in 1999. The fund pooled money from depositors under various small savings schemes (e.g. post office savings, social security schemes, Public Provident Fund). However, NSSF loans were costlier than market loans because they carried higher interest rates than market loans.

State governments also borrow from external sources. These include loans taken from donor agencies (e.g. World Bank, Asian Development Bank (ADB), Asian Infrastructure Investment Bank (AIIB), Kreditanstalt für Wiederaufbau (KfW), Japan International Cooperation Agency (JICA)etc.). These borrowing are in the form of EAP (externally aided projects) loans. The external borrowing are routed through the central government on a back-to-back basis, which means, the loans are passed to the states by the central governments on the same terms and conditions as agreed with the external agency. The repayment of such loans is subject to exchange rate fluctuations.

In addition to these borrowing options, state governments also get a ways and means advances (WMA) window from the Reserve Bank of India (RBI), through which they can borrow funds to meet temporary shortfall in their day-to-day cash flow. These advances have to be paid back to RBI within three months of disbursal. These advances carry a very low rate of interest.

There are situations when state governments have temporary shortfall in their daily cash flow which is over and above the WMA limit. In such situations, states can borrow from the RBI through an overdraft (OD) facility. The OD rate of interest is linked to the repurchasing option (repo) rate as notified by RBI from time to time.

Where a state government is left with a surplus instead of a deficit at the end of the day, the surplus balance is automatically invested in fourteen-day intermediate treasury bills on which the states earn interest income.

4.4 Who Manages SNG Borrowing in India?

The central bank of the country, the RBI, is the debt manager of the SNGs. Borrowing operations are governed by the Government Securities Act 2006 and its rules. However, RBI manages only the market borrowing component of the SNGs. The external borrowing of SNGs is managed by the central government since SNGs cannot borrow directly from abroad. As there is no specialized agency which looks after the borrowing of central government and SNGs in a holistic manner, various experts have argued for the establishment of an independent debt management agency to professionally manage and monitor the borrowing operations. Also, the scope of debt management by RBI is narrow at present as it only covers the market borrowing component. It does not include the management of public account liabilities, and contingent liabilities of the government. The suggestion is that an independent agency could be set up in the form of a debt management office (DMO) to manage both internal and external debt (including liabilities) of the SNGs in a holistic manner and advise the SNGs on minimizing the cost of raising and servicing public debt .

4.5 Controls on SNG Borrowing in India

In section 3.5, we looked at various mechanisms which certain countries have devised to control SNG borrowing. In this section, we will specifically examine the controls on SNG borrowing in India. In India, the dominant (strictest) control mechanism is that of administrative control. The central government controls how much the states can borrow as the states need to obtain permission from the central government when they have outstanding liabilities to the central government as per article 293(3) of the constitution of India. As all states are currently indebted to the central government, the prior approval of central government is a mandatory condition. In the case of borrowing from foreign sources, India follows a system of centralized borrowing with the centre on-lending the borrowing to the states.

In a limited manner, market discipline is also used as a control in India. The fact that states are increasingly reliant on open market borrowing has made this possible. In theory, this would mean that states which are perceived to be performing better fiscally will be able to obtain debt at a lower yield when compared to states that are not performing so well fiscally.

Lastly, rule based controls were implemented in India at the central and state government level through introduction of FRBM Act (2003). These fiscal rules imposes limits on the borrowing of SNGs. However, these controls are self-imposed by the SNGs and their effectiveness depends on the commitments of SNGs to adhere to fiscal targets. A comprehensive discussion on the implementation of the FRBM Act will follow in the subsequent section.

4.5.1   Introduction to the FRBMA (Fiscal Responsibility and Budgetary Management Act) regime

In response to the severe deterioration in the finances of central and state governments after 1997–98, the central government appointed a committee of the then Secretary of Economic Affairs Shri E. A. S. Sharma, to develop a plan to improve the country's finances. The Committee recommended the implementation of fiscal rule legislation, the FRBMA, to gradually move towards fiscal discipline.

The central government, in line with the recommendations of the Committee, enacted the FRBMA in 2003 and the FRBM rules in 2004. By 2010, all states in India implemented the FRBMA. The adoption of a rule-based framework with the objective of achieving macroeconomic stability and intergenerational equity, in line with the golden rule of fiscal policy, was a historical step. FRBMA comprises rules-based controls. FRBM rules at the central level and at state levels typically consists of a budget balance rule in the form of a ceiling on fiscal deficit which is recommended by the Finance Commission and a target for current (revenue) deficit. FRBM rules also typically have a debt rule which defines a target for debt stock.

The FRBM rule had prescribed a target of fiscal deficit of 3 per cent of GDP to be achieved by 31st March 2009, through an annual decline of fiscal deficit by 0.3 per cent of GDP until 2009. However, since its inception there have been a few amendments to the FRBMA.

Due to the global financial crisis in 2008, the central government suspended the fiscal targets which continued until 2013. The FRBMA was again resumed in 2013 with some revisions in the targets. The term 'effective revenue deficit' was introduced in the FRBMA. Effective revenue deficit was defined as the difference between revenue deficit and grants for the creation of capital assets. The target set was to eliminate effective revenue deficit by 2015 and the target for revenue deficit was raised to 2 per cent. FRBM rules were further amended in 2015, which modified the target date for compliance to 2018. FRBMA was again amended in 2018 (Comptroller and Auditor General (CAG), 2018b).The changes relating to SNGs included removal of the term 'effective revenue deficit' and the target for revenue deficit, achieving a fiscal deficit target of 3 per cent of gross state domestic product (GSDP) by 2021 with an annual reduction of 0.1 per cent and debt not to exceed 20 per cent of GDP by the end of 2024–25.

How was the fiscal deficit limit of 3 per cent of GDP determined?

The fiscal deficit limit of 3 per cent was determined based on a simple calculation. It was estimated that the economy will generate savings of around 10 per cent of GDP from the household sector and 2 percent of GDP from external borrowing (current account deficit) . This 12 per cent overall saving would be divided equally between the public and private sectors. This implies that the combined borrowing (fiscal deficit) of the centre and states would be 6 per cent and 6 per cent would be the investment of the private sector. This 6 per cent of the combined borrowing was divided between the centre and the states equally into 3 per cent each.
(FRBM Review Committee, 2017)

With the introduction of the FRBM regime, there has been observable improvements in the state's fiscal position. Barring a few years, the combined gross fiscal deficit of SNGs has been well below the target of 3 per cent of GSDP from FY 2006 up to the Covid-19 crisis in 2020. Also, their combined current (revenue) deficit was virtually eliminated by FY

2015. The trends in subnational debt over the years is covered in detail in Chapter 5.

While the question of whether the controls of SNG borrowing in India are adequate remains to be seen, we can nevertheless look at whether India uses the right control mechanism for SNG borrowing. As mentioned in section 3.5, most countries have moved towards administrative and rules-based controls. This gives credence to the view that the sweet spot of regulation of SNG borrowing lies somewhere between administrative controls and rules-based controls. With recent developments that strengthened the rules-based controls, India uses administrative controls as its dominant (strictest) form of SNG borrowing controls. As such, the Indian system is not too far from the sweet spot of SNG borrowing controls.

4.5.2   Issues and challenges in the FRBM regime

FRBM Act was introduced to instil responsible fiscal management in the central and state governments. However, there are several issues and challenges associated with its implementation. These are discussed below:-

4.5.2.1   Weak link between policy setting and budget implementation

Until FY 2013, when an amendment to the FRBMA at the central level mandated the preparation of a medium-term expenditure framework (MTEF), the link between policy setting and budget implementation was missing. This link is still missing in most states at the time of writing of this book. If all components of the fiscal framework are operating effectively and are well synchronized, an FPS (fiscal policy strategy) statement should be consistent with the overall path to fiscal consolidation and achieving the stated fiscal target in the legislation consistent with the budget (Appropriation Act), while allowing for fiscal breaks to be deployed intelligently on budget implementation (Akin et al., 2017) (see Figure 4.3).

4.5.2.2   Inadequate accountability mechanism for missed targets

Although by virtue of Article 293(3) of the Constitution of India, the borrowing by the SNGs does have a hard budget constraint, this may not remain the case for long. Two states are expected to be completely

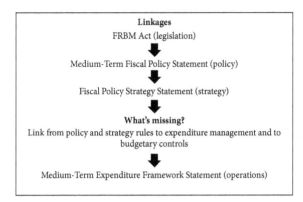

Figure 4.3 Links between policy and budget implementation
Source: Martinez-Vazquez and Vulovic (2016).

non-indebted to the central government and the rest are expected to follow suit by 2030. As this hard budget constraint ceases to exist for the state government, it becomes imperative to increase the penalties for breaching the ceiling. One suggested measure in this regard is having the debt ceiling legislated under Articles 292 and 293 of the Constitution. This would serve as a powerful enforcement tool.

4.5.2.3 Lack of an independent fiscal institution to monitor compliance

Despite the 13th, 14th, and 15th Finance Commissions having recommended for the establishment of an independent fiscal council to review and monitor the FRBM process, currently there has not been any move in this direction. Although the 2012 amendment of the FRBMA introduced the requirement of a periodic review of the implementation of the FRBMA by the CAG, this is a *post facto* review. The solution is continuous *ex ante* monitoring and assessment of the consistency of FRBM targets, and their implementation. The other functions of a fiscal council include conducting debt sustainability analysis, providing independent forecasts of variable such as GDP growth, tax buoyancy, forecasting commodity prices based on certain assumptions, and invoking escape clauses.

4.5.2.4 Lack of flexibility

By nature, a simple budget balance rule (BBR) often tends to be pro-cyclical in the fiscal policy stance. The problem with a pro-cyclical budget balance rule is that it can amplify economic volatility. During economic downturns, when businesses and households are already facing reduced incomes and financial stress, the government's decision to cut spending or increase taxes can worsen the economic situation. Similarly, during economic booms, when the private sector is already growing, the government's decision to increase spending can lead to overheating and potentially speculative bubbles. This is a serious limitation as it is antithetical to one of the goals of fiscal rules. The primary goal of fiscal rules is debt sustainability, with an additional secondary goal of macroeconomic stabilization. It is important to have fiscal rules that address both of these goals. Fiscal rules that place targets for deficits over an economic cycle, or place cyclically adjusted deficit targets gives policymakers room to undertake countercyclical fiscal policy to stabilize the economy in times of economic downturn.

4.6   Suggestions for Strengthening Fiscal Controls on SNG Borrowing in India

While India's fiscal controls on SNG borrowings have been strengthened through the introduction of fiscal rules in the form of FRBMA, there is scope for further improvement. In the subsequent sections, the author offers certain suggestions to improve the controls on SNG borrowings in India

4.6.1   Improving efficacy of market discipline

In principle, markets could exert disciplinary influence on SNGs. However, a number of preconditions are required for them to be effective, as explained earlier. For most countries, many of the preconditions are not met and therefore market discipline alone may not achieve the goal of enforcing fiscal discipline at the SNG level. Nevertheless, market discipline should be an element of the control mechanism for SNG borrowing. In India, we observe that the market does exert some disciplinary influence as the states which are traditionally regarded as poorer performers in terms of their fiscal management get their bonds issued at a higher rate when compared to better performers. This means they pay a price for their poorer fiscal performance. However, the yield spread observed in India is around fifty basis points which some may argue is too insufficient to enforce fiscal discipline. One of the ways to improve the efficacy of market discipline is to improve the information disclosure through more transparent annual financial statements and other statements that reliably captures all off-budget borrowings and other contingent liabilities. Further, steps to make the market for SDLs more free and open may be considered.

4.6.2 Cooperative arrangements

Cooperative arrangements is a system in which the SNG debt targets (and possibly investment priorities) are reached through negotiations between the SNG and the federal government. In this case, the incentive problem,—namely, how to make local politicians accountable,—is addressed through moral suasion and peer pressure (Ter-Minassian, 2007). It promotes a cooperative environment between the different tiers of government and raises the awareness of the SNG politicians to the macro-economic consequences of their budgetary actions. The National Loan Council in Australia, the High Finance Council in Belgium, and the Fiscal and Financial Policy Council in Spain are examples of this system. Such a model could find a place in India as well.

4.7 Conclusion

Since the consequences of reckless borrowing by an SNG is not necessarily limited to itself, there is an incentive problem for the SNGs. It is for this reason that SNG borrowing is controlled using a variety of methods ranging from reliance on the markets to impose discipline in the SNGs to a complete ban on borrowing. A landmark development in the control of SNG borrowing in India was the enactment of the state-level FRBM Acts (2002–10). The FRBMA places a ceiling on the debt stock (debt rule) and targets for fiscal deficit and revenue deficit (BBR). The FRBM regime has had a positive impact on the debt position of the states which will be elaborated in the next chapter. However, there remain challenges with the current FRBM regime such as the weak link between policy and implementation, inadequate accountability mechanism for dealing with missed targets, lack of independent fiscal institution to monitor compliance, and lack of flexibility. It is also a truism that fiscal rules such as FRBM are not a panacea to debt sustainability issues. It performs well when combined with other controls such as cooperative controls and market discipline.

5

Impact of FRBM on Development Expenditure under Capital Account of SNGs

5.1 Context

In the previous chapter, we discussed how and why subnational governments (SNGs) in India borrow. We also discussed the introduction of the FRBM in Indian states and some of the issues and challenges associated with the FRBM regime. In this chapter, we will examine in detail one of the major issues in the FRBM regime which is the lack of flexibility of fiscal controls and its impact on the development expenditure (DEVEX) of states. Before discussing this issue, let us examine how FRBM has contributed in bringing fiscal discipline to SNGs in India.

Following the introduction of the FRBM regime, SNGs witnessed the sharpest ever fiscal consolidation in India (FRBM Review Committee, 2017). There was a significant decline in debt liabilities of the state governments. Although there were other macro-fiscal factors driving fiscal consolidation in India during this period, that is, high economic growth and consequent increase in tax collections of both central and state governments, introduction of VAT, debt relief measures provided by Finance Commissions (FCs); nevertheless, the enactment of the FRBM Act (2003) played a critical role. It is also interesting to note that the states have been more successful than the central government in keeping their fiscal deficit within the target level of 3 per cent of GSDP. In case of states, there are only four years after 2004–05, that is 2009–10, 2015–16, 2016–17 and 2020–21 in which the aggregate fiscal deficit of states was higher than 3 per cent of GDP. In case of central government, there was initial improvement in the fiscal deficit which fell to 2.6 per cent of GDP in 2007–08 but

Debt Sustainability of Subnational Governments in India. Hari Krishna Dwivedi, Oxford University Press.
© Hari Krishna Dwivedi 2024. DOI: 10.1093/oso/9780198903116.003.0005

in all the other years, the fiscal deficit breached the target of 3 per cent of GDP.

However, it can be fairly concluded that the introduction of the FRBM and debt relief support provided by the centre, played a key role in ensuring the debt sustainability of SNGs in India during the period 2003–15. The introduction of fiscal targets through the FRBM Act resulted in augmentation of revenue, and rationalization of expenditure thereby limiting the debt of the state.

Notwithstanding the achievement of improved fiscal discipline due to the enactment of the FRBM Acts, it has been argued in multiple studies that stringent and uniform fiscal targets across the states without taking into consideration the revenue potential, development deficit, levels of poverty, geographical and socio-economic constraints of differing states, may constrain the development in states. In one of the studies of budget deficits in Organisation for Economic Co-operation and Development (OECD) countries, it was observed that governments are more likely to reduce Development Expenditure (DEVEX) for fiscal adjustments in the short run (Alesina & Perotti, 1995). Similarly, in India, the capital expenditure of the central government fell sharply from 23 per cent of total expenditure (TE) in 2004–05 to 10.2 per cent in 2008–09 (Ramu & Gayithri, 2017). This expenditure contraction was as a result of the impact of fiscal rules (Chakraborty & Dash, 2013; Sawhney, 2018). Rangarajan and Subbarao (2007) in their study highlighted that the achievement of the FRBM target is necessary, but not sufficient for sustaining and accelerating growth. Attention has to be paid not just to achievement of the targets in numerical terms, but also with respect to the quality of adjustment. Lalvani (2009) mentioned that although the legislation has lowered the deficit of the states, and FRBM targets have been broadly met, the composition of expenditure has been altered. These studies clearly show that achievement of fiscal targets is necessary, but that it is equally important to see that the DEVEX under capital account is not compromised to the extent that future growth and financial stability are affected negatively.

A one-size-fits-all policy for fixing fiscal targets may not be the most appropriate strategy for achieving fiscal discipline, given the wide divergence of states on socio-economic development and their revenue potential. Successive FCs have tried to factor in this diversity for the purpose of recommending a formula for the horizontal devolution of the shareable divisible pool of central taxes across the states. The FRBM Act does not prescribe different fiscal targets for different states. It is argued that mandating same level of fiscal targets for all states may not be the right approach, as states with low revenue potential and large development needs may be forced to curtail their DEVEX under capital account to achieve their targets. Although 14th and 15th FCs in their recommendations have supported to a certain extent states with very high revenue deficit in the form of revenue deficit grants.

There are counterarguments for fixing different fiscal targets for each state. First, fixing fiscal targets based on a state's socio-economic development and revenue potential would be contentious. Second, fixing higher fiscal targets for some states could entail moral hazard issues. On the one hand, it may encourage these states to be profligate in their spending and they may indulge in more populist policies; on the other hand, it would disincentivize states that follow prudent fiscal policies. Nevertheless, the impact of uniform fiscal targets on the state's ability to invest in its future should be investigated further.

5.2 Why DEVEX under Capital Account Matters?

The role of public expenditure is critical in the economic growth and development of a country. Increase in spending stimulates aggregate demand, which, in turn, increases national output through the mechanism of expenditure multiplier (Mondal and Maitra, 2020). Public expenditure is primarily of two types: developmental and non-developmental. The Reserve Bank of India (RBI, 2023) defines DEVEX as expenditure on social services and economic services (both revenue account and capital account). Non-DEVEX includes expenditure on general services and other services. It normally pertains to expenditure on administrative services, law and order, etc. DEVEX has a more direct impact on the socio-economic well-being of the populace as it includes expenditure on social amenities like education, medical, public health, a combined category of labour welfare, housing, and other social welfare schemes; and expenditure which directly or indirectly promotes economic activity.

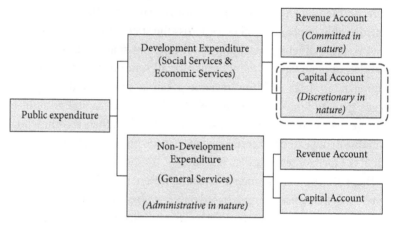

Figure 5.1 Composition of SNG public expenditure

It is also common knowledge that capital expenditure is critical to en-sure that the future is brighter than today. Therefore, DEVEX under cap-ital account is particularly important to improve the future well-being of the people. DEVEX under capital account is also mostly discretionary, thus dependent on the fiscal space of the government. Since expenditure under this head is discretionary in nature (see Figure 5.1), fiscal targets and resource constraints lead to fluctuations in the growth rate of such expenditure.

In order to see whether FRBM has constrained DEVEX of the states, the effect of fiscal consolidation only on DEVEX under capital account has been examined.

Figure 5.2 presents the annual growth in DEVEX under capital ac-count. Barring 2003–04, when the capital expenditure peaked at 65 per cent,[1] in good years the capital expenditure hovered around 20 to 25 per cent, whereas in bad years it fluctuated around 2 to 8 per cent. Thus, DEVEX under capital account has been highly volatile and largely de-pendent on the fiscal space available to governments. This constraint is particularly felt in years of low economic growth where FRBM Act's lack

---

[1] The fiscal year 2003–04, saw a sharp increase in DEVEX, due to the One-Time Settlement Scheme for dues of the state electricity boards (SEBs) and power bonds issued by twenty-six state governments to the Central Public Sector Units in September 2003 (with retrospective date of 1 October 2001) amounting to ₹28,984 cr. (as per RBI records).

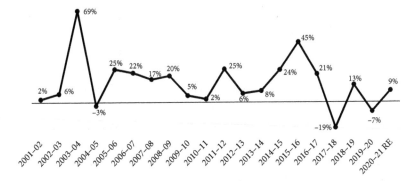

Figure 5.2 Growth in DEVEX under capital account for all GCS
Source: RBI ([state finances] various years: 2002–17) .

of flexibility will force the states from undertaking countercyclical fiscal policies. This has been discussed further in section 4.5.2).

5.3 Has the FRBM Regime Constrained States' DEVEX under Capital Account?

Now that we have seen that DEVEX under capital account of states are typically quite volatile, let us examine whether the DEVEX under capital account has actually been constrained as a result of the stringent targets of the FRBM Acts.

DEVEX under capital account and the fiscal deficit of the General Category States (GCS) have been examined over fifteen years starting from FY 2001. This period has been divided into three phases with each phase coinciding with an FC's award period, starting from the 11th FC. Phase 1 is from 2000–01 to 2004–05 (11th FC period); Phase 2 is from 2005–06 to 2009–10 (12th FC period); Phase 3 covers the period from 2010–11 to 2014–15 (13th FC). Telangana state has not been considered since relevant data is available only from 2014–15 onwards. The launch of Ujjawal Discom Assurance Yojana (UDAY) in 2015 has purportedly increased the average fiscal deficit, expenditure on economic services and outstanding liability of the participating states (RBI, 2016-2019). Hence, the post-UDAY period has not been considered for the analysis.

To understand the effect of the introduction of fiscal targets on DEVEX under capital account of SNGs over the three phases mentioned earlier, scatterplots of the states' average fiscal deficit and DEVEX under capital account (both as percentages of GSDP) were made for each of the three phases. The benchmark for fiscal deficit has been considered as the fiscal deficit target set by the respective FCs. There are no declared benchmark norms for DEVEX under capital account to GSDP ratio, thus the periodic GCS average has been considered.

The states were marked as compliant or non-compliant based on the comparison of the DEVEX under capital account and fiscal deficit to GSDP for all GCS with the decided benchmarks for each phase and the scatterplots were divided into four quadrants as shown in Figure 5.3. The states which comply with FC recommendations on fiscal deficit but are below GCS average for DEVEX under capital account to GSDP ratio, in spite of the fiscal space available, were further analysed. The shortfall in DEVEX under capital account-to-GSDP ratio for these states as against the GCS average has been calculated and added to the net borrowing of the state. The recalculated fiscal deficit-to-GSDP ratio has been compared to the fiscal deficit target of 3 per cent as recommended by the 12th and 13th FCs. If the recalculated fiscal deficit-to-GSDP ratio is more than the fiscal target of 3 per cent, it is inferred that the fiscal targets proved to be binding on the states' DEVEX.

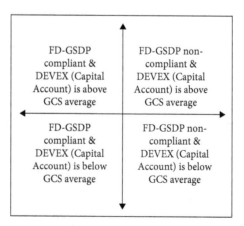

Figure 5.3 Quadrant diagram for state comparison

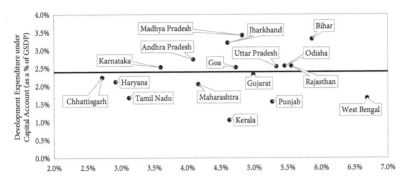

Figure 5.4 Fiscal deficit-to-GSDP ratio compliance vs DEVEX under capital account-to-GSDP ratio (Phase 1)

Source: RBI ([state finances] various years: 2002–07).

5.3.1 Key observations

A phase-wise analysis of DEVEX under capital account and the fiscal deficit for the GCS is set out below.

5.3.1.1 Phase 1 (2000–2001 to 2004–2005)

Figure 5.4 shows the fiscal deficit-to-GSDP ratio and the DEVEX under capital account-to-GSDP ratio of GCS in Phase 1. Since there was no fiscal deficit target during this phase, the analysis is based on the states' DEVEX under capital account. It can be seen that eight states among the seventeen GCS are below the assumed benchmark at 2.4 per cent (which is the GCS average for the concerned period). As the first fiscal target recommendations were made in the 12th FC report for the period 2005–06 to 2009–10, no fiscal deficit targets were assumed for this year.

From 2000 to 2005, only certain states like Karnataka (2002), Kerala (2003), Punjab (2003), Tamil Nadu (2003), and Uttar Pradesh (2004) had passed their FRBM Acts. Major fiscal consolidation initiatives across states started only in Phase 2, i.e. after 2005–06. During Phase 1, some states like West Bengal (WB), Punjab, and Kerala were running a very high revenue deficit which occluded a considerable part of borrowing to finance the deficit on revenue account.

Bihar and WB were the two states which had the highest fiscal deficit-to-GSDP ratio during this phase. WB had the highest fiscal and revenue

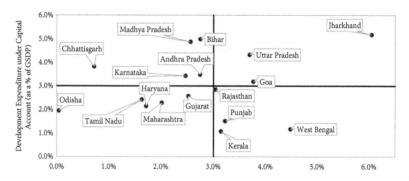

Figure 5.5 Fiscal deficit-to-GSDP ratio compliance v/s DEVEX under capital account-to-GSDP ratio (Phase 2)
Source: RBI ([state finances] various years: 2008–12) .

deficit leaving very little scope for DEVEX. On the other hand, Bihar had the second highest fiscal deficit and a moderate revenue deficit thus providing fiscal space for a high DEVEX.

5.3.1.2 Phase 2 (2005–2006 to 2009–2010)

In the second phase, as seen in Figure 5.5, Maharashtra, Haryana, Gujarat, Odisha, and Tamil Nadu had met the fiscal deficit target but failed to undertake DEVEX under capital account above the GCS average. In this phase, all GCS, except Haryana, registered a negative growth rate in DEVEX under capital account. After the Electricity Act of 2003, Jharkhand formed its own regulatory commission, the Jharkhand State Electricity Regulatory Commission in 2004, which resulted in an increase of 128 per cent in loans and advances to the power sector. The high loans and advances in economic services led to both high DEVEX under capital account and high fiscal deficit.

On the other hand, the finances of WB were still stressed with extremely high committed expenditure, comprising on average 70 per cent of revenue expenditure during the period. This continued to constrain the fiscal space for any significant increase in DEVEX under capital account. Interestingly, during the same period, Odisha had contracted its revenue and capital expenditure to lower the deficit of the state and maintain DEVEX under capital account-to-GSDP ratio at around 2 per cent only although it had the fiscal space to enhance it.

Figure 5.6 highlights fiscal deficit patterns of the states that failed both the original fiscal deficit target (of 3 per cent of GSDP) and DEVEX under capital account benchmark (GCS average of 3 per cent) in Phase 2. It is further seen from Figure 5.7 that if these four states undertook additional DEVEX under capital account up to the GCS average for the period, the fiscal deficit would have further gone up for Kerala, Punjab, and Rajasthan under recalculated fiscal deficit figures during the period. For example, while Punjab had a fiscal deficit-to-GSDP ratio of 3.2 per cent during Phase 2, had Punjab undertaken DEVEX under capital account up to the GCS average, the projected ratio could have been as high

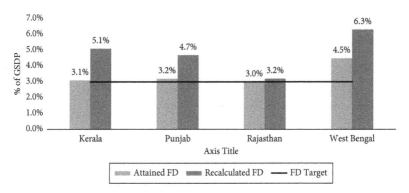

Figure 5.6 Phase 2 calculated fiscal deficit-to-GSDP v/s FC target of states that failed FC targets
Source: RBI ([state finances] various years: 2008–12).

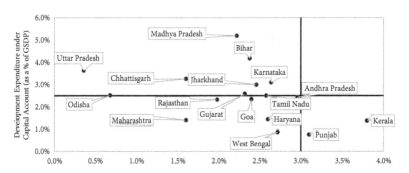

Figure 5.7 Fiscal deficit-to-GSDP ratio compliance v/s DEVEX under capital account-to-GSDP ratio (Phase 3)
Source: RBI ([state finances] various years: 2013–17).

as 4.7 per cent. Thus, it is clear that stringent fiscal targets had constrained states ability to make discretionary expenditure.

5.3.1.3 Phase 3 (2010–2011 to 2014–2015)

In Phase 3, among those states that failed to exceed the GCS average (of 2.5 per cent of GSDP) for DEVEX under capital account but met the original fiscal deficit target (of 3 per cent of GSDP), only WB and Rajasthan registered a considerably high average year-on-year growth rate of 28 per cent and 24 per cent, respectively on DEVEX under capital account.

During this phase, Kerala with the highest fiscal deficit-to-GSDP ratio and Madhya Pradesh with the highest DEVEX under capital account-to-GSDP ratio are at two extremes. During the period, Kerala was burdened with a very high revenue deficit, and consequent increase in the fiscal deficit restricted its DEVEX under capital account. On the other hand, during the same period Madhya Pradesh had a high revenue surplus of 2.1 per cent of GSDP thus enabling the state to undertake higher DEVEX under capital account and maintaining the fiscal deficit within FRBM limits.

Figure 5.8 highlights those states that met the original fiscal deficit target of 3 per cent of GSDP but failed the DEVEX under capital account benchmark of 2.5 per cent of GSDP. The DEVEX under capital account of these states is compared with the GCS average. The difference is added to the fiscal deficit of the states with lower than average DEVEX under

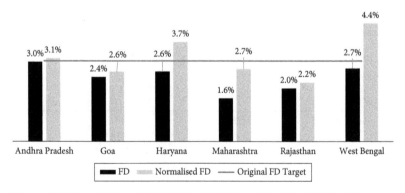

Figure 5.8 Phase 3 Actual fiscal deficit v/s Normalised fiscal deficit (states meeting original 3% target)

Source: RBI ([state finances] various years: 2013–17).

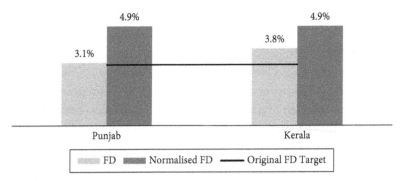

Figure 5.9 Phase 3 Actual fiscal deficit v/s Normalised fiscal deficit (states not meeting original 3% target)
Source: RBI ([state finances] various years: 2013–17).

capital account to arrive at their normalized fiscal deficit. This would have been their fiscal deficit had these states been investing in DEVEX as per the GCS average. The normalised fiscal deficit of these states do not meet the original fiscal deficit target of 3 per cent (except Goa, Maharashtra, and Rajasthan) as shown in normalised fiscal deficit to GSDP figures in Figure 5.9. In Phase 3, Andhra Pradesh, Haryana, and WB had spent less on DEVEX under capital account in order to meet the fiscal targets.

It can also be seen that states like Punjab and Kerala had failed in achieving the original fiscal deficit target along with the DEVEX benchmark targets. As evident from normalised fiscal deficit-to-GSDP ratio, both states would also have failed the original fiscal deficit target by a large margin had they undertaken DEVEX under capital account up to the GCS average level. Punjab's fiscal deficit-to-GSDP ratio could have been as high as 4.9 per cent had it undertaken DEVEX under capital account up to the GCS average for the period.

5.4 Conclusion

While it is certainly important to have a framework for fiscal responsibility at the state level like the FRBM regime, it is nevertheless crucial to understand what its effect is on the socio-economic health of the populace measured by the DEVEX under capital account that the government can make. Previous literature has analysed the impact of fiscal rules on capital account and the impact on DEVEX independently. However, DEVEX under capital account has a more direct impact on the well-being of the population, and is an investment for a better tomorrow. The analysis of fiscal targets as per the FRBM Act and DEVEX of states shows that for a fifteen-year period (starting from 2000–01) various states had to cut back their DEVEX under capital account in order to achieve fiscal targets mandated by the FRBM Acts.

6

Debt Situation of SNGs in India

Historical Trends

6.1 Context

Previously, we discussed the impact of the introduction of FRBM Act
(2003) on the development expenditure (DEVEX) of states. In this
chapter, we look at how much the subnational governments (SNGs) have
borrowed over the years and the manner in which the debt position of
states in India has evolved from the 1980s up to the early 2020s.

Interestingly, in the first three decades following independence, the
fiscal position of state governments in India like central government was
stable in terms of risks that arise from exposure to debt as the revenue
account was never allowed to be in deficit until 1979. During this period, India's fiscal policy can be termed 'conservative' as the deficits were
kept under control. It is only from the 1980s that fiscal indicators started
showing signs of stress. The reasons for increased fiscal stress and growing
debt during this period are detailed in the sections that follow, along with
trends in state governments' debt in India. Debt position here refers to all
outstanding debt, including government liabilities on public funds.

6.2 Trends in the Debt Position of SNGs in India

In India, different state governments under the Indian Constitution have
clearly delineated powers of taxation and development responsibilities.
They are empowered to raise capital through borrowing. We have discussed that the fiscal condition including the debt of SNGs greatly impacts the debt situation of the country and its overall macroeconomic
stability. Any debt crisis or debt-stressed situation in SNGs as a whole

Debt Sustainability of Subnational Governments in India. Hari Krishna Dwivedi, Oxford University Press.
© Hari Krishna Dwivedi 2024. DOI: 10.1093/oso/9780198903116.003.0006

or in a group of SNGs will severely affect the financial stability of the country.

An RBI study entitled *Subnational Government Debt Sustainability in India: An Empirical Analysis* shows that although SNGs in India account for around one-third of all receipts of the government, they collectively spend more than three-quarters of all expenditure on social services and greater than half of all spending on economic services (Misra et al., 2020). The ability of the state governments to spend on DEVEX and welfare schemes is determined by their fiscal position. If the fiscal position of SNGs is poor, then the SNGs will not be able to spend on revenue-generating capital assets which in turn will hamper the growth of economy and vice versa. Therefore, it becomes very important to examine the historical debt position of SNGs in India and how they have managed their debt.

The debt and deficit indicators of SNGs follow a similar trajectory as that of the national government during the period that we are covering in the book (1980s–2020s). The trend in debt position of SNGs in India can be divided into three phases. Phase I is the period of rising debt from 1982–83 to 2002–03, Phase II is the period of falling debt from 2003–04 to 2014–15, and Phase III is another period of rising debt-to-GDP ratio from 2015–16 to 2020–21. These three phases are discussed sequentially.

6.2.1 Phase I (1982–2003)

From 1982 to 2003, the fiscal health of the states continuously deteriorated. The debt-to-GSDP ratio of states taken together increased from about 18 per cent in 1980–81 to about 32.6 per cent in 2002–03 (see Figure 6.1). The sharp increase in debt-to-GDP ratio of the state governments was due to reasons similar to that of the central government. In 1987–88, the country was faced with drought and floods in different parts. This not only affected the revenues but also imposed an extra financial burden on the states from relief and rehabilitation work. The implementation of a revised pay structure in some states in the 1980s also resulted in increase in expenditure on salaries and pensions. The resultant gap between revenues and expenditure increased state governments' borrowing. Due to increased borrowing by the states and the centre, the interest rates went

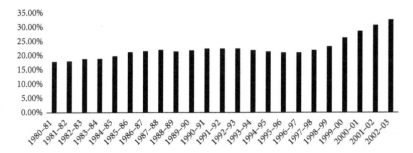

Figure 6.1 Phase I—Period of rising debt (1982–83 to 2002–03) (SNGs)
Source: author's calculation based on RBI ([state finances] various years).

up which further increased the debt-servicing obligations. The coexistence of both revenue and fiscal deficit during the second half of the 1980s implied that substantial borrowing was used to finance revenue expenditure. This affected the outlay of the states on capital projects which further hampered the development prospects of the states. The high levels of revenue and fiscal deficits of the states worsened the balance-of-payment (BoP) crisis of 1991 in India.

Although, the debt position of the states improved from 1992 to 1996, due to macroeconomic and structural reforms undertaken by the central government, the improvement was short-lived and could not be sustained. The period from 1998 to 2003 was the worst period for state finances. State deficits reached record levels with average revenue deficit climbing to 2.5 per cent of GSDP and average fiscal deficit to more than 4 per cent of GSDP (see Figure 6.2). Also, the average debt-to-GSDP ratio of states increased during this period from about 21 per cent in 1996–97 to 32.6 per cent in 2003.

There were several reasons for the precarious condition of state finances during this time. One of the reasons was the increased burden of additional expenditure liabilities on state governments due to the implementation of the Fifth Pay Commission's recommendations during the second half of the 1990s. The implementation of the pay commission resulted in sharp rise in salaries and pensions expenditure by about 60 per cent over next three years. In addition, poor performance of public sector undertakings (PSUs) had a major bearing on the fiscal health of the states (RBI, 2012). Also, this period saw a sharp decline in central transfers to states due to reduced collection of revenues by the central government. The central transfers to the states declined from 32.7 per cent of total receipts of the centre in 1996–97 to 15.8 per cent in 2004–05. These factors resulted in high revenue and fiscal deficit of states which forced state governments to accumulate debt at high interest rates. 'The cost of loans as measured by weighted average of interest rates on SDLs was in the range of 12–14 per cent over 1995–96 to 1999–2000' (Raju, 2009,p.3). Due to increased fiscal stress, SNGs extended guarantees to state PSUs leading to an increase in outstanding guarantees of the SNGs (see Figure 6.3). The increase in outstanding guarantees during this period further added to the rising debt of the states.

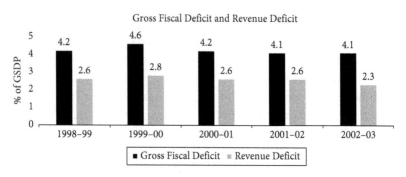

Figure 6.2 Gross Fiscal Deficit and revenue deficit as % of GSDP
Source: RBI ([state finances] various years).

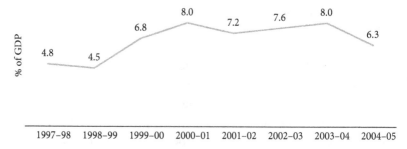

Figure 6.3 Outstanding guarantees as % of GDP (SNGs)
Source: RBI ([state finances] various years).

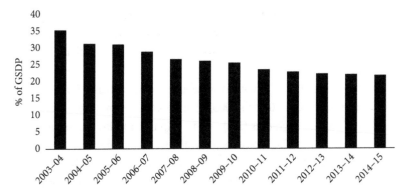

Figure 6.4 Phase II—Period of falling debt (2003–4 to 2014–15) (SNGs)
Source: author's calculation based on RBI ([state finances] various years).

6.2.2 Phase II (2003–2015)

From 2003 to 2015, the fiscal health of the states improved considerably. This phase saw a marked improvement in aggregate debt-to-GSDP ratio of states from 35.4 per cent in 2003–04 to 21.7 per cent in 2014–15 (see Figure 6.4). The steep decline in debt-to-GSDP ratio was largely due to the enactment of the FRBM Act, expenditure rationalization measures adopted by state governments and implementation of VAT in 2005 helped states to augment their revenues. Apart from this, high economic growth and recommendations of the FC for debt consolidation also helped the states in a major way. The 12th FC (2005–10) recommended a debt write-off scheme which was linked to the reduction of revenue deficit by the states. However, the benefit of the scheme was conditional on states adopting a rule-based adherence to fiscal limits through legislation. The two-fold strategy for fiscal consolidation, called Debt Consolidation and Relief Facility (DCRF), as per the recommendations of the FC was: (1) consolidation and rescheduling of all central loans contracted up to 31 March 2004, and outstanding as at 31 March 2005, for a fresh term of twenty years at a reduced interest rate of 7.5 per cent; (2) debt waiver to states based on fiscal performance of states which was linked to the reduction of revenue deficits and control of fiscal deficit. The 13th FC (2010–15) further continued with the debt consolidation. It allowed the consolidation of National Small Savings Fund (NSSF) loans contracted until 2006–07 at 9 per cent interest in place of 10.5

per cent or 9.5 per cent and recommended waiver of central government loans administered by ministries other than the Ministry of Finance. It also extended the DCRF of central loans and reset the interest chargeable on such loans to 7.5 per cent.

The centre had also launched a debt-swapping scheme (DSS) which was operational from 2003 to 2005, to support states in tackling the huge burden of interest payments (IPs) and to help them in fiscal consolidation. The scheme covered high-cost loans which were outstanding with interest rate of 13 per cent and above (Sucharita & Sethi, 2011). It enabled states to benefit from the low-interest regime, to prepay high-interest loans given by the centre by swapping with the low-interest-bearing small savings and open market loans. These measures significantly reduced the burden of the states on account of interest payment (IP). The ratio of IPs to revenue expenditure and the state's own tax revenue (SOTR) fell significantly during this period.

The IPs as a percentage of revenue expenditure of all states declined from 22 per cent in 2003–04 to 13 per cent in 2014–15. Further, IPs of all the states as a percentage of SOTR also declined from 50 per cent in 2003–04 to 24 per cent in 2014–15 (see Figure 6.5). This improvement reflects the combined impact of a reversal in the interest rate cycle and central government policy initiatives, namely, debt swap scheme and DCRF.

With the implementation of the FRBM Act, on the one hand, and debt and interest relief measures, on the other, there was also a change in the composition of borrowing of states. With regard to the composition of debt, the contribution of NSSF decreased while market loans increased. In this context, it may be noted that the Committee headed by Shyamala Gopinath (former Deputy Governor of RBI) on Comprehensive Review of National Small Savings Fund (2011) had recommended reducing the

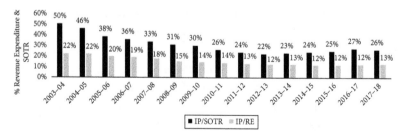

Figure 6.5 Interest payments of all states (as % of revenue expenditure and SOTRs)
Source: author's calculation based on RBI ([state finances] various years).

share of state governments in net collections of small savings under the NSSF from 80 to 50 per cent so as to reduce the burden on the states as the interest rates on borrowing from the NSSF was higher than market rates (see Figure 6.6). From 2016 to 2017, NSSF borrowing has been completely discontinued for all states except four.

The impact of central government policies, efforts of state governments and recommendations of the FCs is also reflected in the declining effective interest rate on state borrowing. Between 2003–04 and 2014–15, while the indebtedness of the states grew at a compound annual growth rate (CAGR) of 12.32 per cent, IPs saw a CAGR of only 10.76 per cent. The effective rate of interest on state borrowing also declined from 10.2 per cent in 2003–04 to 7.7 per cent in 2014–15. The decline in the effective interest rate between 2003–04 and 2014–15 is shown in Figure 6.7.

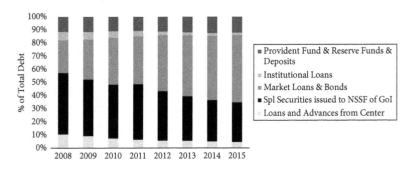

Figure 6.6 Change in composition of SNG borrowing
Source: RBI ([state finances] various years).

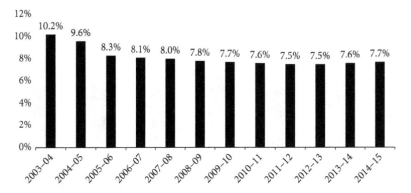

Figure 6.7 Effective interest rates of all states (2004-2015)
Source: RBI ([state finances] various years).

6.2.3 Phase III (2015–2021)

Covid-19 period

The fall in debt-to-GSDP ratio of the states could not be sustained beyond 2014–15. It increased from 23.7 per cent in 2015–16 to 31.1 per cent in 2020–21 (see Figure 6.8). This was for multiple reasons. First, with the introduction of Ujjwal DISCOM Assurance Yojana (UDAY), there was a rapid increase in states' debt and fiscal deficit. The scheme was launched in 2015 to support state power distribution companies (DISCOMs) which were reeling under huge financial stress. They had accumulated huge losses of approximately ₹3.8 lakh Crore and had an outstanding debt of approximately ₹4.3 lakh crore (as of March 2015) (PRS, 2019). Under the UDAY scheme, most of the state governments, barring a few, absorbed 75 per cent of DISCOM debt as on September 2015 over two years—50 per cent in 2015–16 and 25 per cent in 2016–17 and the rest of the debt was to be issued by DISCOMS in the form of bonds. While UDAY reduced the debt stock problem of the DISCOMs, the large interest outgo was merely transferred from the DISCOMs to the state governments. The increased debt and IPs by the states resulted in an increase in revenue deficit. The fiscal deficit of states taken together exceeded the FRBM target of 3.0 per cent. With UDAY, the fiscal deficit of all states was 0.7 per cent of GDP higher in 2015–16 and 0.8 higher per cent in 2016–17 as compared to states' fiscal deficit without UDAY (15th FC, 2020).

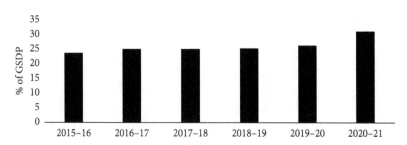

Figure 6.8 Phase III—Period of rising debt (2015–16 to 2020–21) (SNGs)
Source: author's calculation based on RBI ([state finances] various years).

Case study 1—Impact of UDAY on the fiscal position of Rajasthan

Rajasthan was one of the states that participated in the UDAY scheme through a tripartite agreement between the central government, the state government, and the respective DISCOMs. The state took over 75 per cent of the DISCOM debt in 2015–16 and 2016–17 amounting to ₹62,414 crores. Against this borrowing, the state government issued bonds (SDLs) with maturity of ten to fifteen years. The borrowing from the UDAY scheme increased the fiscal deficit of the state from just over 3 per cent in 2014–15 to 9.3 per cent in 2015–16 and 6.1 per cent in 2016–17. The revenue deficit of the state increased from 0.5 per cent in 2014–15 to about 2.4 per cent in 2016–17 and 2.2 per cent in 2017–18 due to an increase in IPs on account of taking debt. The resultant outstanding debt-to-GSDP ratio of the state government shot from 24 per cent in 2014–15 to over 33 per cent in 2016–17 (see Figure 6.9). The state missed the debt ceiling of 25 per cent as mandated by the 14th FC and has made the task of achieving target of 20 per cent as recommended by the FRBM review committee for 2025 more difficult. This scheme has disturbed the fiscal balance of the state and it will continue to strain state finances in future due to increased debt-servicing costs .

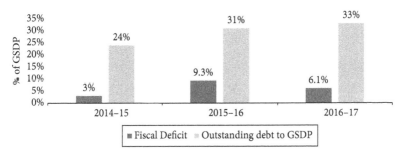

Figure 6.9 Worsening debt situation of Rajasthan post UDAY
Source: author's calculation based on RBI ([state finances] various years).

Case study 2—Impact of UDAY on the fiscal position of Punjab

Punjab joined the UDAY scheme in March 2016. As per the report of the Institute of Economic Growth (IEG), Delhi, the total outstanding debt of Punjab State Power Corporation Limited (PSPCL) was ₹20,837.68 crore on 30 September 2015. Out of this, the state of Punjab had taken over ₹15,628.26 crore (75 per cent of total debt on 30 September 2015) in two years, meaning 50 per cent of the outstanding debt (₹10,418.84 crore) in 2015–16 and 25 per cent of the outstanding debt (₹5,209.42 crore) in 2016–17 (IEG, 2018). Due to the absorption of DISCOM debt the fiscal position of the state deteriorated significantly. The fiscal deficit of the state increased from 2.9 per cent of GSDP in 2014–15 to 4.4 per cent in 2015–16 and then to 12.3 per cent of GSDP in 2016–17. In 2016–17, the fiscal deficit of Punjab was the highest among all the states and that too by a very high margin. The second highest fiscal deficit in 2016–17 was that of Rajasthan (6.1 percent of GSDP), which is more than six percentage points lower than Punjab. As a result, outstanding debt-to-GSDP ratio of the state government shot from 32 per cent in 2014–15 to over 43 per cent in 2016–17 (See Figure 6.10).

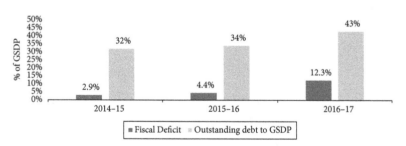

Figure 6.10 Worsening debt situation of Punjab post UDAY
Source: author's calculation based on RBI ([state finances] various years).

Second, the economic slowdown also contributed to rising debt-to-GDP ratio of the states. Since 2016–17, the growth rate of the economy decelerated, falling well below 4 per cent. A slowdown in the economy, in turn negatively affected the revenue collection, thus leading to divergence in revenue and expenditure.

The final blow to the rising debt-to-GDP ratio of the states was the pandemic which hit the country in 2020, leading to a situation of degrowth of 7.3 per cent. Apart from the decline in revenue collection, the expenditure commitments increased owing to support extended through schemes to boost the economy both on the demand and supply side. The governments had to address issues at multiple levels, assuring basic needs of people through cash transfers and food support to vulnerable sections of the society, address supply bottlenecks to control inflation through interest subsidy to micro, small, and medium enterprises, etc. This worsened the fiscal position of the states. The fiscal deficit of the states reached an all-time high since 2003–04 at 4.7 per cent. The revenue deficit in 2020–21 expanded to 2 per cent of GSDP which was 'zero per cent' in 2018–19. The central government provided additional fiscal space to the states by increasing the borrowing limits by an additional 1 per cent of GSDP (out of which 0.5 per cent earmarked for capital expenditure). In 2021, the 15th FC provided a revised fiscal consolidation roadmap for states. The revised roadmap requires states to gradually reduce their fiscal deficit limit back to 3 per cent of GSDP by 2025–26.

Inflation is on the rise, and with increased inflation, the governments run the risk of increasing borrowing cost. The weighted average yield of state government securities has increased from 6.55 per cent in 2020–21 to more than 7.5 per cent at the end of September 2022. With GST compensation ending in July 2022, the debt-to-GSDP ratio of the states is expected to go up. Until July 2022, the centre had compensated all states whose revenue growth was lower than 14 per cent of the projected amount, but this has now been discontinued. So, with a multitude of issues already plaguing the fiscal space of the SNGs, the discontinuation of the GST compensation could further worsen the debt levels of the SNG unless there is buoyancy in GST collection which may offset the loss of compensation. In addition, the states now have limited manoeuvrability over the tax rates since major sources of tax revenue of the SNGs have been subsumed under GST.

6.3 Interstate Comparison of Debt Position

Before the Covid pandemic, the average fiscal deficit as a percentage of GSDP of the states from 2011–12 to 2019–20 was modest at 2.5 per cent, below the Fiscal Responsibility Legislation (FRL) threshold of 3 per cent (RBI, 2022b). However, there were significant interstate differences. Among the general category states (GCS), Gujarat, Maharashtra, and Odisha had fiscal deficit to GSDP ratios less than 2 per cent whereas Haryana, Andhra Pradesh (AP), Kerala, Punjab, Rajasthan, and Telangana had average GFD above 3.5 per cent of GSDP (RBI, 2022b) (see Figure 6.11).

Similarly, on the revenue deficit side, states like Rajasthan, Tamil Nadu, West Bengal (WB), Andhra Pradesh (AP), Haryana, Kerala, and Punjab had high revenue deficit from 2011–12 to 2019–20 (see Figure 6.12).

Also, among these eighteen GCS states, AP, Kerala, Punjab, Rajasthan, WB, and Haryana were not only running revenue deficits but also had high fiscal deficits during 2011–12 to 2019–20. This is mainly due to a significant increase in revenue expenditure in these states much higher than the growth in their own revenues.

Thus, the fiscal position of some states was already poor even prior to the pandemic. The outbreak of the pandemic in 2020 has only aggravated their already stressed fiscal condition. A state-wise comparison of the deterioration of fiscal position in 2020–21 shows that all the states breached the FRBM limit of 3 per cent of GSDP in 2020–21. However, there are

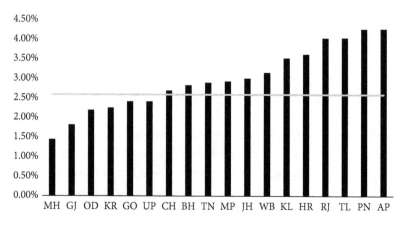

Figure 6.11 State-wise average GFD-to-GSDP ratio (2011–20)
Source: author's calculation based on RBI ([state finances] various years).

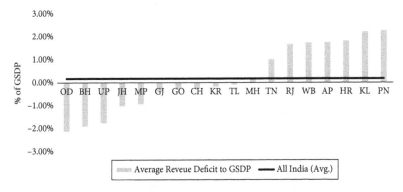

Figure 6.12 State-wise average GRD-to-GSDP ratio (2011–20)

Source: author's calculation based on RBI ([state finances] various years).

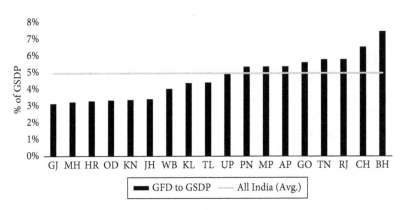

Figure 6.13 State-wise GFD to GSDP ratio (2020–21 RE)

Source: author's calculation based on RBI ([state finances] various years).

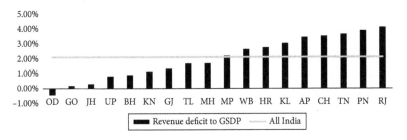

Figure 6.14 State-wise GRD to GSDP ratio (2020–21)

Source: author's calculation based on RBI ([state finances] various years).

significant variations among states. Some states are under severe stress whereas other states are in a relatively comfortable position. States like Rajasthan, Chhattisgarh, Punjab, AP, and Tamil Nadu not only had revenue deficit much higher than the national average of 2 per cent of GSDP, but they also had a fiscal deficit of more than 5 per cent (national average) in 2020–21 (see Figures 6.13 & 6.14). Among all the GCS, except Odisha which was in revenue surplus for 2020–21, all the other states had revenue deficit.

In its recent study, *State Finances: A Study of Budgets of 2022–23* (2023), the RBI categorized some states as 'fiscally vulnerable' based on a set of fiscal indicators. According to the IMF (2000), states in this situation face the prospect of falling short of both overall fiscal policy objectives and long-term debt sustainability targets. The study showed that the ten states with the highest debt–GSDP ratio in 2021 were eventually found to be with the highest debt burden. These included Rajasthan, Kerala, WB, Punjab, Bihar, Jharkhand, AP, Uttar Pradesh (UP), Madhya Pradesh, and Haryana. These states incidentally account for more than 50 per cent of the total expenditure (TE) incurred by all Indian states (See Table 6.1).

The gross fiscal deficit (GFD)–GSDP ratio for these 'fiscally vulnerable' states in 2020–21 was either equal to or higher than 3 per cent. In addition to this, all of these states—with the exception of Jharkhand and UP—saw revenue deficits. Moreover, it was found that in eight of the ten states, the IP to revenue receipts (RR) (IP–RR) ratio was greater than 10 per cent. From among the ten states identified by the required benchmark, that is, the debt-to-GSDP ratio, the RBI study identified a core group of severely stressed states considering the warning signs that many indicators were showing. WB, Bihar, Kerala, Punjab, and Rajasthan were found to be under most stress. The debt-to-GSDP ratio of these states was more than 35 per cent in 2020–21 which is far above the target of 20 per cent set for state governments for 2022–23 by the FRBM review committee in 2017. These five states have also breached the targets set by the 15th FC both for outstanding debt liabilities and fiscal deficit for state governments for 2020–21.

Table 6.1 Debt–GSDP and IP–RR ratio of GCS states

State	2020–21	2021–22 RE	2021–22 RE
	Debt–GSDP (%)	IP–RR (%)	
AP	35.5	32.5	14.3
Bihar	36.7	38.6	8.6
Chhattisgarh	26.3	26.2	8
Gujarat	21.0	19.0	14.2
Haryana	28.0	29.4	20.9
Jharkhand	34.4	33.0	8.4
Karnataka	22.4	26.6	14.3
Kerala	37.1	37.0	18.8
Madhya Pradesh	31.0	31.3	11.7
Maharashtra	19.6	17.9	11.4
Odisha	20.0	18.8	4.3
Punjab	49.1	53.3	21.3
Rajasthan	40.5	39.5	14.9
Tamil Nadu	26.9	27.4	21
Telangana	25.2	24.7	11.3
UP	29.1	34.9	11.2
WB	37.1	34.4	20.8

Source: RBI (2022b).

6.4 Reasons for Poor Condition of State Finances of Ten Stressed States

6.4.1 Declining own revenues

State's own revenue (SOR) accounts for about 50 to 60 per cent of the total RR of the state governments. The rest is the transfers from the central government. For most of these stressed states except for Jharkhand and Rajasthan, SOR as a percentage of GSDP has declined since 2015–16 (see Table 6.2).

6.4.1.1 High proportion of revenue expenditure
As pointed out earlier, the TE of these ten states account for almost half of the TE undertaken by all states and UTs. Interestingly, the revenue

Table 6.2 Own revenue-to-GSDP ratio for stressed states (%)

State	2015–16	2016–17	2017–18	2018–19	2019–20	2020–21 RE
AP	7.42	7.21	7.15	7.22	6.31	5.98
Bihar	7.44	6.21	7.09	6.63	5.81	7.25
Haryana	7.20	7.16	7.98	7.26	6.59	7.16
Jharkhand	8.39	7.89	8.28	7.53	8.22	11.16
Kerala	8.44	8.17	8.46	7.97	7.59	6.80
Madhya Pradesh	9.02	8.20	8.12	7.87	7.05	6.44
Punjab	7.52	7.87	7.60	7.69	6.82	6.58
Rajasthan	7.87	7.36	8.42	8.42	7.50	8.35
UP	9.16	8.92	8.99	9.66	12.03	8.23
WB	5.56	5.55	6.24	5.94	5.29	4.79

Source: author's calculation from RBI (various years).

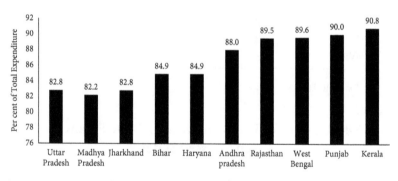

Figure 6.15 Ratio of revenue expenditure-to-total expenditure-5years (2017-18 to 2021-22) average
Source: RBI (2022b)

expenditure of these states' ranges from 80 to 90 per cent of TEs (RBI, 2022b) (see Figure 6.15).

What is worrying is that out of the revenue expenditure, committed expenditure accounts for around 35 per cent. As the committed expenditure is very high, it becomes increasingly difficult for the government to cut back on revenue expenditure and increase the capital outlay (CO), the ratio of which is used as an indicator for the quality of expenditure. In other words, high committed expenditure eventually led to poor expenditure quality of such states, which is reflected in high revenue expenditure-to-capital outlay (RECO) ratio (RBI, 2022) (see Figure 6.16). These states are hardly left with any fiscal space to undertake capital expenditure. Fewer resources utilized for capital expenditure implies that there is a lower multiplier effect on the economic growth which in turn leads to lower revenue generation in the future. For most of the stressed states, Punjab, Kerala, WB, Rajasthan, AP, Haryana, the CO-to-GSDP ratio is much lower than the other states (see Figure 6.17).

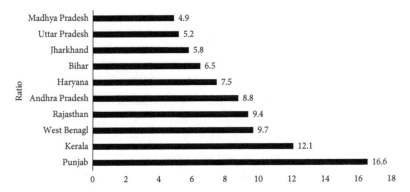

Figure 6.16 Revenue expenditure-to-capital outlay ratio (RECO) -5years (2017-18 to 2021-22) average
Source: RBI (2022b)

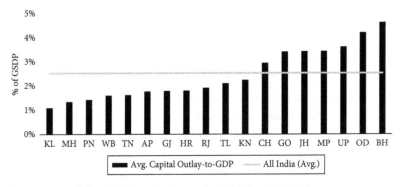

Figure 6.17 CO to GSDP ratio-5years (2017-18 to 2021-22) average
Source: author's calculation based on RBI ([state finances] various years).

6.5 Conclusion

This chapter discussed how the debt position of the SNGs in India has evolved since the 1980s. They follow a similar trend with an initial period of worsening debt indicators starting from the 1980s until 2003. From the 1980s to early 2000s, there was a significant accumulation of debt for a variety of reasons: some due to external factors such as the oil shock in the 1990s and some due to internal factors such as the reforms introduced from the mid-1980s towards trade liberalization and increased investment in modern technologies. Moreover, many parts of the country witnessed droughts and floods in the late 1980s. All these factors contributed to an increase in the debt of both the central government and the SNGs over this period. However, beginning in the 2000s, it was recognized that this burgeoning debt had to be reined in before it could spiral out of control: the FRBM Act was therefore passed at the central level and at the SNGs during the period from 2002 to 2010. Also, the steps taken by the central government and recommendations of the respective central finance commissions to restructure states debt and reduce borrowing cost cannot be ignored. As such, there was a noticeable improvement in the debt position of both the central government and SNGs in this period up to 2015–16. From 2015 to 2016, there was a significant worsening of the debt indicators of the SNGs due to the states taking on the debt of the DISCOMs which was earlier off-budget borrowing through PSUs. This brought all that debt onto the books of the state government as a result of which the debt indicators associated with the SNGs showed high stress. The hope was that, since the states have taken over the debt of these DISCOMs, there would be an effort to reduce this debt to a manageable limit in the medium-term future with better visibility of the problem.

However, the Covid-19 pandemic further affected the debt position of the states as the states now had the huge responsibility of ensuring that their public health infrastructure remained resilient. This high expenditure along with a lower revenue collection on account of reduced economic activity due to the strict lockdowns pushed the states to taking on higher levels of debt. Similarly, the central government debt also increased due to the pandemic and its debt as a percentage of GDP reached 61 in 2020. The average debt–GSDP ratio of the states crossed 30 per cent and reached the same levels as in 2004–05. However, as we discussed earlier, the fiscal position of the states was already stressed due to the tendency to undertake borrowing through PSUs (DISCOMS in particular).

There are, however, large variations in the debt position of the states. States like Rajasthan, Chhattisgarh, Punjab, AP and Tamil Nadu not only had revenue deficit much higher than the national average of 2 per cent of GSDP, but they also had a fiscal deficit of more than 5 per cent (national average) in 2020–21. Among all the GCS, except Odisha which was in revenue surplus for 2020–21, all the other states had revenue deficit. It is important to note that the pandemic only aggravated the already stressed debt position in many of these states. Further, there are certain emerging risks to the sustainability of the debt position of the SNGs which are covered in Chapter 9. The concept of debt sustainability and the various approaches to studying debt sustainability are covered in the next chapter.

7

Debt Sustainability of SNGs

7.1 Context

The previous chapter discussed the manner in which the debt position
of subnational governments (SNGs) has evolved over time. It was observed that the debt-to-GSDP ratio of SNGs in India today has returned
to the peak levels of 2003–04. Is this debt level alarming for SNGs in
India? What are the chances that SNGs in India will fall into debt crisis?
We will address these questions in the next chapter. Before we answer
these questions, it is important to examine the concept of debt sustainability. Once the concept of debt sustainability is explained, the chapter
delves deep into the different approaches to assess debt sustainability. The
chapter ends with a review of some of the important studies that have
been undertaken on the debt sustainability of SNGs in India.

7.2 Introduction to Debt Sustainability

In simple words, debt sustainability means the government's ability to
service its debt obligations without going to external agencies for rescue.
As per the World Bank, debt sustainability refers to a situation where the
ratio of outstanding debt and debt servicing to GDP is not increasing
over time. The IMF defines sustainable debt as where a government can
meet all its present and future payments without defaulting (IMF, 2020).
While a debt limit may act as an indicative ceiling, it is necessary to assess
whether the debt undertaken is sustainable under the changing macroeconomic and fiscal conditions.

Unsustainable debt might lead to a situation of a debt trap where all additional borrowing goes into servicing earlier debt leading ultimately to insolvency and default. This underscores the significance of examining debt

Debt Sustainability of Subnational Governments in India. Hari Krishna Dwivedi, Oxford University Press.
© Hari Krishna Dwivedi 2024. DOI: 10.1093/oso/9780198903116.003.0007

sustainability. Over the years, various models or approaches have been used to measure whether government debt is sustainable. In determining debt sustainability, these approaches take into account the revenues and expenditure of governments and whether the revenues are enough to provide fiscal space to meet debt obligations after meeting all expenditure.

7.3 Debt Sustainability: Existing Approaches

The existing approaches broadly employ four ways of assessing debt sustainability. These include the Domar model of debt sustainability, present value budget constraint (PVBC), fiscal response function (FRF), and the indicator-based approach. These approaches are discussed in the subsequent sections.

7.3.1 Domar model of debt sustainability

The core tenet of government financing is that when expenses surpass revenue, the deficit is covered through government borrowing. This is known as government budget constraint. So:

$$D_t - D_{t-1} = G_t - R_t \tag{1}$$

Where D_t is outstanding debt stock, G_t, is government expenditure, and R_t is the government revenue in year t.

$$D_t - D_{t-1} = F_t = P_t + IP_t \tag{2}$$

Where P_t is primary deficit (PD) and IP_t is interest payment in year t. The interest payment can be redefined as the rate of interest for the year t on the outstanding debt stock for year t-1 ($Dt-1$):

$$D_t = P_t + (1+i)^* D_{t-1} \tag{3}$$

$$D_t - D_{t-1} = P_t + i^* D_{t-1} \tag{4}$$

Equation (4) is normalized by GSDP as for an SNG as in Equation (5):

$$d_t = p_t + \frac{(1+i)^* D_{t-1}}{GSDP_t} \qquad (5)$$

Where the GSDP in time t can be redefined as growth of GSDP in time t(n) on GSDP in time t-1 ($GSDP_{t-1}$):

$$d_t = p_t + \frac{(1+i)}{(1+n)} {}^* d_{t-1} \qquad (6)$$

Where, d_t is outstanding debt stock–GSDP ratio in year t, p_t is PD–GSDP ratio in year t, n is the growth rate of GSDP in year t, i is the rate of interest in year t.

The relationship between the change in debt stock and interest rate and GSDP growth rate can be understood if is subtracted on each side of Equation (6):

$$\Delta d_t = p_t + \frac{(1+i)}{(1+n)} {}^* d_{t-1} - d_{t-1} \qquad (7)$$

$$\Delta d_t = p_t + \frac{(i-n)}{(1+n)} {}^* d_{t-1} \qquad (8)$$

According to the Domar model of debt sustainability, for debt to be sustainable, the debt should eventually converge to the initial level. For this to happen, Δd_t should be negative. As in Equation (8), Δd_t is negative if:

- $p_t < 0$

- Since $d_{t-1} > 0$; $(i-n) < 0$

Debt is said to be sustainable if the outstanding debt stock converges to zero. According to the Domar model, debt in time period t is less than outstanding debt stock in time period t-1, if: p_t

1. *Growth rate of nominal GSDP should be greater than the rate of interest*
2. *PD/GSDP < 0 (i.e. the government should maintain primary surplus (PS))*
3. *The growth–interest differential is greater than the PD, i.e. $(n-i)>p_t$*

In the short run (SR), a growth–interest differential greater than PD may result in a lower debt-to-GSDP ratio. However, for debt to become sustainable and to maintain a positive growth–interest differential, a PS is desirable.

Even though the Domar model of debt sustainability has been widely studied in literature, the model has certain shortcomings. One of the main drawbacks of the Domar approach is that it does not consider the interdependencies existing between the elements involved, namely the interest rate, the volume and the structure of public expenses, the degree of public indebtedness and the economic growth rate (Bilan, 2010). Also, it is important to consider the type of expenditure which results in increased public spending and hence borrowing (Sardoni, 2008). If the debt-to-GDP ratio is growing because more and more public resources are directed towards capital expenditure and a smaller amount is going into current expenditure, a primary deficit may become sustainable due to the multiplier effect of capital expenditure on economic growth and hence on revenue receipts (RR) of the government.

7.3.2 PVBC (empirical approach)

The PVBC approach to measure debt sustainability is also known as the government intertemporal budget constraint (IBC) approach. This approach implies that the discounted present value (PV) of all future budget surpluses must equal the value of the current stock of debt. Thus, the fiscal variables are tested to see whether it is consistent with IBC.

Sustainability analysis is based on the IBC which is a basic accounting identity:

net borrowings = interest payments − primary balance − seigniorage   (9)

This identity (1) can be written as:

$$D_t - D_{t-1} = I_t - PB_t - \left(M_t - M_{t-1}\right) \tag{10}$$

For an SNG, there's no role of seigniorage, so it can be redefined as:

$$D_t - D_{t-1} = I_t - PB_t \tag{11}$$

Assuming that time is discrete, and all borrowing has a maturity of one year, and that Equation 3 is expressed in real terms, i.e. the face level is indexed to the price level. The rate of interest is assumed to be constant at r:

$$d_t - d_{t-1} = r * d_{t-1} - pb_t \tag{12}$$

$$d_t = \left(1+r\right)* d_{t-1} - pb_t \tag{13}$$

Rearranging Equation (5):

$$d_{t-1} = \left(1+r\right)^{-1} * d_t + \left(1+r\right)^{-1} pb_t \tag{14}$$

Equation (6) can be updated for time period t as in Equation (7):

$$d_t = \left(1+r\right)^{-1} * d_{t+1} + \left(1+r\right)^{-1} pb_{t+1} \tag{15}$$

Equation (7) can be used to replace in Equation (6):

$$d_{t-1} = \left(1+r\right)^{-2} * d_{t+1} + \left(1+r\right)^{-1} pb_t + \left(1+r\right)^{-2} pb_t \tag{16}$$

The same procedure can be used to replace in Equation (8) and then for and so forth in a recursive fashion. After several iterations Equation (8) can be rewritten as:

$$d_{t-1} = \left(1+r\right)^{-(j+1)} * d_{t+j} + \sum_{i=0}^{j} \left(1+r\right)^{-(i+1)} pb_{t+i} \tag{17}$$

Equation 9 shows the link between government debt in time t-1 and t+j. In particular, the amount of debt government has on date t+j is a function of the debt it initially had at date t-1 as well as PS, it ran during these dates.

On imposing the below condition:

$$\lim_{j \to \infty} (1+r)^{-(j+1)} d_{t+j} = 0 \tag{18}$$

This condition is often called the no-Ponzi scheme condition.

This reveals the lifetime budget constraint:

$$d_{t-1} = \sum_{i=0}^{j} (1+r)^{-(i+1)} pb_{t+i} \tag{19}$$

Intuitively, the PVBC constraint requires that a government should be able to meet its initial debt by running PS in the future, whose PV is equal to its initial debt obligations. The solvency condition for government debt implies that future budget surpluses would be sufficient to meet current debt liabilities.

The time series properties can be tested to check whether the IBC is satisfied. To test the time series properties of the IBC, many studies have carried out tests on unit root and cointegration properties of fiscal data.

Unit root test: the stationarity of revenue and expenditure is tested sep-arately to ensure that the statistical properties of the parameters do not change over time. In other words, this approach checks whether revenue and expenditure are stable and there are no sudden spikes over time.

Cointegration test: this is used to study the long-term relationship be-tween revenue and expenditure for ascertaining sustainability.

One of the oldest papers that proposed the use of the cointegration test to study fiscal sustainability was Hakkio and Rush (1991). 'The under-lying idea behind the cointegration framework is that government ex-penditure, inclusive of IP, and total revenue should not diverge from each other in the long run' (Galvao et al., 2011,p.6). If there is a divergence between government revenues and expenditure, then the fiscal condition of the government is not sustainable.

Globally, studies have tested for cointegration between government revenues and expenditure but found debt to be unsustainable or weakly sustainable in South Africa (Lusinyan & Thornton, 2009), most of the West (African Monetary Zones Oshikoya & Tarawalie, 2010) and Sri Lanka (Deyshappriya, 2012). While debt was found to be unsustainable in India when applying the IBC approach (Buiter & Patel, 1992), it was found to be weakly sustainable when considering India as a whole and not states and centre individually (Goyal et al., 2004).

7.3.3 Fiscal response function

Another approach often used for assessing debt sustainability is the use of fiscal response function (FRF) of the government. It tests whether fiscal policy responds to the accumulation of debt. If the Primary Surplus PS as a percentage of GSDP has a positive relation with debt as a percentage of GSDP, then it means that the increase in debt accumulation by the government is followed by increase in PS in the subsequent year. It means that the government is taking steps to reduce its borrowing in subsequent year if it borrows more in the current year. This act of the government helps in maintaining the debt at sustainable levels. First, Trehan and Walsh (1991) and then Bohn (1998), started the work in this area which aimed at assessing the debt sustainability of government by examining it in a time series context for the USA (Ferrarini et al., 2012). Bohn used the simple fiscal reaction function:

$$Primary\, Surplus_t = \beta_0 + \beta_1 \frac{Debt}{GDP} ratio_t + \varepsilon_t$$

That is, a statistically significant positive response of PS to an increase in the lagged stock of debt (both as a ratio of income or as a ratio of output) in a 'fiscal reaction function' constitutes a sufficient condition of stability. This tests whether a government takes corrective action when there is a sudden increase in net borrowing by reducing expenditure or increasing revenue in the next period, that is, with an increase in primary balance (PB).

Several studies have assessed debt sustainability using FRF either for individual economies or for a panel of countries. Di Lorio et al. (2022) examined debt sustainability in advanced economies from 1961 to 2019 using FRF in a panel data set. Turan et al. (2022) examined debt sustainability by estimating FRFs for developing and developed countries. A recent RBI study, entitled *State Finances: A Risk Analysis, Debt Sustainability of Vulnerable States of India* (RBI, 2022b) is assessed using FRF.

7.3.4   Indicator approach to debt sustainability

Another widely used approach to measure debt sustainability is the indicator approach which is an extended version of the Domar condition. It examines several macro-fiscal indicators which reflect growth, liquidity conditions, creditworthiness, fiscal burden, fiscal space, etc. Indicators are assessed to understand government's ability to service its debt repayment obligations through regular sources of revenue without relying on temporary or incidental revenues (Dwivedi & Sinha, 2021).

The indicator-based approach considers the movement of various fiscal indicators to assess sustainability such as: rate of growth of public debt (D) should be lower than rate of growth of nominal GSDP (G), real rate of interest (r) should be lower than real output growth (g), PB and primary revenue balance (PRB) should be in surplus, IP as a percentage of RR and GSDP should decline over time. This is shown in Table 7.1.

The indicator-based approach to assess debt sustainability has been used in multiple studies. In a 2012 RBI paper titled, 'Threshold Level of Debt and Public Debt Sustainability: The Indian Experience', the public debt sustainability of India has been examined using the indicator-based approach for the period 1981–2013 (Kaur, B. and Mukherjee, A. 2012). In another RBI study entitled 'Subnational Government Debt Sustainability in India: An Empirical Analysis', the debt sustainability of Indian states was assessed for the period 1992–2019 using the indicator approach (Misra, S., Gupta K. and Trivedi P. , 2020). Similarly, in a study published

Table 7.1 Indicators used to assess debt sustainability for indicator-based approach

Serial no.	Indicators	Symbolic representation
1	Rate of growth of public debt (D) should be lower than rate of growth of nominal GSDP (G)	$D - G < 0$
2	Real rate of interest (r) should be lower than real output growth (g)	$r - g < 0$
3 (a)	PB should be in surplus	$PB / GSDP > 0$
3 (b)	PRB should be in surplus	$PRB / GSDP > 0$
4 (a)	RR as % of GSDP should increase over time	$RR / GSDP \uparrow\uparrow$
4 (b)	Public debt- to-RR ratio should decline over time[*]	$D / RR \downarrow\downarrow$
5 (a)	Interest burden defined by IP as % of GSDP should decline over time	$IP / G \downarrow\downarrow$
5 (c)	IP as % of RR should decline over time	$IP / RR \downarrow\downarrow$

[*] Definition of public/outstanding debt – cumulative of net borrowing + liabilities in public fund = loans from the centre + internal liabilities + ways and means advances from GOI + small savings and state provident funds.

by Dwivedi and Sinha (2021), the debt sustainability of West Bengal was assessed using the indicator-based approach.

7.4 Studies on Assessment of Debt Sustainability of SNGs in India

Multiple studies have been undertaken to examine debt sustainability of SNGs in India. These studies examined debt sustainability of SNGs using different approaches as discussed earlier.

In an RBI study entitled 'State Finances: A Risk Analysis' (2022), the debt sustainability of eighteen large Indian states was assessed. The study used FRF to assess debt sustainability and fiscal stress of SNGs. The FRF assesses the solvency by linking the PB to debt, while accounting for current economic conditions to reflect the impact of business cycle fluctuations. The data used is panel data from 2001–02 to 2021–22 for variables such as debt-to-GSDP ratio (debt includes contingent liabilities in the form of explicit guarantees), primary expenditure, and deviation of actual output from its trend. There were three regressions run: one with all the states, second with the ten most indebted states, and a third regression with the five most indebted states. The results show that debt is sustainable and the results statistically significant in the regressions with all the states and the ten most indebted states. When the regression is run with data from the five most indebted states, the results are not statistically significant, and the sign on the coefficient indicates that it does not satisfy the sustainability condition. From this analysis, it was concluded that while the combined debt of state governments in India is still sustainable, for the five most indebted states, it may not be sustainable. The study further assesses debt sustainability of the five debt-stressed states using the Domar condition, that is, the real rate of interest should be less than real GDP growth rate for the sustainability condition to be satisfied. The study found that this condition is fulfilled for all the states for all the years except for 2020–21. The study further highlights that the rate of growth of public debt is higher than GSDP growth mostly in the last five years, which led to accumulation of huge debt in these states.

In an RBI paper by Kaur et al. (2014), the debt sustainability of twenty Indian states was examined using the indicator-based analysis and empirical exercises on time series data. The indicator-based analysis shows that while most of the debt sustainability indicators witnessed significant improvements during the period from 2005 to 2013 in comparison to the previous phase of 1998 to 2004, debt repayment capacity and IP indicators worsened in comparison to the period from 1982 to 1992. The results from the estimation based on panel data also revealed that in India there is a positive significant relationship between government revenue and expenditure. Moreover, from the estimated fiscal policy response function, the study also found that the PB for state governments in India responds to the rise in debt in a stabilizing manner. Thus, the results from both the approaches lead to the conclusion that there is long-term sustainability of debt at the state level.

Nayak and Rath (2009) examined debt sustainability using Domar sustainability criteria for eleven special category states (SCS) for the period 1991–2009. The study used data on various fiscal parameters from RBI. The indicators used for this study are the nominal growth rate of debt stock (%), average nominal interest rate paid (%), average nominal interest rate paid (%). The results revealed that the Domar sustainability condition is met for all states except for Arunachal Pradesh. The study further revealed that average nominal interest paid by the SCS (except Mizoram) during the period is higher than the non-special category states (NSC). The study also stresses the challenges to debt sustainability of the states due to excessive issuance of guarantees by the state governments to public sector entities. The guarantees known as contingent liabilities become direct liabilities of the state when the borrower defaults.

Narayan (2016) analysed the public debt and fiscal sustainability of Haryana for the period 1980–81 to 2014–15 using indicator-based analyses and the PVBC approach. The indicator-based analyses show that while most of the debt sustainability indicators witnessed significant improvements from 2004–05 to 2009–10 but the period after 2009–10 showed signs of fiscal stress and increasing debt burden. The study further revealed that while both traditional debt sustainability indicators and cointegration analysis supported the opinion that debt liabilities of Haryana were sustainable but in comparison to General Category States (GCS), the debt position of Haryana on sustainability indicators for the time period 2010–11 to 2014–15 had deteriorated.

Das (2016) estimated the relationship between debt and fiscal deficit in a panel data framework using data from seventeen GCS over thirty-four years (1980–2013). The study used panel unit root tests to examine the relationship between various fiscal variables. The results of the tests indicate that the change in debt ratio is significantly more sensitive to revenue expenditure than capital expenditure at the subnational level. The increase in the states' OTR did not significantly improve the debt situation of the state governments. The elasticity of debt due to revenue expenditure is significantly higher than the elasticity of capital outlay. The results also indicate that state-specific unobserved factors, mostly related to the budget management capabilities of the state governments, had a decisive impact on the rise in government borrowing and on economic growth of the states.

Maurya (2013) assessed the debt sustainability of the state of Uttar Pradesh (UP) from 1990–91 to 2011–12 in terms of standard debt sustainability indicators in the post-FRBM period as the state finances during this period were highly vulnerable. The sustainability analysis has been done to examine the impact of reforms on debt position and to measure debt sustainability before and after FRBM years. The study has used three approaches, namely, the Domar sustainability condition, PVBC approach and sustainability indicators analysis. The study found that the Domar condition for debt sustainability is satisfied strongly for UP in the post-FRBM period except for the year 2011–12 but it is weakly satisfied in the pre-FRBMA period. From the PVBC approach which has been tested for stationarity by applying unit root test, the study found that for the pre-FRBM period, the debt sustainability was highly unsustainable, becoming weakly unsustainable in the post-FRBM period. These conclusions were reached by observing the statistical significance of the coefficients of the equations. Using the indicator-based analysis, the debt position of the state in the pre-FRBM period was found to be above comfort level. Nevertheless, the results of different approaches suggested that the position on debt sustainability of the state improved in the post-FRBM period. The study, however, warned that the growth parameters may moderate post 2011–12 and suggested that the state needed to implement measures to increase revenue and curtail inefficient expenditure without reducing expenditure on productive purposes.

A large volume of literature examining the sustainability of debt of SNGs in India presents no clear pattern (Narayan, 2017). Some studies have found evidence of unsustainability of public debt in the long run whereas some studies have found debt to be sustainable. Nevertheless, the results of these studies differ due to the differences in the approaches adopted to measure debt sustainability.

However, it is pertinent to note that while several studies tested the debt sustainability of SNGs by undertaking the cointegration between revenues and expenditure in the Indian context, structural breaks and cross-sectional dependence in panel setting were not considered. This may lead to erroneous results. Previous literature on fiscal sustainability considering structural breaks have been undertaken in fifteen EU nations (Afonso & Rault, 2007), twenty developed countries (Habib et al., 2016), and Turkey (Kuştepeli & Önel, 2005). In the Indian context, sustainability of the combined public debt of states and the centre has been tested. No cointegration was found between government revenues and expenditure without structural breaks and with a single break. However, testing with two structural breaks confirmed a relation between the variables (Asif & Husain, 2018).

7.5 Conclusion

The recent episodes of debt crises have again brought to the fore the discussion on debt sustainability. Leading institutions such as the IMF and World Bank have defined debt sustainability in different ways. IMF (2020) defines sustainable debt as where a government can meet all its present and future payments without defaulting. The World Bank defines debt sustainability as a situation in which the ratio of outstanding debt and debt servicing to GDP is not increasing over time.

Multiple studies have examined the issue of debt sustainability for SNGs in India. Different studies have used different approaches to measure SNG debt sustainability. While most studies have shown that currently the cumulative SNG debt situation remains sustainable, a few have found that the sustainability criteria were not met, albeit with a lower statistical significance. Studies which look at the historical debt position of the SNGs however tend to agree that the SNG debt position was not sustainable in the period immediately before the implementation of the FRBM regime.

These studies have used various different approaches to look at the question of debt sustainability. The existing literature on debt sustainability does not rate one approach as better than other approaches. However, they do suggest that the combination of results from these approaches should provide additional information on government debt sustainability (Marini & Piergallini, 2007).

The studies which look at the cointegration of expenditure and revenue of the SNGs in India do not consider structural breaks and cross-sectional dependence. While such studies have been done globally and also with regard to central government debt in India, there has not been a similar study of SNG debt sustainability using the same approach. Such an approach which accounts for structural breaks and cross-sectional dependence is used in the alternative approach presented in the next chapter.

8

An Alternative Approach to Measure SNG Debt Sustainability

8.1 Context

In the previous chapter, we examined the concept of debt sustainability and the approaches to measure it. The results from various studies on debt sustainability of SNGs in India using multiple approaches were also explored. In this chapter, we present an alternative approach that attempts to address the limitations of the existing approaches. The debt sustainability of SNG in India is tested using this approach.

8.2 An Alternative Approach to Assess Debt Sustainability of SNGs

Various approaches have been applied to study the sustainability of subnational debt in India. The Domar model of debt sustainability has been exceedingly popular among researchers who have highlighted that the primary deficit path can be sustained as long as real growth of the economy continues to be higher than the real interest rate. However, as pointed out earlier, the Domar function does not consider the interdependencies that may be present between interest rates, public spending, outstanding public debt, and the GDP growth rate. The alternative approach moves away from the focus on primary surplus (PS) and attempts to explore whether the fiscal policy of general category states (GCS) have been sustainable over a time period. Debt sustainability studies which have been undertaken for SNGs in India have focused on revenue receipts (RR), revenue expenditure, and total expenditure (TE). In the present chapter, the debt sustainability has been examined using state's own revenues (SOR) and TE as indicators.

Debt Sustainability of Subnational Governments in India. Hari Krishna Dwivedi, Oxford University Press.
© Hari Krishna Dwivedi 2024. DOI: 10.1093/oso/9780198903116.003.0008

The use of total RR as one of the variables for measuring debt sustainability has its own set of limitations. This is because RR of state government comprise SOR and central transfers. SOR, which comprise 55 per cent of the total RR, is within the legislative and administrative domain of the state while the transfers from the centre which contribute to around 45 per cent of the RR of the states comprise tax devolution, Finance Commission (FC) grants, and other discretionary grants.

The share of central transfers in states' RR has been fluctuating over the years primarily due to external factors which are not in the control of the state governments. Some of the factors which have caused volatility in central transfers are discussed below.

1. Increasing share of central cesses and surcharges

The transfers received by the states from the centre include FC transfers which is a percentage of the divisible pool. The divisible pool consists of net of all taxes collected by centre, excluding cesses and surcharges levied for specific purposes. Article 270 of the Indian Constitution provides that cesses and surcharges that are levied do not form part of the divisible pool. It has been observed that the share of cesses and surcharges in the divisible pool of the central government has been rising over the years.

As can be seen from Figure 8.1, the share of the central cesses and surcharges in gross tax revenues (GTR) has risen from 10.4 per cent in

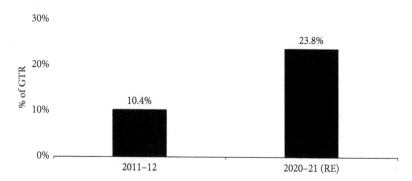

Figure 8.1 Percentage share of cesses and surcharges in GTR of Union government

Sources: Government of India (2020) and Union Budget documents 2021–22.

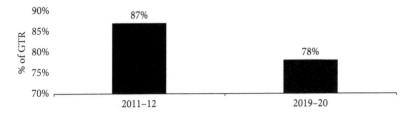

Figure 8.2 Divisible pool to GTR ratio
Source: Government of India (2020).

2011–12 to 23.8 per cent in 2020–21 (RE). Since 2011–12, the cesses and surcharges have grown at the CAGR of 19 per cent as against 9 per cent growth rate (CAGR) of gross tax revenue. This is despite recommendations of the 13th FC Report to review and reduce the cesses and surcharges. Owing to huge increase in cesses and surcharges, the divisible pool-to-GTR ratio has reduced consistently from about 87 per cent of the total tax collection of the central government in 2011–12 to about 78 per cent in 2019–20 (Fifteenth Finance Commission , 2020).(See Figure 8.2)

2. Revenue foregone in the divisible pool and huge amount of unrealized taxes

The central government offers various incentives such as tax holidays, tax credits, rebates to attract new investment and promote industry. This revenue foregone accounts for 25 per cent of the taxes collected. Apart from tax exemptions, the central government data shows that there is a huge amount of tax which is raised but not realized. The revenue from unrealized taxes has increased from ₹90,255.88 crores in 2005–06 to ₹16,19,391 crores in 2020–21, recording a yearly growth of 21 per cent. Additionally, the tax arrears which were not under dispute have grown at 22 per cent from ₹19,875.74 crores lu 2005 06 to ₹4,05,583 crores in 2020–21. A staggering 40 per cent of the total taxes collected by the centre is arrears. This has a major bearing on the total divisible pool.

Owing to the tax exemption in the form of conditional exemptions, tariff concessions, etc., and tax arrears, the gap in the central government revenue forecasted by the FCs and the revenue collected has risen

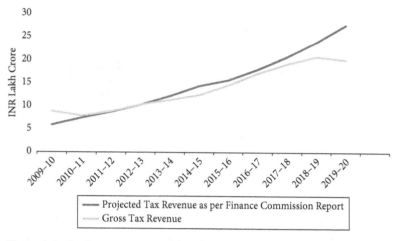

Figure 8.3 Gap between projected and actual GTR of central government
Source: FC reports and Union budget documents.

sharply over the years. Since 2013–14, the gap between the projected tax revenue and the actual tax revenue of the centre has been on average 14.92 per cent. This divergence has increased from 2016–17 onwards (see Figure 8.3).

3. Grants from the centre

The other component of transfers is the grants from the centre which comprise grants given as per the recommendation of the FC and for central sector (CS) schemes and centrally sponsored schemes (CSS) by different central ministries. There is an element of predictability in the FC grants but grants under CS and CSS are highly volatile. Even in respect of FC grants, where release of funds is conditional upon the state fulfilling the conditions precedent to get the grants, there is an element of volatility.

In 2014–15, grants for CSS increased significantly. This is because since 2014–15 grants for CSS are routed through the state budgets which earlier bypassed state budgets. This resulted in an increase in the flow of grants to states reflected in one-off hike in the amount of grants during 2014–15. This was mainly an accounting change.

For the period 2015–20, as per the recommendations of the 14th FC, the share of tax devolution was increased from 32 per cent of the

divisible pool to 42 per cent. The tax devolution is a form of general purpose transfer. This increase in general purpose transfers was offset by two
ways. First, there was a discontinuation of discretionary grants with the
abolition of the planning commission. Second, through a reduction in
matching share of the centre in the CSS. The combined effect was a decline in overall grants to the states by 5.73 percentage points. However,
since 2019–20 there has been an increasing trend in grants from the
centre to the states. This is primarily on account of increase in FC transfers (mainly transfers to local bodies) and transfers to the states in the
form of GST compensation cess.

Figure 8.4 captures the rate of growth of grants from the centre for the
period 2006–07 to 2020–21. It can be seen, the grants from the centre
have been volatile. The spike in 2014–15 has been mainly due to CSS
grants being routed through state budget which hitherto were credited
to bank accounts bypassing the state budget. Similarly, the growth in
transfer beyond 2018–19 was due to FC grants and GST compensation.

Thus, it can be seen that transfers from the centre are extremely volatile, unpredictable, and not under the control of the states. Thus, a debt
sustainability of SNGs which considers total RR (includes transfers from
the centre) as one of the variables may not provide a correct assessment of
the debt situation. Given the volatile nature of RR, a state can ensure sustainability primarily through controlling its own revenue collection and
TE. Portrafke and Reischmann (2015) in their study also argue that empirical tests based on RR may not be a reliable indicator for assessing debt

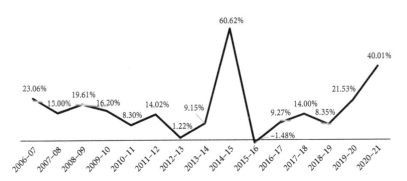

Figure 8.4 Year-on-year growth rate of grants from centre
Source: RBI ([state finances] various years).

sustainability. For instance, when a government with below par fiscal performance receives central transfers, the empirical tests may predict that the fiscal policy of the government is sustainable owing to the central transfer, whereas in fact the fiscal policy of the state may not be sustainable.

8.3 Is India's SNG Debt Sustainable as per Alternative Approach?

The new approach uses the SOR and TE of the states for assessing debt sustainability of SNGs. This study assesses debt sustainability for GCS using an alternative approach. The new approach also introduces newer econometric methods to test the sustainability of fiscal policy. Additional checks such as structural breaks, cross-section independence, and panel cointegration with structural breaks and cross-sectional dependence have been undertaken. The sustainability of fiscal policies of fourteen Indian states for the period 1980–2020 is estimated through a new lens and with more robust checks. The revenue, expenditure, and fiscal indicators of all GCS (except Jharkhand, Chhattisgarh, Goa, and Telangana) has been considered for a period of forty years (560 observations) from 1980 to 2020. For some tests, a lagged variable of outstanding liabilities has been considered, reducing the total observations to 546. All data has been taken from RBI publications on state finances across years.

The debt sustainability analysis using this new approach has been undertaken as follows:

Empirical analysis (PVBC): this includes analysis to test for debt sustainability, which is the ability of a government to sustain its current spending, tax, and other policies in the long run without threatening government solvency. The following tests have been undertaken:

Panel unit root test: the panel data on debt is tested using Levin–Lin–Chu (LLC) and Im–Pesaran–Shin (IPS) tests for the presence of unit roots.

Panel cointegration: the debt sustainability in India is analysed through testing for cointegration of SOR and TE. The underlying theory for the test is that increases in expenditure must be financed through increases in borrowing or increases in own revenue. Thus, to ensure that the increase in expenditure doesn't lead to unreasonable increase in borrowing, the own revenue and TE should be *cointegrated*.

Cross-sectional dependence: to check the possibility of *cross-sectional dependence* within this panel, the Lagrange multiplier (LM) test developed by Breusch and Pagan (1980) has been used, as T (panel's time dimension) > N (cross-sectional dimension) in the panel.

Structural break test: considering the long time period of the study (1980–2020), the existence of structural breaks in the hypothesized relationship between the two variables is highly probable. The Karavias and Westerlund (2021) test has been used to identify the location of the *structural breaks*.

Panel cointegration with structural breaks and cross-sectional dependence: a panel cointegration test that considers both structural breaks and cross-section dependence was developed by Westerlund and Edgerton (2008). Apart from cross-sectional dependence and unknown structural breaks in both the intercept and slope, heteroskedastic and serially correlated errors, as well as cross unit-specific time trends are allowed for, in this test. Moreover, the structural breaks may be located at different dates for different panel members. The study uses this test to determine the cointegration between SOR and TE in the panel set.

Dynamic panel regression: the robustness of the model is tested using dynamic panel regression.

Vector error correction model (VECM): if SOR and TE is found to be cointegrated, short-term variations are analysed through the VECM.

8.4 Results

8.4.1 Unit root test

The stationarity properties of the state governments' outstanding liabilities, SOR, and TE are tested through panel unit root tests. Panel unit root tests are regarded as more powerful than the unit root test applied on a single series. This is because the information content of the individual time series gets enhanced by that contained in the cross-section data within a panel set up (Ramirez, 2006). There are different methods to carry out panel-based unit root tests. While the panel unit root methodology of LLC (Levin et al., 2002) assumes that there is a common unit root process across the relevant cross-sections, the test suggested by IPS assumes individual unit root processes (Im et al., 2003). Some select descriptive statistics under both panel unit root tests are presented in Table 8.1.

The required condition in the unit root approach is that the debt series needs to be a mean-reverting process. The results of panel unit root tests on relevant fiscal variables (outstanding liabilities, SOR, and TE) at level are furnished in Table 8.2.

It may be seen that the IPS test failed to reject the null hypothesis of a unit root for outstanding liabilities, SOR, and TE in level form. However, the null hypothesis was rejected for all variables at level form under LLC. The stationarity of the variables at first difference has also been tested under both tests.

Table 8.1 Select descriptive statistics

	LLC	IPS
Null hypothesis	H_0=Panels Contain unit root$_s$	H_0=All Panels Contain unit roots
Alternate hypothesis	H_a=Panels are stationary	H_a=Some Panels are stationary
Number of panels	14	14
Number of periods	40	40

Table 8.2 Panel unit root tests at level form

Variable	LLC-adjusted t statistic	IPS-z statistic
Outstanding liabilities	−5.6872*	−0.8188
SOR	−3.4640*	1.3558
TE	−6.0700*	0.7988

*&** The rejection of the null hypothesis of non-stationarity at 1% and 5% levels of significance.

Table 8.3 Panel unit root tests at first difference

Variable	LLC-adjusted t statistic	IPS-z statistic
Outstanding liabilities	−9.2040*	−11.0239*
SOR	−9.4825*	−12.9799*
TE	−12.7846*	−14.7316*

*&** The rejection of the null hypothesis of non-stationarity at 1% and 5% levels of significance.

The result for both tests at first difference for all three variables, i.e. outstanding liabilities, SOR, and TE are presented in Table 8.3.

Both the tests reject the null of a unit root in the first difference for all variables. Overall, the results reveal that the three variables, i.e. outstanding liabilities, SOR, and TE are stationary in order one, i.e. I (1).

Since the SOR and TE were found to be integrated at the same order, we look at whether there exists a long-term equilibrium between the two through a panel cointegration test (Dutta & Dutta, 2014; Kaur et al., 2017; Maurya, 2014).

8.4.2 Cointegration test

Cointegration has been considered in the context of a single equation specification with only two variables, i.e. SOR and TE. In this case, an equilibrium or long-run relationship will be unique if cointegration exists. Several tests have been proposed for panel cointegration like Pedroni (1999; 2004; see also Kao, 1999) and a Fisher-type test using an underlying Johansen methodology.

The Pedroni and Kao tests are based on two-step (residual-based) cointegration tests (Engle & Granger, 1987) while Fisher's cointegration test combines individual cross-sections. The Fisher method uses two ratio tests: trace test and maximum eigenvalue (max-eigen) test. This panel cointegration test may be more robust than the conventional cointegration tests based on the Engle–Granger two-step approach. However, Pedroni is widely accepted for panel data regression analysis as it is more comprehensive. Further, the Kao test may be conducted as a robustness check to Pedroni.

The Pedroni test employs four panel statistics and three group panel statistics to test the null hypothesis of no cointegration against the alternative hypothesis of cointegration. In the case of panel statistics, the first-order autoregressive term is assumed to be the same over all the cross-sections, while in the case of group panel statistics the parameter is allowed to vary over the cross-sections. If the null is rejected in the panel case, then the variables are cointegrated. The statistics generated by the test include variance ratios, rho statistics (non-parametric), Augmented Dickey Fuller (ADF), and Phillips and Perron (non-parametric) (Pedroni, 1999).

The two tests were undertaken to check the cointegration between TE and SOR, and the results are presented in Table 8.4 and Table 8.5.

Both tests above reject the null hypothesis of no cointegration at 1 per cent significance level, indicating a long-run relationship between TE and SOR.

Table 8.4 Cointegration results conducting Pedroni tests

	Ha=Common AR coefficients	
	Statistic	Weighted statistic
Panel v-Statistic	11.37173*	7.314066*
Panel rho-Statistic	−7.592678*	−6.387255*
Panel PP-Statistic	−6.783943*	−5.693085*
Panel ADF-Statistic	−4.858215*	−4.912583*
	Ha=Individual AR coefficients	
Group rho-Statistic	−5.916278*	
Group PP-Statistic	−7.961124*	
Group ADF-Statistic	−6.327541*	

*&** The rejection of the null hypothesis at 1% and 5% levels of significance.

Table 8.5 Cointegration results conducting Kao tests

	t-statistic
ADF	−7.123654*

*&** The rejection of the null hypothesis at 1% and 5% levels of significance.

Table 8.6 Cointegration results conducting Johansen–Fisher tests

6	Fisher Stat (from trace test)	Fisher Stat (from max-eigen test)
None	42.88**	43.55**
At most 1	30.49	30.49

*&** The rejection of the null hypothesis at 1% and 5% levels of significance.

Further, the Fisher test has also been conducted. Maddala and Wu, with the help of Fisher (1932), adjusted the Johansen test to panel data (Stojkoski & Kristina, 2016). The Johansen–Fisher test statistic is computed as cross-sectional trace or maximum eigenvalue cointegration tests. The null hypothesis tests for no cointegration and at most one cointegration. The results of both tests are presented in Table 8.6.

As per Table 8.6, the null hypothesis of no cointegration has been rejected under trace test as well as maximum eigenvalue tests at 5 per cent significance level thus indicating cointegration between the two variables through Johansen–Fisher test.

8.4.3 Structural breaks

It is very crucial to identify structural change in the analysis of panel data. Structural changes are basically disruptive events which cause significant movements in the data set. The longer the time period of the data, the more is the likelihood of unexpected changes (or structural breaks) in the data. The balance-of-payment crisis of 1991, the 2007–08 global financial crisis, and the Covid outbreak are examples of disruptive events. These events may have caused significant changes in fiscal variables of the state. If ignored, they may give biased or unexpected results. Identification of structural changes and treating them using appropriate tests is therefore very important to ensure robustness of the results. Structural breaks in the hypothesized relationship of SOR and TE are as mentioned below.

The test detects five structural breaks at years 1988, 1994, 2000, 2008, and 2014 (see Table 8.7).

Table 8.7 Structural breaks estimated using the model

Null hypothesis | Alternative hypothesis	Test statistic
H0: No structural break | Ha: One structural break	73.76*
H0: One structural break | Ha: Two structural break	46.87*
H0: Two structural break | Ha: Three structural break	51.05*
H0: Three structural break | Ha: Four structural break	48.45*
H0: Four structural break | Ha: Five structural break	22.20*
Estimated structural break in year	[95% confidence interval]
1988	[1987, 1989]
1994	[1993, 1995]
2000	[1999, 2001]
2008	[2006, 2010]
2014	[2011, 2017]

8.4.4 Cross-sectional dependence test

A growing body of the panel data literature concludes that panel data models are likely to exhibit substantial cross-sectional dependence in the errors, which may arise because of the presence of common shocks and unobserved components that ultimately become part of the error term, spatial dependence, and idiosyncratic pairwise dependence in the disturbances with no particular pattern of common components or spatial dependence. When T (panel's time dimension) > N (cross-sectional dimension), the recommended test is the LM test developed by Breusch and Pagan (1980). The test considers all the pair-wise correlations of the ordinary least squares (OLS) residuals from the individual regressions in the panel data model:

$$y_{it} = \alpha_i + \beta_i x_{it} + \mu_{it}$$

where $i = 1, ..., N$ represents the cross-section member, $t = 1, ..., T$ refers to the time period and x_{it} is a $(k \times 1)$ vector of observed regressors. The intercepts, α_i, and the slope coefficients, β_i, are allowed to vary across the panel members.

The results of the cross-sectional dependence test are presented in Table 8.8.

Table 8.8 Results of cross-sectional dependence test

	LM statistic
SOR	406.58*
TE	599.37*

*&** rejection of null hypothesis of non-stationarity at 1% & 5% levels of significance.
Source: author.

The test for both variables rejects the null hypothesis of no cross-sectional dependence, as expected. Thus, in addition to the cointegration tests suggested for panel data, it is important to undertake the test proposed by Westerlund who considers cross-sectional dependence among panels (Westerlund & Breitung, 2009).

8.4.5 Panel cointegration with structural breaks and cross-sectional dependence

Westerlund and Edgerton (2008) proposed two versions to test for the null hypothesis of no cointegration which can be used under those general conditions. Their test is derived from the LM-based unit-root tests developed by Schmidt and Phillips (1992), Ahn (1993), and Amsler and Lee (1995).

Cointegration between the variables has also been tested for considering cross-sectional dependence and structural break. The results are presented in Table 8.9.

The null hypothesis of no cointegration under both tests has been rejected. The alternate hypothesis of some panels being cointegrated under the first test and all panels being cointegrated under the second test is accepted using the Westerlund test.

8.4.6 Granger causality

The cointegration test results presented imply that SOR and TE variables have a relationship. In order to test the direction of the relation, i.e.

Table 8.9 Results of panel cointegration with cross-sectional dependence and structural break

	H_a – Some panels are cointegrated	H_a – all panels are cointegrated
Variance ratio	−3.9147*	−3.2319*

Source: author.

Table 8.10 Results of the Granger causality test

	F-Statistic
SOR does not Granger Cause TE	45.2018*
TE does not Granger Cause SOR	−5.13339*

unidirectional from SOR or TE, bidirectional or no causality, the Granger causality test is performed (Granger, 1969). The test has been applied to the first difference form of the two variables, and the results are presented in Table 8.10.

As seen above, the null hypotheses of SOR does not Granger Cause TE and TE does not Granger Cause SOR are rejected at 1 per cent significance. Thus, the Granger causality analysis reveals that there is a bidirectional relationship between the two variables. This implies that an increase in SOR leads to an increase in TE in the ensuing time period and vice versa. The direct connotation of this fact is that the increase in SOR provides the fiscal space to SNGs to undertake additional expenditure in the next time period. Similarly, additional expenditure leads to an increase in the SOR in the next period.

8.4.7 VECM

Along with long-term behaviour, it is also necessary to examine short-term behaviour of the variables because in the short term, there may be disequilibrium between the fiscal variables. Keeping this fact in mind, the VECM is also incorporated in this analysis to examine short-term behaviour among the variables (Engle & Granger, 1987; Pradhan, 2014).

Table 8.11 Results of VECM

	D (TE)	D (SOR)
Error Correction	−0.040483*	−0.020538**
Constant	0.112714*	0.137179*
Adjusted R^2	0.219002	0.16996

The estimation of the cointegration relationship will provide a series (i.e. series of residuals) which is stationary at levels. This series of residuals can be used to estimate the error-correction model to analyse the long-run and short-run effects of the variables as well as to split the long-run cointegration vector into a vector of adjustment parameters and a vector of long-run coefficients.

Thus, the results in Table 8.11 help us infer that the LR model, cointegrating equation is:

$$ect_{t\text{-}1}=1.000\,Total\ Expenditure_{t\text{-}1}-0.65\,States\ own\ revenue_{t\text{-}1}-3.90$$

Now, estimating the VECM with SOR as the target variable shows that:

$\Delta States'sOwn\ Revenue_t$

$$=-.0205ect_{t\text{-}1}-0.000076\Delta States'sOwn\ Revenue_{t\text{-}1}$$
$$-0.117628\Delta Total\ Expenditure_{t\text{-}1}+0.137$$

VECM with TE as the target variable shows that:

$\Delta Total\ Expenditure_t$

$$=-.04048ect_{t\text{-}1}+0.3240\Delta States'sOwn\ Revenue_{t\text{-}1}$$
$$-0.2747\Delta Total\ Expenditure_{t\text{-}1}+0.1127$$

It is evident from Table 8.11 that the error correction variable is negative and significant when considering TE to be dependent, suggesting that deviation from equilibrium is corrected at 4.04 per cent per year (Dutta & Dutta, 2014). Similarly, error correction variable is also found to be negative and significant when considering SOR to be dependent, with the deviation from equilibrium corrected at 2.05 per cent annually.

8.5 Summary

The summary of all the tests undertaken and subsequent results are presented in Table 8.12.

Table 8.12 Summary of all tests undertaken

	Result
Unit root tests—at level—LLC	• Outstanding liabilities and TE are stationary • SOR is not stationary
Unit root tests—at level—IPS	• All variables are not stationary
Since the variables are not stationary at level under either test, stationarity is tested for at first difference.	
Unit Root Tests—at first difference—LLC	• All variables are stationary
Unit Root Tests—at first difference—IPS	• All variables are stationary
Since TE and SOR are stationary at the same level, i.e. at order one, cointegration between the variables may be tested for.	
Cointegration—Pedroni	• The test generates 11 test statistics, of which at least half are required to be statistically significant. All statistics are significant at 1%.
Cointegration—Kao	• The test rejected the null hypothesis of no cointegration at 1% significance.
Cointegration—Fisher	• Null hypothesis of cointegration rejected at 5%.
There exists cointegration between TE and SOR.	
Structural break	• The test identified the years of structural break which are 1988, 1994, 2000, 2008 and 2014.
Cross-sectional dependence	• The test rejects the null hypothesis of no cross-sectional dependence.
Cointegration—Westerlund	• The test rejects the null hypothesis of no cointegration between the two variables
There exists structural breaks and cross-sectional dependence in the panel set. Considering the same, there also exists cointegration between TE and SOR.	
Granger causality	• There is a bidirectional relationship between TE and SOR • An increase in SOR leads to an increase in TE in the ensuing time period • An increase in TE leads to an increase in SOR in the ensuing period
VECM	• The error correction term is negative and significant with the TE correcting at 4.04% p.a. and SOR correcting at 2.05% p.a.

8.6 Conclusion

Earlier there has not been an expenditure–revenue cointegration study that looks at the debt sustainability of the SNGs in India, and which also accounted for structural breaks and cross-sectional dependence. Structural breaks and cross-sectional dependence can introduce many errors and need to be sufficiently accounted for.

The model first tests for stationarity of the variables: state's outstanding liabilities, SOR, and state's TE using two different tests. Both the tests conclude that the variables are stationary in first order. The preliminary cointegration tests (Pedroni, Kao, and Fisher) that does not account for structural breaks and cross-sectional dependence shows that there exists cointegration between the SOR and state's TE. Further, tests for structural breaks and cross-sectional breaks reveal that there are five structural breaks and there is evidence for cross-sectional dependence.

The panel cointegration tests accounting for structural breaks and cross-sectional dependence, proposed by Westerlund and Edgerton shows that there is cointegration between SOR and state's TE indicating that the debt is sustainable in the long run. Further, the relationship between the SOR and TE of the state is found to be bidirectional in nature. Further, in the case of any deviation in one of the two variables from the equilibrium path, there is presence of an automatic stabilizer which corrects the error. This makes the relationship between SOR and TE quite stable giving further credence to the sustainable nature of SNG debt in India.

Despite the models presenting a positive scenario for SNG debt sustainability in India, there are some emerging issues which have the potential to upset states' finances in coming years. These are discussed in detail in the next chapter.

9

Emerging Issues in Debt Sustainability of SNGs in India

9.1 Context

All the approaches, including the alternative approach discussed in the previous chapter, for assessing the debt sustainability of Indian states, have found that although some states are debt stressed, the present debt levels of Indian states are sustainable. However, there are clear signs of worry for SNGs in ensuring debt sustainability in the future. RBI (2022b) has warned that India will face a similar fate as that of Sri Lanka if corrective measures are not undertaken to avert the crisis. According to the RBI 'the slowdown in own tax revenue, a high share of committed expenditure and rising subsidy burdens have stretched state government finances already exacerbated by Covid-19' (RBI, 2022b:115). The SNGs' combined debt in India surpassed 31.1 per cent in 2020–21, significantly higher than the FRBM Review Committee recommended target of 20 per cent by 2022–23. States are also likely to miss the debt-to-GDP ratio target of 20 per cent in 2022–23 by a huge margin. As per the forecast, the debt stock has become unsustainable in the five states with the highest indebtedness and there is no sign of improvement in their debt–GSDP ratio. The ratio is expected to remain above 35 per cent in 2026–27 (RBI, 2022b). Moreover, for all states taken together, the projected average debt-to-GDP ratio in 2026–27 would be around 27 per cent which is still higher than 26 per cent in 2019–20 (pre-Covid).

What is more worrying is that the quality of borrowing has worsened in recent years. Revenue deficit-to-fiscal deficit ratio is one of the indicators that assesses the quality of spending of the government. It can be observed that due to limited borrowing capacity, a large part of the borrowing is being utilized by SNGs to finance their revenue expenditure.

Debt Sustainability of Subnational Governments in India. Hari Krishna Dwivedi, Oxford University Press.

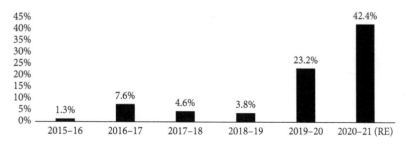

Figure 9.1 Quality of expenditure (states combined)- Revenue Deficit-Fiscal Deficit ratio

Source: author's calculation based on RBI ([state finances] various years).

This ratio which was 1.3 per cent in 2015–16 increased to 42.4 per cent in 2020–21 (see Figure 9.1).

One of the reasons for the decline in quality of spending is fiscal profligacy. Grand political commitments in the form of transfer payments, which have evolved into the mainstay of discretionary spending at the subnational level, are driving this expenditure. It is evident that the political class is tempted by electoral calculations to prioritize short-term benefits above long-term sustainability.

The opportunity cost is that when SNGs spend more on transfer payments, they have less money available for investing in social infrastructure, such as education, health, etc. as well as physical infrastructure, such as power, roads, etc. which has the potential to boost growth and create employment.

Nonetheless, concerns are raised about the sustainability of borrowing and spending on these transfers.

There are additional factors which are adding to the risks to debt sustainability of state governments in India. These factors include, rising outstanding guarantees, significant losses of the state power distribution companies (DISCOMs), end of GST compensation beyond June 2022, increase in inefficient subsidies, poor financial performance of state-level public sector enterprises (SLPEs) and massive inflationary pressures causing an increase in bond yields. These factors are likely to put severe strain on already poor state finances. Each of these factors are discussed below.

9.2 Rising Outstanding Guarantees of State Governments Adding to Debt Risk

A key factor which can pose a massive risk to the debt sustainability of Indian states is an increase in guarantees issued by the state governments. Sovereign guarantees issued by state governments constitute a part of the contingent liabilities of the state governments. ADB in one of its reports titled 'The Sustainability of Asia's Debt' observes that, the contingent liabilities of SNGs in India accounts for about 24 per cent of GDP' (Ferrarini et al., 2022:19).

A state government can issue guarantees as per Article 293(1) of the Constitution of India. However, the number of guarantees issued by the state government should not breach the limit as determined by the state legislature based on the security of the consolidated fund of the state. The state Government Guarantees Act, FRBM/FRL, or Ceiling Acts prescribe the norms set by the SNGs on the permissible level of guarantees. These acts prescribe a ceiling on the annual growth of guarantees as a ratio to GSDP or revenue receipts (RR). Following the enactment of the FRBM Act in 2005, the guarantees issued by state government as a percentage of GDP had continuously declined until 2017. But thereafter, the guarantees issued by state governments as a percentage of the GDP has been increasing, indicating early signs of fiscal risks. The total guarantees outstanding as a percentage of GDP has climbed from about 2 per cent in 2017 to about 3 per cent in 2020. Of these guarantees, about 60 per cent of them are given to the power sector, followed by the transport sector at a less than 5 per cent (see Figure 9.2).

Since guarantees account for a significant share of GDP, if invoked they can pose a massive risk to the debt sustainability of Indian states. If one adds up the guarantees given by state governments in the outstanding debt, then the outstanding debt-to-GDP of state governments in 2020–21 increases from 31.1 per cent to about 34 per cent.

The state issues guarantees mainly for off-budget borrowing. This borrowing is not made directly by the state or central government. This borrowing is made by the public sector undertakings (PSUs) or an implementing agency (special purpose vehicle (SPV)) and such borrowing does not form a part of government borrowing, hence off-budget.

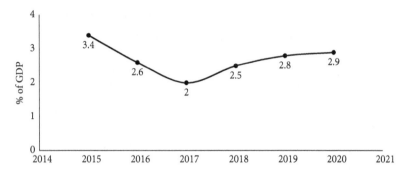

Figure 9.2 Outstanding guarantees as % of GDP (all states and UTs)
Source: author's calculation based on RBI ([state finances] various years).

As this borrowing does not enter the consolidated fund of the centre and states, it is not included in the fiscal deficit targets mandated under FRBM. In many cases of off-budget borrowing, the government raises resources for itself by requiring a PSU or an SPV to issue bonds or take loans with sovereign guarantee. For example, in the case of food subsidy, the central government provided for only half the budgeted amount and required Food Corporation of India to take out loans from the National Small Savings Fund to make for the shortfall.

Also, sometimes PSUs require financial grants from the government for meeting operational needs or incurring capital expenditure. In such cases, instead of providing budgetary grants, the government allows PSUs to raise loans, the repayment of which may become a liability of the government. The FRBM committee has flagged this issue in its report and observed that while such borrowing by PSUs or SPVs typically do not enter government accounts, state governments' reimbursement of such borrowing is recorded as a debit, leading to an accounting discrepancy where repayments exceed the loans advanced.

The off-budget borrowing of the state governments during the period 2019–20 to 2021–22 ranges from 0.07 to 10.21 per cent of GSDP. As can be seen from Figure 9.3, states like Telangana, AP, and Kerala have very high off-budget borrowing of more than 1 per cent of their GSDP. AP has the highest level of off-budget borrowing at 10.21 per cent of GSDP.

There are two reasons why state governments in recent years have relied more and more on off-budget borrowing. First, due to rising revenue

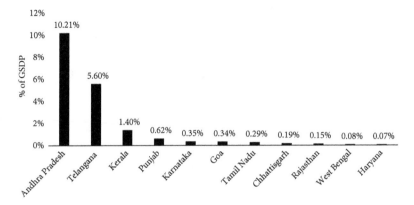

Figure 9.3 State-wise off-budget borrowings (2019–20 to 2021–22)
Source: author's calculation based on Gupta & James (2023) and MOSPI (2023).

expenditure of the states there is a severe mismatch in the revenue and expenditure. This shortfall cannot be made up through borrowing within the fiscal deficit limits. Therefore, the states are relying more on off-budget borrowing to bridge this gap as these are outside fiscal deficit targets mandated under FRBM. The guarantees provided by the state governments help the public sector agencies to borrow from the market. Second, states do not need approval from the central government to give guarantees on off-budget borrowing taken by these public sector entities which in case of borrowing to the consolidated fund of the state is mandatory. Also, the ceilings for guarantees are set by states themselves, and hence, they find it easier to borrow through this route.

Considering rising guarantees of the power sector which is extremely stressed, suggestions have made recommendations on including guarantees for assessing fiscal risk.

The Group to Assess the Fiscal Risk of State Government Guarantees had recommended in July 2002 that repayment provisions for guarantees with 100 per cent risk should be provided. For the rest of the guarantees, credit rating should be undertaken, and devolvement probability should be worked out. In order to determine the annual fiscal burden of debt and guarantees, the devolvement probability could then be applied to the underlying liabilities for which the guarantees have been extended. The report additionally suggests changes in the norm to keep the interest payment within 20 per cent of Revenue Receipts (RR), in tandem with the 11th FC recommended threshold of interest payments of 18 per cent of RR in the medium term.

The 14th FC also discusses the need for expanding the definition of debt. It recommended that the government's risk exposure should be considered by taking into account the guarantees extended by the state government. The Commission defined extended debt as the amount of public debt plus the weighted sum of guarantees provided to high-risk PSEs, such as those in the electricity and transport sectors. A weight of 90 per cent was given to the power sector guarantees during the analysis of this extended debt, while a weight of 10 per cent was given to other guarantees, including the transport sector guarantees.

The Comptroller and Auditor General (CAG), the chief government auditor, has in its many audit reports of the state governments suggested that:

> If any State government borrows money in the name of any PSU, which has no independent source of income, and the loan is to be repaid by setting apart a share of the Government's own resources, then for that reason, the loan is not a contingent liability but a liability on its own income. In fact, such borrowings for all practical purposes, represent fiscal deficit of the State and should be treated as such. Creating such liabilities, without disclosing them in the budget, raises questions both of transparency, and of inter-generational equity. Merely because the borrowing is not shown in the budget does not mean that the liability of discharging it from the State revenues will disappear.
>
> (Government of Kerala, 2020:43)

Although there are measures in place to prevent over dependence on guarantees, such as setting up the Guarantee Redemption Fund (GRF). However, only a few states have adhered to the rules of the GRF. The corpus of the GRF is generally less than 1.5 per cent of the outstanding guarantees, which is a very small share.[1] Another mechanism to limit guarantees issued by state government is the ceiling on outstanding guarantees mandated in their FRBM Acts, whereby the total outstanding

---

[1] https://www.rbi.org.in/Scripts/PublicationsView.aspx?id=19710

government guarantees as on 1 April of any year shall not exceed a particular percentage of the state's total receipts or its RR. However, there are variations across states in terms of their understanding of the fiscal risk involved in the issuance of these guarantees and the implementation of an effective procedure to reduce the impact of guarantees on state budgets.

9.3 Losses of DISCOMs Not Reflected in State Deficits

The deficit of SNGs does not reflect the real picture as the debt of DISCOMS is not taken into account. In the last twenty years, there have been three cases in which state governments have taken over the debt of the DISCOMs. This has had a severe impact on state finances (RBI, 2022b).

The power sector's financial situation has again deteriorated. As of 2018–19, the losses of DISCOMs exceed by 0.4 per cent of GDP compared to what it was before implementation of UDAY. In 2019–20, the aggregate losses of DISCOMs of five heavily indebted states, namely Bihar, Kerala, Punjab, Rajasthan, and West Bengal accounted for about 25 per cent of the total DISCOM losses. According to projections by Subramanian et al. (2022), in 2020–21 the aggregate losses of the DISCOMs amounted to ₹2,10,000 cr without subsidies and grants and ₹3,00,000 cr when arrears are considered. Additionally, the overdue amount of DISCOMs to power generation companies (GENCOs) have increased significantly in the last three years to over ₹1,00,000 cr in 2020-21. The total outstanding debt stock of state DISCOMs have risen to about ₹5,90,000 cr in 2020-21 (see Figure 9.4).

The state governments in 2015 had faced a similar situation of unprecedented rise in losses of DISCOMs. The state DISCOMs had accumulated total losses of about ₹3,80,000 cr and a total debt of about ₹4,20,000 cr and were reeling under severe financial stress. To rescue them, the UDAY scheme was introduced to financially restructure the DISCOMs. Under the UDAY scheme, the state governments had to absorb the debt of the DISCOMs to improve the operational and financial efficiency of DISCOMs. In addition, the states were expected to start initiate reforms

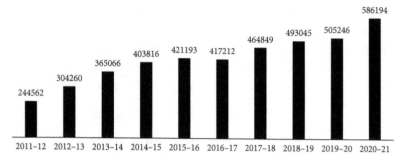

Figure 9.4 Outstanding debt stock of DISCOMs (₹ Cr)
Source: Power Finance Corporation (2022)

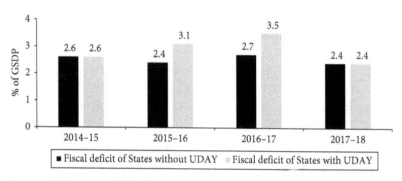

Figure 9.5 Impact of UDAY
Source: Government of India (2020).

to cut down on aggregate technical and commercial losses and hike tariffs to levels that would prevent the problem from recurring.

With the introduction of UDAY, the deficits of the state governments increased significantly. With the states taking over the debt of DISCOMs, the combined state fiscal deficit was 3.1 per cent of GDP in 2015–16 and 3.5 per cent in 2016–17. When the UDAY impact is removed, the fiscal deficit equals 2.4 per cent of GDP in 2015–16 and 2.7 per cent in 2016–17 (15th FC, 2020) (see Figure 9.5).

Although, the outstanding debt of the DISCOMs declined immediately post UDAY, the financial situation has again worsened. If steps are not taken by the DISCOMs to curtail their losses, there may be a recurrence of the situation prevailing in 2015 when the state governments had to step in to bail out the DISCOMS due to an unprecedented rise in losses. If a similar rescue package is to be provided by the state governments to DISCOMs again, then it will significantly increase the burden on the exchequer. As per the RBI study, the cost of bailout of DISCOMs for eighteen major states taken together is about 2.3 per cent of their combined GDP. Punjab, Madhya Pradesh, Tamil Nadu, and Rajasthan are the states most at risk from a potential future bailout (RBI, 2022b). Thus, going forward, state DISCOMs must initiate necessary reforms (e.g. appropriate tariff revisions) to avoid bankruptcy, otherwise it will adversely affect the state finances as has happened in the past.

9.4 End of GST Compensation

The central government, as per the agreement arrived at with the states in the GST Council, had been compensating states for any shortfall in their actual GST revenues vis-à-vis the merged taxes in 2015–16 increased by 14 per cent every year, for a period of five years starting from 2017. This five-year period ended in June 2022. The compensation was financed by a separate cess on the demerit and luxury items.

It is apprehended that the discontinuation of GST is likely to burden the state finances because states are heavily dependent on GST compensation. To determine the extent of dependency on GST compensation, the share of the GST compensation fund in the total GST revenue[2] for General Category States (GCS) is calculated as per the data availability. The greater the share of GST compensation of a state in its total GST revenue, the greater is the dependency of that state on GST compensation.

The share of GST compensation in total GST revenue for GCS for FY 2017–18, 2018–19, and 2019–20 is shown in Table 9.1.

It can be observed that from FY 2017–18 to FY 2019–20, all GCS had received GST compensation from the central government for the loss arising due to GST implementation. Punjab, Chhattisgarh, and Karnataka had the highest dependency on GST compensation from FY 2017–18 to FY 2019–20. In the state of Haryana, Karnataka,

---

[2] Total GST revenue is the sum of SGST collection (including revenues from IGST) and GST compensation

Table 9.1   GST compensation analysis

States	GST compensation in total GST revenue (%)		
	(A) 2017–18	2018–19	(B) 2019–20*
Punjab	31.03	34.54	47.55
Chhattisgarh	18.62	20.69	32.15
Karnataka	18.57	20.13	30.35
Odisha	17.56	21.15	27.21
Kerala	11.45	9.82	25.43
Madhya Pradesh	15.37	12.67	25.28
Haryana	9.39	13.06	25.12
Bihar	18.59	13.32	23.47
Gujarat	13.64	15.37	23.30
Tamil Nadu	2.44	7.45	21.77
Rajasthan	14.32	8.39	20.76
Jharkhand	19.75	11.76	18.39
Maharashtra	2.69	9.10	18.20
WB	7.46	6.56	16.96
UP	5.35	0.63	13.99
AP	2.00	0.00	13.02

* Total GST revenue for FY 2019–20 includes RE of GST collection and actual estimates of GST compensation for FY 2019–20.

Source: author's calculation from state budget documents.

Maharashtra, Chhattisgarh, Goa, Odisha, Punjab, and Tamil Nadu, the dependency had been rising over a period at an increasing rate. For such states, discontinuation of GST compensation is likely to have a more serious impact leading to significant decline in their overall tax revenues. In order to tide over the shortfall, these states may have to either increase their borrowing or in the absence of borrowing curtail their capital expenditure.

9.5   Rising Inefficient Subsidies

Government subsidies tend to drive resources away from useful and productive expenditure to non-income-generating ones. It is pertinent

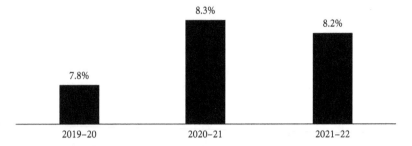

Figure 9.6 Share of subsidy expenditure to total revenue expenditure
Source: RBI (2022b)

to note that Sri Lanka which defaulted on its debt and Pakistan which was on the brink of default had significantly large shares of subsidies in total expenditure (TE). The public debt-to-GDP ratio of Pakistan and Sri Lanka would have been 25 percentage points and 10 percentage points of lower respectively, if these countries would not have followed a free electricity policy (Ferrarini et al., 2022).

The expenditure on subsidies by state governments in India has witnessed growth at 12.9 per cent and 11.2 per cent during the FY 2019–20 and FY 2020–21, respectively. Similarly, subsidies' share in revenue expenditure has grown from 7.8 per cent in 2019–20 to 8.2 per cent in 2020–21 (see Figure 9.6). In some circumstances, it is necessary to spend on transfer payments so that social protection is provided for the most vulnerable groups of the population. However, these transfers should be funded through revenue and not debt.

An analysis of state expenditure on subsidies shows that there are significant variation among states. For states such as Chhattisgarh, Karnataka, Punjab, Gujarat and Rajasthan, the subsidies as a percentage of revenue expenditure is much higher than the national average. These states spend in excess of 10 per cent of their revenue expenditure on subsidies (see Figure 9.7).

Going forward, the headroom for spending on welfare schemes will be significantly diminished with the discontinuation of GST compensation. In such a scenario, inefficient subsidies will prove to be a significant financial strain on state governments' finances.

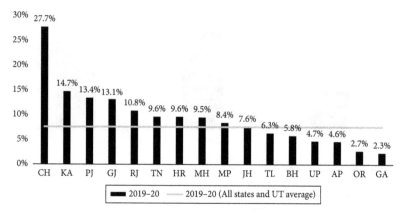

Figure 9.7 State-wise Subsidy to revenue expenditure ratio: 2019–20
Source: author's calculation based on RBI ([state finances] various years).

9.6 Poor Financial Performance of SLPEs

State Level Public Enterprises (SLPEs) form an important part of the public enterprise system of the country. The role of SLPEs includes mobilization of institutional finances to meet social objectives, acting as drivers for growth for backward regions, and supporting the state governments in the implementation of public policy. The SLPEs mainly act as a support system to state governments and contribute to about 5 per cent of GDP of the country. Without SLPEs, it is not possible to successfully implement the reform programmes of the government. Most of the SLPEs are in the energy and power sector followed by the manufacturing and transport sectors. Over the years, the SLPEs have provided employment in India when unemployment has been a significant economic and social problem.

However, at a time when state governments are under financial stress, the financial performance of SLPEs has been an area of concern. The SLPEs are plagued with problems of mismanagement and poor governance. Due to lack of autonomy and operational independence, these SLPEs are not able to compete with the private sector.

The poor financial performance of the SLPEs has been analysed based on the latest CAG reports on the functioning of the SLPEs. The analysis has been carried out for the states of Punjab, Kerala, Rajasthan, and West Bengal.

In Punjab, there are thirty-three working SPSEs of which thirteen earned profit. Of the latter, only three declared dividends, of about 3.9 per cent, which is much less than the lower limit of 5 percent recommended by the 13th FC. Further, only five SPSEs had an interest coverage ratio above 1 per cent from 2020 to 2021. The interest coverage ratio reflects the ability of the PSU to service its debt out of its revenues. The interest coverage ratio of less than 1 indicates that the PSUs are not generating enough resources to meet their interest payment expenses.

In Kerala, from 2018 to 2019, the total dividend paid by the SLPEs was about 0.57 per cent of the paid-up capital. From 2015–16 to 2018–19, the net income of all the SLPEs (including the power sector) was negative. Out of the sixty-two working SLPEs having loan liability, forty PSUs had an interest coverage ratio below 1 which indicates that these PSUs could not generate sufficient revenues to meet their expenses on interest.

In Rajasthan, from 2019 to 2020, there were forty-one SLPEs. Of these, about ten had interest coverage ratio of less than 1. Moreover, four SLPEs defaulted on their debt repayments during 2019–20. Of the forty-one SLPEs, fifteen had net worth fully eroded and accumulated losses of about ₹93,721.74 cr. A negative net worth means that the entire investment by the stakeholders is eroded on account of accumulated losses and deferred revenue expenditure.

In West Bengal, out of sixty-six working SPSEs, only two had paid dividends to the state government. The total dividend paid by the working SLPEs to the government is only 0.11 per cent of the profit earned which is much lower than the dividend of 5 per cent recommended by the 13th FC (2009). What is worrying is that the power sector accounts for about 75 per cent of the total borrowing by SLPEs and these borrowing by SLPEs are backed by guarantees from the state government. Therefore, there exists a substantial risk that this liability may ultimately be borne by the state.

As many of the SLPEs have huge losses, the state governments have to support them by extending grants or loans, which is a heavy drain on state resources. Many of the SLPEs are operating in sectors which now have a thriving private sector. There is an urgent need for the state governments to restructure SLPEs in core areas so as to run them on commercially sound principles and exit from those sectors where private sector can provide the public services presently rendered by SLPEs. This would greatly reduce the burden on state finances arising due to inefficient and loss-making SLPEs.

In addition to this, the usual practice for states has been to borrow on the books of SLPEs, often with the promise of future state earnings as a guarantee. The state exchequer actually bears the burden of debt, albeit skilfully concealed. If we look at just the state budgets, we observe that all of the states are adhering to the FRBM goals and that the state finances are in a good, if not robust, condition.

However, this picture can be misleading. A large portion of the borrowing used to fund many schemes and programmes takes place off-budget. Even the CAG had highlighted that in respect of some states 'if extra-budgetary borrowings are taken into account, the liabilities of the government are way above what is acknowledged in the official books'. Comprehensive information available to evaluate the magnitude of this off-budget debt is lacking in the public domain. However, anecdotal evidence indicate that it may be of a similar scale to the debt officially acknowledged in the Budget documents (Subbarao, 2022).

9.7 Massive Inflationary Pressure and Consequent Rise in Bond Yields

There are massive inflationary pressures created in the economy due to a rise in global fuel prices and disruption of global food and fuel chains since the war in Ukraine. RBI had targeted inflation in the range of 4±2 per cent from 2017 to 2022 and decided to continue the same range for the next five years as well. As can be seen from Figure 9.8, consumer price index (CPI) inflation has exceeded the ceiling limit targeted by RBI in the first quarter of 2022–23. Inflation in April 2022 was the highest for eight years at 7.8 per cent.

With increased inflation, RBI has been revising the monetary policy by raising the interest rate to cool down the economy. This has pushed the interest rates on all debt instruments including state development loans (SDLs). Likewise, the interest on SDLs has been rising which is making debt servicing costlier for the state governments. The weighted average yield of state government securities increased from 6.03 per cent in 2020–21 to more than 7.3 per cent in September 2022 (see Figure 9.9).

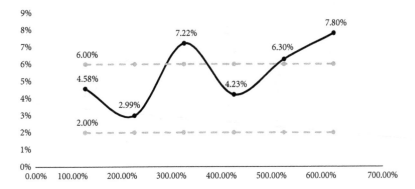

Figure 9.8 Rising inflation rate
Source: RBI ([state statistics] various years).

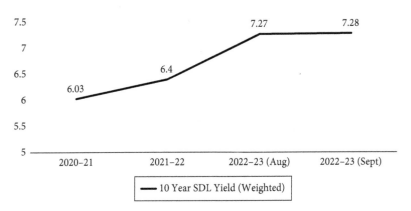

Figure 9.9 Rising bond yields of SNGs
Source: RBI.([National Summary Data Page] various years)

9.8 Decline in Share of Tax Devolution

Tax devolution in the form of central transfer from the shareable taxes to SNGs forms about 25 per cent of their total revenues. This form of transfer from the centre is unconditional in nature. However, the actual tax devolution to the states as a percentage of gross tax revenues (GTR) of the central government has declined over the years. This has been on account of the increase in the cesses and surcharges and low collection of the revenues by the central government. In the 2022–23 budget, states'

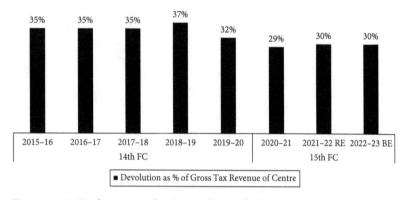

Figure 9.10 Decline in tax devolution (as % of GTR)
Source: author's calculation using data from Union Budget Documents (2017-18 to 2022-23).

share in central taxes is estimated to be only 30 per cent of the GTR of the centre (see Figure 9.10).

As discussed earlier, cesses and surcharges as a percentage of GTR has increased from about 10.4 in 2011–12 to a significantly higher figure of 23.8 in 2020–21 RE. With the increase in cesses and surcharges as a share of GTR, the divisible pool has shrunk over the years.

The decrease in devolution out of the GTR will continue to put pressure on the state finances.

9.9   Conclusion

The states face many new challenges which will put significant pressure on SNG finances, on both the revenue front as well as on the expenditure front. These could derail the fiscal health of the SNGs in India.

On the revenue side, SNG revenues are likely to take a serious hit due to the discontinuation of GST compensation and declining actual tax devolution to the states from the divisible pool. Over the years, the devolution to the states as a percentage of centre's GTR has declined from 35 per cent in 2015–16 to 30 per cent in 2020–21. Moreover, the GST compensation arrangement that ended in June 2022 now deprives the states of valuable resources that helped tide over the shortfall in tax collection due to implementation of GST. However, the tax collection has not yet returned to the pre-GST trend level, and with the end of GST compensation, the states may find themselves in a difficult fiscal position.

On the expenditure side, SNGs have exposed themselves to significant risks, namely, rising outstanding guarantees of SNGs, huge losses of DISCOMs, rising subsidies, poor performance of SLPEs, and increasing debt-servicing costs due to inflationary pressures of SNGs. If not timely addressed, these challenges may further worsen the already debt-stressed situation of SNGs.

10

How Can SNGs in India Avoid Debt Crises?

10.1 Context

We have seen that although the debt levels of SNGs is sustainable, going forward they face challenges. Even though collectively the debt situation of SNGs is not serious, some of the SNGs are debt stressed. We have also seen that many of the SNGs in order to achieve fiscal targets had to compromise their development expenditure (DEVEX) on capital account. This low creation of capital assets may in the long run affect their revenue generation capacity. So, the question that arises is: how can SNGs in India avoid a situation of debt default? What measures should the state governments take to improve their fiscal management? We now attempt to address these questions.

10.2 Measures for Sound Fiscal Management by SNGs

Sound fiscal management by SNGs would entail prudent policy interventions on both revenue and expenditure sides. Figure 10.1 shows the two-pronged strategy which states can adopt.

10.3 Revenue Augmentation Strategy

SNGs in India can augment their resources through higher collection of tax and non-tax revenues. The own tax and non-tax sources of revenues of SNGs are presented in Figure 10.2.

Debt Sustainability of Subnational Governments in India. Hari Krishna Dwivedi, Oxford University Press.
© Hari Krishna Dwivedi 2024. DOI: 10.1093/oso/9780198903116.003.0010

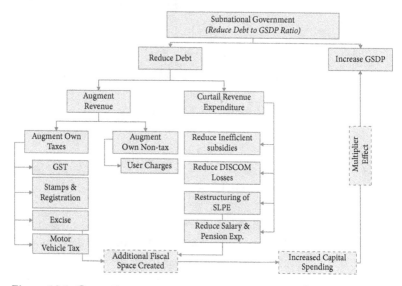

Figure 10.1 Corrective measures state governments in India can exercise

Within the tax revenues, collection is primarily from four sources, namely, the state Goods and Services Tax (GST), excise (on alcohol for human consumption), stamp duty and registration fees, and motor vehicles taxes. Together, these taxes generate more than 70 per cent of the state's total tax revenue. The state GST itself accounts for almost 40 per cent of the state's own tax revenue (SOTR) collection. The states do not have much leeway in augmenting GST revenues through changes in the tax structure and rates as it is exclusively the domain of the GST Council.[1] However, apart from evasion of tax, there are inefficiencies in the collection of state GST. The state governments should adopt measures aimed at increasing GST compliance. After GST, the second major source of tax revenue for the state governments is revenue from excise on alcohol. The excise duty on alcohol can be augmented through effective regulation and control of the liquor trade. As alcohol is a demerit good with social consequences, there are limitations on increasing revenue from this source. In fact, some states have adopted policies banning the sale and

---

[1] Formed following the introduction of GST in 2016. The Council consists of members from both state and central governments. It recommends important aspects of GST like rates, exemptions, special provisions.

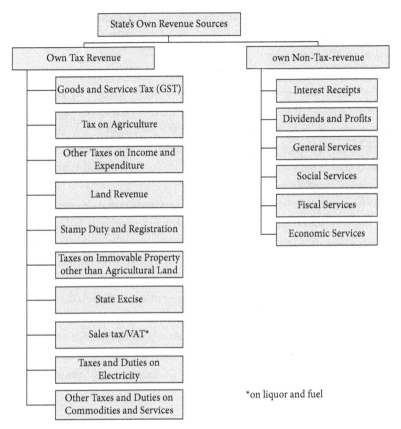

Figure 10.2 Components of own revenue of states

consumption of alcohol. The other major sources of revenue include revenue from stamp duty and registration fees on property and certain transactions and motor vehicle taxes. Stamp duty and registration fees account for about 10 per cent of states' OTR collection. This source of revenue has huge potential which state governments can tap by bringing in reforms in the valuation of circle rates (minimum rate fixed by government for registration of transaction) of properties and efficiency in collection. Revenue from motor vehicles largely depends on the size and structure of states' economy. In other words, the number of vehicles sold and registered depends upon the per capita income of the people of the state and their propensity to consume taxable goods. Apart from improving efficiency of collection and curbing evasion, states can consider imposition of green taxes on older vehicles. This will not only generate additional revenue for the government but will also help to control pollution by discouraging the use of older vehicles.

In addition to tax revenues, states also receive non-tax revenue through collection of user fees or charges for providing goods and services to the public. Less than 2 per cent of the nation's GDP comes from non-tax revenues and this ratio has not changed in the past eight years. This source of revenue has huge potential to increase in future. However, there is a reluctance on the part of political executive to align the user charges with the cost of providing services.

While traditional tax and non-tax revenue sources remain pivotal for the financial health of SNGs, the evolving economic landscape has necessitated innovative strategies of revenue mobilization. As environmental and technological challenges become more pronounced, the need for measures such as carbon emission taxes, tourism levy, congestion pricing, and the monetization of government-owned assets and data becomes more pronounced. Exploring these novel avenues not only offers new financial streams but also aligns revenue generation with broader societal goals and contemporary challenges. In susbsequent sections of this chapter, we will delve into these potential strategies and examine their viability and impact for SNGs.

10.4 Expenditure Rationalization Strategy

On the expenditure side, states may focus on reducing revenue expenditure through rationalization of workforce and reduction in expenditure on salaries and pensions, curtailing inefficient expenditure on subsidies, taking steps to reduce DISCOM losses, restructuring and disinvestment or strategic sale of loss-making public sector enterprises, reducing guarantees, rationalizing expenditure on schemes through targeted programmes and channelling public resources to capital expenditure. By taking these measures, SNGs in India can generate enough fiscal space which can be invested back into revenue-generating capital assets resulting in a positive multiplier effect on economic development. This would also help states to avoid excessive borrowing.

Each of these measures is discussed in detail in the subsequent sections.

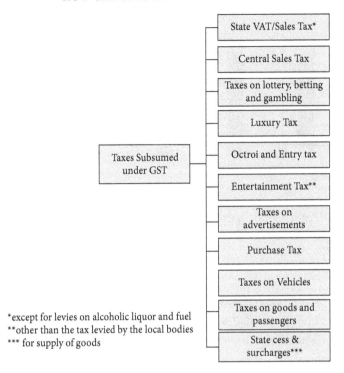

Figure 10.3 Taxes subsumed under GST

10.5 Augmenting Revenues

10.5.1 Increasing GST compliance at the state level

GST was introduced in India in 2017. It subsumed major central and state indirect taxes (see figure 10.3) and introduced seamless flow of credit across the boundaries of the state and across goods and services, thereby reducing multiplicity of taxes and the cascading effect of tax. Its introduction was expected to bring buoyancy in the indirect tax collection within a couple of years of implementation. However, even after five years of implementation of GST, the expected buoyancy still eludes the centre and the states. Although the last two years were badly affected by Covid, GST is still in the process of getting fully stabilized.

The 15th FC noted in its report that the proposed GST tax compliance system is inoperable. GST collection was 5.1 per cent of GDP in 2019–20

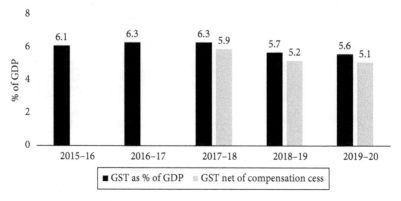

Figure 10.4 GST efficiency gap (total collection vis-à-vis collection from taxes subsumed under GST)

Source: Government of India (2020)

(a non-Covid year), compared to collection of 6.1 per cent of GDP in 2016–17 of all taxes subsumed into GST (see figure 10.4). This implies that the benefits of the GST system have not yet been fully realized.

A state-wide analysis of the comparison of collections from GST from 2017 to 2020 and collections from taxes subsumed under GST (pre-GST era 2012–17) shows significant differences among states. The largest decline in the average of tax collection-to-GSDP ratio is in Punjab (decline of 2.06 percentage points) followed by Gujarat (0.82), Goa (0.81), and Karnataka (0.78) (see Table 10.1). Only in respect of Rajasthan and Uttar Pradesh (UP), the state tax-to-GSDP ratio increase marginally. This very nominal increase or decrease reflect the inherent structural deficiencies in GST and inefficiencies in collection.

There are several reasons for low compliance of GST. The technology-driven tax has been administered leniently in the initial years by central and state tax officials, giving firms and dealers time to adjust to the new system. However, this has encouraged businesses to indulge in unfair trade practices for the purpose of evasion of tax.

GST tax evasion has been widely observed at the retail level. The common practice resorted to by the retailers is to sell goods and services either without invoices or fake invoices.

Selling without invoices typically happens when the buyer is the ultimate consumer and cannot utilise any input tax credit (ITC) and is

Table 10.1 Average tax collection-to-GSDP ratio (general states)

States	(A) 2012–17[*]	(B) 2017–20[**]
	GSDP (%)	
AP (Divided)	2.31[1]	2.29
Bihar	3.09	3.21
Chhattisgarh	3.19	2.69
Goa	4.17	3.36
Gujarat	3.09	2.27
Haryana	3.09	2.49
Jharkhand	3.06	2.80
Karnataka	3.50	2.73
Kerala	3.06	2.57
Madhya Pradesh	2.93	2.38
Maharashtra	3.34	3.07
Odisha	3.39	2.63
Punjab	4.58	2.51
Rajasthan	2.43	2.44
Tamil Nadu	2.63	2.34
Telangana[2]	2.86[7]	2.63
UP	3.04	3.14
WB	2.62	2.51

[*] Taxes subsumed in GST.

[**] SGST (after IGST settlement).

[1] Since Telangana was separated from Andhra Pradesh as a newly formed state on 2 June 2014, we have considered the data for FY 2015–16 and 2016–17 for the pre-GST era for AP.

[2] The state of Telangana was formed on 2 June 2014 and as per data availability, we have taken the data for FY 2015–16 and 2016–17 for Pre-GST era.

Source: author's calculation based on data from RBI state finances.

generally not interested in tax invoices. In these cases, though the amount of tax is collected by the retailer from the customer, it is not deposited with the government. The sale is also not recorded officially in the accounts. This is common in cases where the supplier is the manufacturer or a service provider. In the case of retailers, inventory is needed for sales without invoices in addition to what is indicated in the records. This is usually done by reusing the same e-way bill (an electronic permission for the carriage of goods).

With regard to selling fake invoices without any supply, it is seen that invoices generated out of sale (where no invoice is given to the consumer) are sold by the retailer to another manufacturer or service provider at a negotiated price by raising proper invoices but without any supply in reality. The full value of the invoice is received from the buyer through banking channel and refunded by cash after retaining the price negotiated for the fake invoice. Though the manufacturer or service provider or retailer pays off the full tax this time, the next buyer in the chain utilises the credit without receiving any goods or service and uses that credit for paying tax, which would have otherwise been paid from his current account. So, the government loses out revenue at the end of the cycle.

Another practice which is commonly adopted is that a registration is taken with fake identity proof of random people (like a labourer, domestic helper). It typically functions for a period of two to three months during which fake invoices are sold to various manufacturers or service providers who utilises the credit on the basis of this document while the tax has not been deposited by the fake invoice supplier. Commonly they close their business after a short period, and during their period of operation, they evade huge amount of tax.

Another crucial element for improving efficiency of compliance is improving the capacity of state tax officials to administer GST, especially tax on services, as they have no experience of handling service tax prior to the introduction of GST, as it was a central tax. Also, in order to distinguish between the three components of the compliance verification system—'return scrutiny' (to ensure accuracy of assessment), 'audit' (to reconcile the tax return with the financial records), and 'intelligence-based investigations'—it is also crucial to streamline the state tax departments in each of the states.

Advanced technology should be used to help identify fraudulent activities. To that end, each state needs to develop tax analytic units and train the state tax officers to properly use the unit to identify patterns of fraud and to perform analysis for mass detection of evasion in a systematic manner. Stemming tax evasion along with capacity building of tax officials will improve GST compliance.

10.5.2 Expanding the coverage of GST

There are several goods and services which are still outside the ambit of GST. The two most important among them is petrol and diesel and supply of electricity.

Subsumation of petroleum products in GST

Petroleum products like diesel and petrol are among the most consumable items and constitute a major part of India's GDP. Currently, the central government levies excise duty on petroleum products while the state governments impose value-added tax (VAT), sales tax (and cesses and surcharges) on petrol, diesel, and other petroleum products. The rate of state tax on petrol and diesel ranges from 12 per cent to more than 30 per cent (state-wise rates on petrol and diesel are provided in Table A.1 in the Appendix). Taxes and duties on petroleum products roughly account for 20 to 25 per cent of the total revenue receipts of the centre and 15–20 per cent of the OTR of the states. Given the huge dependency of the centre and the states on the revenues collected from petroleum products, the GST Council at the time of the introduction of GST decided to keep petroleum products out of GST until such time as GST stabilizes. This was primarily to give comfort to the states who were apprehensive of their loss of autonomy and decline in revenues.

Over time, the government's revenue from taxes on petrol and diesel has climbed dramatically. The collection from central excise duties including cesses collected from petroleum products has increased from ₹99,068 cr. in 2014–15 to ₹3,63,305 cr. in 2021–22 (see figure 10.5).

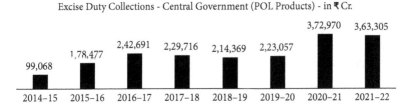

Excise Duty Collections - Central Government (POL Products) - in ₹ Cr.

Figure 10.5 Excise collection of central government on POL products (in ₹ Cr.)
Source: PPAC (2023a).

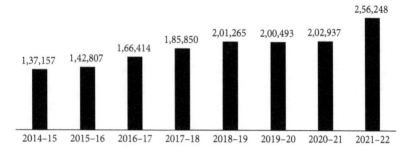

Figure 10.6 Sales tax or VAT collection of states (aggregate) on POL products
Source: PPAC (2023a)

Similarly, the aggregate collection of the states from VAT or sales tax on petroleum products has climbed (see figure 10.6) significantly from ₹1,37,157 crores in 2014–15 to ₹2,56,248 crores in 2021–22.

The burden of the increasing fuel prices affects the daily lives of the common people in addition to contributing to rising inflation rates. The increasing fuel prices also have a cascading effect on various sectors since the cost of transport and logistics goes up.

If, going forward, petrol and diesel are brought under the ambit of the GST regime, it may benefit the overall economy. Even if a higher rate of GST along with cesses and surcharges is charged on these products, petrol and diesel will be sold at much cheaper than current rates. The ITC on the tax paid on these products will be available to the industry thereby reducing the cost which at present is embedded in the price of the final goods. Lower fuel prices would greatly reduce the transport costs of all products giving a huge fillip to the economy through increased demand and production. Such a salutary effect on the economy would not only offset any possible initial loss of revenue due to subsumation of petroleum products in GST but in the long run will increase revenues. However, as the states collect substantial taxes from these two items, the central government may explore putting in place a compensation mechanism à la GST to provide comfort to the states for any loss of revenue arising out of subsummation. This comfort is essential as the desired buoyancy in GST collections is yet to be achieved coupled with discontinuation of GST compensation. It may be mentioned that many SNGs wanted the central government to continue with the compensation for a couple of years more.

Supply of Electricity

The power to levy tax on the consumption or sale of electricity is with the states as per the Seventh Schedule of the Constitution of India. As this tax has not been subsumed in GST, states continue to levy taxes on the consumption or sale of electricity.

Almost all the states collect charges on consumption of electricity which is a major source of revenue for them. In 2019–20, total collection of all states from taxes and duties on electricity was more than ₹40,000 crores which is about 3 to 4 per cent of the total states' OTR (see Figure 10.7). Across the states, this ratio ranges from 3 to 9 per cent.

Electrical energy is considered as 'goods' under the GST and is exempted from levy of tax. While GST is leviable on provision of services of supply of electricity distribution services', but transmission or distribution of electricity by an electricity transmission or distribution utility is exempted from levy of GST. The Central Electricity Authority, a state electricity board, the Central Transmission Utility, a state transmission utility notified under the Electricity Act 2003, or a distribution or transmission licensee under the said Act, or any other entity entrusted with such function by the central government or, as the case may be, the state

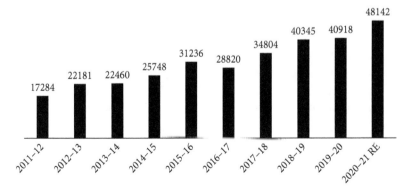

Figure 10.7 States' collections from taxes and duties on electricity (in ₹ Cr.)
Source: RBI ([state finances] various years).

government are all included in the definition of an electricity transmission or distribution utility.

A main contention of the power-generating companies is that such exemptions to electricity actually denies the power companies the benefit of ITC on the major input 'coal' which in turn increases the power tariff. The argument in this regard is that imposition of GST would actually help in reducing the cost of production and in turn the power tariff.

By including the electricity supply under GST, there would be multiple benefits to the overall economy which would boost economic growth and hence revenue collections. These include reduced cost of manufacturing, increase in export competitiveness, and smooth flow of ITC across the supply chain.

So, there are distinct gains for the states in the long run if both petroleum products and supply of electricity is brought under GST. The boost in economy that will result will translate into higher GST collections. However, given the fiscal position of the states and their ever-increasing expenditure responsibilities, the country may wait for a couple of years to subsume these two items into GST. Hopefully, in a couple of years, GST will stabilize and the states will be confident in coping with any related revenue loss.

10.5.3 Revenue mobilization through stamp duty and registration fees

Stamp duty and registration fees are taxes levied and collected by the states. These taxes are levied on transactions mainly involving the sale of immovable property, registration of wills, powers of attorney, shares and debentures, insurance policies, etc. Together, this is the third highest source of revenue collections after GST and state excise for most of the states in India. In states, such as Gujarat and Bihar, where there is prohibition on the sale and consumption of alcohol, this is the second highest source of revenue. As seen from Figure 10.8, in terms of its share in SOTR collections, revenue from stamp duty and registration fees has hovered around 10 per cent. This source of revenue has a large untapped potential for state governments to augment their tax revenues.

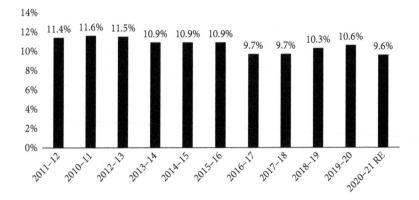

Figure 10.8 Stamp duty and registration fees as % of SOTR (all states aggregate)
Source: author's calculation based on RBI ([state finances] various years).

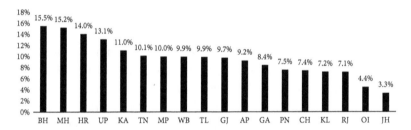

Figure 10.9 State-wide stamp duty and registration fees as % of SOTR (2019–20) (GCS)
Source: author's calculation based on RBI ([state finances] various years).

A state-wise comparison of stamp duty and registration fees shows that some states have much higher collection from stamp duty and registration fees than other states (see Figure 10.9). This variation is mainly due to differences in the level of urbanization, system of valuation and inbuilt inefficiencies in collection.

It is seen that many states which are more urbanized and have buoyant property transactions have their revenue from stamp duties and registration lower than the combined average of all states. Notably among them are Gujarat, Punjab, Chhattisgarh, and Rajasthan. One of the primary reasons, as cited by the Comptroller and Auditor General of India (CAG), is the persistent undervaluation of properties at the time of registration.

This is mainly due to four reasons - market value databases not kept up to date to reflect the real market value, inability of database to capture the influence of locational attributes (e.g. proximity to road, markets) in a systematic manner, limited data validation at the time of registration, and excessive human element in determination of market value of properties.

Also, in many states the rate of stamp duty and registration fees is high which encourages undervaluation by the prospective buyers of property leading to evasion of tax. In such cases, the value of property is shown to be lower than the exact transacted value and difference between the two is transacted in the form of cash payments. The amendment in 2013 to the Income Tax Act, which stipulates that income tax is payable on the amount of the difference in the value of the property as declared by the buyer and seller of the property and the circle rate, has to a large extent prevented undervaluation of the property. However, cash transactions occur where the circle rate is less than the transacted value. In such cases, undervaluation still remains an issue. There is a need to rationalize the stamp duty rates to prevent such types of evasion.

It is necessary for the state governments to streamline the methodology for valuation of immovable properties, so that the real market value can be captured which will enhance revenues from property registrations. Also, state governments should digitize their market value databases, property records, transaction records, and make available digitized cadastral maps for effective revenue collection by the department.

10.5.4 Enhancing state excise duty revenue collections

State excise taxes apply to all alcoholic beverages manufactured for human consumption. Alcohol-containing toiletries and medicines are also subject to this tax. As alcohol is a demerit good with negative health effects its use is regulated by governments through licensing of manufacture and sale. The manufacture and sale of alcohol is subject to state excise taxes. It is a major own source of revenue for the SNGs in India. The importance of this tax source can be gauged by the fact that in order to raise more funds during the recent pandemic, twenty-five states and Union Territories(UT) raised the taxes on the sale of alcohol by 10 to 120

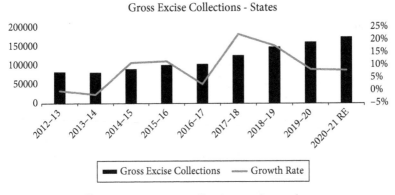

Figure 10.10 All states gross excise collections and growth rate
Source: author's calculation based on RBI ([state finances] various years).

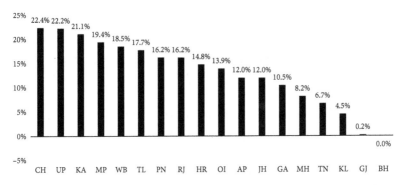

Figure 10.11 Statewide collection of excise duty as % of SOTR (2019–20) (general states)
Source: author's calculation based on RBI ([state finances] various years).

per cent (RBI, 2022). The gross excise collection has increased over the years(see figure 10.10).

A statewide comparison reveals that share of excise revenue collection in GSDP varies widely across the states from 4.5 per cent in Kerala to 22.4 per cent in Chhattisgarh (see Figure 10.11). This shows that states which have lower excise revenues have scope to significantly increase their revenues by undertaking appropriate reform measures.

Since this is a state matter, efficient regulation and control of the liquor trade should be a top priority for SNGs. Alcohol regulation is a lot more complex. The challenge is to reduce societal consumption of fake and subpar intoxicants through regulated sale of licit liquor. Total prohibition raises the cost for law enforcement, judicial application of law and public healthcare (e.g. to deal with alcohol-related abuse, accidents).

Duty, licence fees, label registration fees, and import/export fees are the main sources of excise revenue. SNGs should adopt an excise policy that clearly lays down the direction the state should pursue in order to successfully increase revenue and at the same time impose effective controls on the negative externalities arising out of alcohol consumption.

The excise policy should encourage prevention of cartelization or monopolies and open up the market to new participants, a streamlined pricing and tariff system that is frequently evaluated, a microbrewery policy to encourage the use of low-alcohol drinks, systemic controls to prevent smuggling and bootlegging, cover underserved areas or areas with few legal outlets to prevent consumption of illicit and spurious liquor, encourage customer choice and discourage unethical behaviour like brand pushing and bringing transparency in the entire excise value chain.

10.5.5   Additional mobilization of motor vehicles tax (MVT) through green tax on older vehicles

Taxes on vehicles is one of the key sources of revenue for the state. It primarily comprises of receipts under the Indian Motor Vehicle Act, and receipts under state Motor Vehicle Tax Acts. Motor Vehicle Tax (MVT) levied by states under their own motor vehicle taxation acts, is mainly been for revenue purposes, whereas licence fees, registration fees, national permit fees, etc. collected under the Indian Motor Vehicles Act are for regulatory purpose of road transport. Out of the total collection under taxes on vehicles, MVT forms a substantial proportion. It is a road tax levied by state governments on the owners of a vehicles who are liable for paying the tax at the time of purchase of a vehicle. Each state has its own Motor Vehicle (MV) Act, with states imposing different tax rates on different type of motor vehicles.

The collection of motor vehicles tax has a direct relation to the per capita income of the people residing in a particular state. The number of new vehicles registered in a particular year is dependent upon people's spending power. The size of the state and the transport infrastructure along with the status of development of other modes of transport like railways, inland waterways also impact to a large extent the potential for collection of motor vehicles tax. Motor vehicles tax has not been very buoyant. Although the collections of SNGs from MVT in absolute figures has increased since the 1990s from ₹1,500 Cr. in 1990–91 to ₹60,681 Cr. in 2020–21, however, the collection as a percentage of SOTR has stagnated at 5 per cent since the 1990s. Hence, there is a lot of scope for states to mobilize revenues from this tax.

A state-wide analysis of collection of taxes on motor vehicles shows a wide variation among states. The collection of the motor vehicle tax as a proportion of GDP differs widely among states, from as low as 4.3 per cent in West Bengal (WB) to as high as 9 per cent in Bihar (see Figure 10.12).

One of the ways to increase collections from motor vehicle tax is by imposing a green tax on older vehicles which will not only mobilize additional revenues for governments but will also control air pollution. Vehicle exhaust fumes are one of the biggest causes of air pollution. Although the commercial vehicle segment, which includes trucks, buses, taxis, and three-wheelers, make up for only around 5 per cent of the whole fleet of vehicles, it contributes roughly 65–70 per cent of all vehicular emissions. The older fleet, which often date back to before the year 2000 or even before, make up less than 1 per cent of the overall fleet but accounts for 15 per cent of the total vehicle pollution. These older

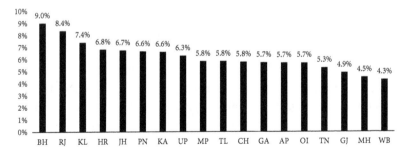

Figure 10.12 Statewide tax collections of motor vehicles as % of SOTR (2019–20) (general states)

Source: author's calculation based on RBI ([state finances] various years).

automobiles emit ten to twenty-five times more pollution than the new ones. (Ministry of Road Transport & Highways, 2021)As a result, operating older vehicles has a negative externality, and as a result, society must pay for this pollution rather than individuals. Therefore, levying a green tax on the usage of outdated cars is meant to deter their excessive use by making the owner of the vehicle responsible for the financial cost of adding to pollution .

In 2021, the Ministry of Road Transport & Highways issued draft guidelines for the imposition of a green tax by state/UT governments. In the meantime, some states have imposed green taxes on older vehicles while some already had a similar tax in place (see Table A.2 in Appendix for rate of green taxes levied by states).

It is observed that, except for Maharashtra, practically all other states have very low rates of green tax. Also, as the rate of green tax is not uniform across the states, the expected results are not achieved as automobiles may be registered in a state without or low rate green tax. Furthermore, the rate is also insufficient to deter the use of older vehicles on the road.

10.5.6 Augmenting non-tax revenues through effective collection of user charges

The government collects 'user charges' from the general, social and economic services as non-tax revenues. Interest on loans extended by the government, dividends from equity investments and earnings from general economic, social and government services are all examples of non-tax revenues. About 80 per cent of states' own non-tax revenue comes from the three main administrative non-tax receipts heads: general services, social services, and economic services. General services like police, jails, supplies and disposals, stationery and printing, public works and other administrative miscellaneous services are the main sources of receipts. Receipts from social services mainly include services like water supply and sanitation, education, sports, arts and culture, health, urban development. Receipt from economic services include receipts from mines and mineral, irrigation, forest and wildlife and industries.

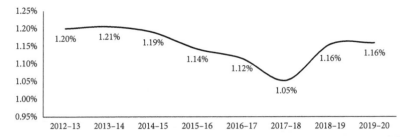

Figure 10.13 Trends in tax and non-tax receipts of all state governments (including UTs)
Source: author's calculation based on RBI ([state finances] various years).

User fees are typically fixed at very low levels or continue to be almost non-existent in most states (Purohit et al., 2009). Due to this, non-tax revenues of the state governments have suffered over the years.

About 18 per cent of the state governments' total own revenues come from sources of non-tax revenues (including UTs).[2] This is a significant portion. However, the ratio of non-tax revenue-to-GSDP, which measures how effectively these funds are mobilized, is less than 1.2 per cent and has been stagnant since 2012-13 (see Figure 10.13).

A state-wide study of non-tax revenue shows that the share of non-tax revenues to GSDP significantly differs across the states in the range of 0.3 per cent to 4.8 per cent. While this ratio is highest in UP at 4.8 per cent, it is lowest in WB and Andhra Pradesh (AP) at 0.3 per cent (see Figure 10.14). Therefore, it may be argued that there is scope for some states with lower collection to boost the non-tax revenue source.

The effective collection of user fees for the many public services offered by the government is hampered by a number of factors and issues.

First, the most important impediment to realizing the full potential of non-tax revenue via levying and collecting user charges is the consideration of political economy. Elected governments are generally reluctant to impose user charges on the people to avoid antagonizing them. So political will to impose and periodically revise the user charges with the increase in input cost of providing services is necessary to increase the collection of non-tax revenues.

---

[2] Author's calculations based on data from RBI state finances—study of budgets across years.

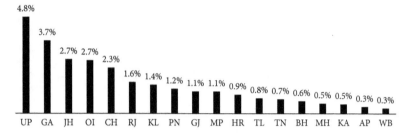

Figure 10.14 State-wise collection of non-tax revenue (GCS)
Source: author's calculation based on RBI ([state finances] various years).

Second, there are issues in setting the right price for user charges. State government's user fee collection is not utilized to its full potential nor connected with the provision of services. As a result, both the quality and quantity of service provided steadily deteriorate. The failure of departments or agencies to fairly price the services they offer to consumers of public infrastructure is one of the more important contributing factors to the bad status of services. It is necessary to recover costs adequately in order to sustain services in line with the cost incurred to provide these services. This will minimize neglect of these services and will lead to better maintenance of assets. Lack of asset maintenance leads to subpar service delivery, and it fuels lack of willingness to pay which further worsens asset formation.

As a result, a vicious cycle of subpar public infrastructure and insufficient cost recovery is created, which further leads to the deterioration of the service life, quality and coverage of infrastructure assets. User fees for public services are effective instruments when benefits are quantifiable and beneficiaries are identified according to Bahl and Linn (1992). Therefore, it is important that the agencies levy user charges appropriately to recover the costs such that the resources gathered are sufficient to fulfil the commitments of expenditure. User charges are generally notified by the concerned departments, and it is difficult to change such user charges levy from time to time. While input costs keep rising due to rising inflation, the user charges typically do not reflect the increasing cost of inputs.

Third, there are issues in designing appropriate user charges: though the general case for charging users is clear, it is difficult to determine the appropriate domain and design of user charges in practice. It is important not just to impose user charges but also to 'get the prices right' and impose the correct charges. Even where the user charges are levied, its design could often be improved from an efficiency perspective. Economic theory demonstrates that the ideal prices are equal to the marginal cost of providing the required good or service, that is, the marginal cost price.

The fees/user charges for various services supplied by the state governments must be modified to increase additional revenues from non-tax sources. However, it is necessary to increase collection efficiency while simultaneously protecting the interests of vulnerable population through cross-subsidies and lifeline tariff systems.

10.5.7 Leveraging Innovative Sources of Revenue

10.5.7.1 Carbon Emission Tax

Carbon Emission Tax is based on the idea of penalising polluters for their greenhouse gas emissions. The aim is to shed light on the 'invisible' societal costs associated with carbon emissions. This approach aims to not only diminish the demand for high carbon emission products and services but also encourage the development of more environmental friendly alternatives. Also, this fiscal instrument seeks to drive investments into cleaner energy solutions and generate revenue for governments. For SNGs, a carbon tax can be both a sustainable revenue strategy and a move toward environmental conservation.

Several regions across the globe have showcased the viability and success of this approach. **British Columbia, Canada**, for instance, introduced carbon tax for a period of 10 years from 2008 to 2018. The legislation brought in 2008 in British Columbia has set a carbon price of $10 (Canadian) for every metric ton. This amount saw an annual rise of $5 per ton from 2008 to 2012, stabilizing at $30 per ton from 2012 onwards[3]. This tax was applied directly to the acquisition of fossil fuels.

A 2015 review of the greenhouse gas (GHG) emissions in British Columbia, conducted by Komanoff (2015), revealed that the province has registered a significant decrease in GHG emissions compared to the rest of Canada. Between 2008 and 2015, British Columbia recorded a 6.1% net decrease in GHG emissions, while other parts of Canada saw

---

[3] Carbon tax amount in British Columbia has been evolving over the years

an increase of 3.5%. When broken down on a per person basis, the emissions in British Columbia decreased by 12.9%, in contrast with a 3.7% reduction in the rest of Canada. Though various initiatives played a role in decreasing emissions, the carbon tax certainly deserves recognition for its contribution to the success.

Likewise, **California's Cap-and-Trade Program**, initiated in 2012, places a cap on greenhouse gas emissions and facilitates the trading of emission allowances. This program has not only slashed carbon emissions but also yielded billions in revenue, which the state channels into further greenhouse gas reduction projects (California Air Resources Board, 2023). In essence, the carbon emission tax represents more than just a financial mechanism, it shows how fiscal policies can seamlessly integrate with environmental stewardship at the sub-national level.

10.5.7.2 Asset Monetisation

Asset monetization, where public sector assets are transformed into economic resources, has emerged as a promising strategy in several nations. SNGs in India can bolster its revenues through asset monetisation without leaning on debt or increased taxation.

In India, this concept has been particularly pivotal. Given the expansive array of public sector assets in the country, ranging from vast stretches of land and infrastructure to railways and buildings, there has been a concerted effort to tap into these resources more effectively over the last few years.

Beyond the obvious assets like roads, airports, mobile towers, and transmission lines, there lies an immense untapped potential in some of the country's less conspicuous public resources (Ahluwalia, I.J., 2000). Public sector school grounds, for instance, can be rented out for community events or sports activities during weekends or holidays, creating a dual benefit of community engagement and revenue generation (Desai, M., 2002). Similarly, auditoriums, often lying vacant in off-school hours, can be leased for cultural or corporate events.

Furthermore, the digital era has ushered in a significant opportunity with government-owned data centers. As businesses pivot towards digital operations and data-driven strategies, these centers can be leased out, catering to the surging demand for data storage and management solutions.

One of the landmark initiatives in this direction has been the National Monetization Pipeline (NMP). This ambitious framework, rolled out by the Indian government, seeks to monetize a slew of state-owned assets over a multi-year period, channeling the resultant revenues towards vital infrastructure and developmental projects, thereby sidestepping the pitfalls of an enlarged fiscal deficit (Ministry of Finance, Government of India, 2021). The assets in this purview are diverse: from roads, highways, and railways to airports, sports facilities, power transmission infrastructure, and sprawling real estate properties. The modalities adopted to realize this are equally varied, incorporating mechanisms such as the Toll-Operate-Transfer (TOT) model for highways, the innovative Infrastructure Investment Trusts (InvITs) for power assets, and straightforward lease or sale models for underutilized real estate. The aim of these is to strike a balance between asset management and the ambitious developmental goals of the country. SNGs could adopt similar strategies for asset management and resource mobilisation.

10.5.7.3 Data monetization

As people increasingly use digital services for communication, gathering information, purchase goods and services, pay bills, file taxes, and access welfare services, data is being generated at an unprecedented scale. Concurrent with this data explosion, the marginal cost of data has declined exponentially and the marginal benefit to society of using this data is higher than ever [Economic Survey 2018–19].

Data monetization is a process where data is sold to third parties for commercial use. This not only creates profits for the private sector, but also helps to ease the pressure on government finances.

The Economic Survey 2018–19 suggested that the government could monetize citizens' data as part of its larger plan to use data as a public good. Given that sophisticated technologies already exist to protect privacy and share confidential information, governments can create data as a public good within the legal framework of data privacy.

Data monetization has been implemented in the past.

Data monetization by the Ministry of Road Transport & Highways
The Ministry of Road Transport and Highways collects and holds data as part of issuance of vehicle registration certificates (RCs) and driving

licences (DLs). On 8 March 2019, the government approved a bulk data sharing policy, enabling it to monetize a database of vehicle RCs with specified law enforcement agencies and with automobile industries, banks, finance companies, etc. at specified rates for each data set. It is recognized that sharing data for other purposes, in a controlled manner, can support the transport and automobile industry. The sharing of data will also help in service improvements and wider benefits to citizens and government. Examples of data monetization are as follows:

1. Police department
    (a) Employee verification: at the time of recruitment of a new employee in any organization, the employer initiates a background criminal verification. The police department checks the name of the prospective employee against their multiple databases and provides the result to the employer. The charges per verification ranges from ₹500 to ₹1,000, and is a great source of revenue generation.
    (b) Insurance documentation: whenever an accident takes place, a First Information Report (FIR) needs to be registered. To process the insurance claim, the insurance companies require a set of documents. By paying a fee to the police department, the insurance companies can directly download these documents from the department's portal for further processing. The usual charges for a document download per claim is around ₹1,000. This can be revenue earner for the SNGs.
2. Power distribution companies
    (a) Credit organizations: the power consumption and payment history provide a lot of insight on repayment pattern to a credit issuing organization if the person availing credit does not have any previous credit history. This source of revenue has been already used in few countries in Africa.
    (b) Fast Moving Consumer Goods companies: anonymised consumption data provides a lot of market insights to the companies. This includes economic status of the residents of a particular area, their usage pattern location wise, repayment history, etc.

3. Department of Agriculture
   (a) Credit organizations: the availability of the cadastral map and
       the crop data maintained by the revenue department and agri-
       culture department are of immense value to banking organiza-
       tions while providing credit to farmers against the produce.
       The above examples are only illustrative. There are a large
       number of such opportunities available with SNGs which can
       not only generate additional revenue but also give data access
       to non-government actors.

10.6 Curtailing Revenue Expenditure

10.6.1 Curtailing inefficient subsidies

Subsidies must be distinguished from merit or public goods, like the
state assistance for education and health, the public distribution system,
and employment guarantee programmes, which have associated social
and economic benefits. In contrast, provision of free unmetered electricity, farm loan waivers, free public transport, free water, waiver of utility
overdues, etc. are considered inefficient subsidies. Some cash transfers
may help the poor if they are effectively targeted, but their advantages
must be evaluated against the considerable financial costs and inefficiencies they produce by inefficiently allocating resources and distorting
prices. A subsidy is considered inefficient if it does not reach the targeted
group, or excludes the deserving, or has negligible cost recovery from the
beneficiary, or is not withdrawn from people who no longer need it, or
has negative consequences like environment degradation and water table
depletion caused by free water and free electricity schemes.

There has been a steady growth in state expenditure on subsidies.
For the general category states (GCS), subsidies witnessed a growth of
18.1 per cent and 12.1 per cent during the FY 2019–20 and FY 2020–
21 (RE), respectively. This growth varies across the states, from a low of
3.2 per cent in Odisha to a high of 77.2 per cent in Chhattisgarh. For the
2018–21 period, the states of Chhattisgarh, AP, Telangana, Goa, Kerala,
Madhya Pradesh, UP, and Jharkhand have seen the highest increase in
subsidies(see Figure 10.15).

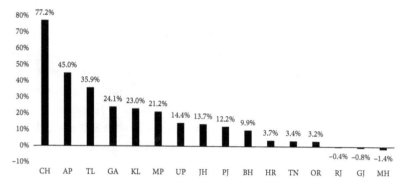

Figure 10.15 State-wide Growth rate of subsidy expenditure (2018-21 RE)
Source: author's calculation based on RBI ([state finances] various years).

It is crucial for state governments to reprioritize their spending, cut down on inefficient subsidies, and move towards efficient delivery mechanisms in order to get the biggest long-term welfare benefits by making sure the recipients get lasting empowerment and give up such short-term benefits. For instance, free unmetered electricity for farmers, as is well known, causes financial losses where even misuse or theft is passed off as agricultural and excessive water use. Even with concessions, prepaid metering, can prove to be a critical mechanism to counter inefficiency in this form of subsidy. Additionally, states should also make sure that each social sector programme has a sunset provision. The reduction in subsidies by SNGs will free money for capital expenditure and reduce borrowing.

10.6.2 Reducing DISCOM losses

In the previous chapter, we highlighted the poor financial condition of DISCOMs. In 2020–21, the overall losses of DISCOMs crossed ₹2 lakh crores (excluding arrears). The total outstanding debt of DISCOMs is close to ₹6 lakh crore which accounts for roughly 3 per cent of GDP. High aggregate technical and commercial (AT&C) losses put severe strain on DISCOMs' finances. As shown in Figure 10.16, the losses in some states are much higher than the national average.

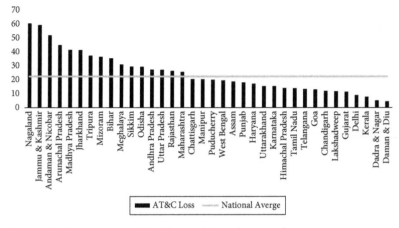

Figure 10.16 State-wise AT&C losses (%) and national average
Source: Power Finance Corporation (2022)

Power theft, overloading of existing lines, lack of timely upgradation of equipment, low billing efficiency, faulty meters contribute to huge AT&C losses. Another very significant reason for the poor state of DISCOMs' finances is delay and non-payment of subsidies from state governments. The DISCOMs sell electricity at prices lower than the cost of electricity procurement to benefit customers. The difference is paid by the state governments as subsidies. As per the report on performance of state power utilities 2020–21, tariff subsidy released by state governments as a percentage of tariff subsidy billed by distribution utilities decreased from 95.08 per cent in 2019–20 to 84.54 per cent in 2020–21 (Power Finance Corporation, 2022). Due to political economy consideration and for other reasons, DISCOMs have been unable to revise power tariffs periodically to absorb the increasing costs of providing electricity.

DISCOMs have two types of costs – fixed and variable. Similarly, tariffs have two components- fixed charge and energy charge. Ideally fixed charges should be able to recover the fixed cost fully and energy cost to match the variable cost. However, only a portion of fixed costs are recovered through fixed charges. This leads to a mismatch in the cash flow as DISCOMs need to pay fixed monthly charges to the generation company and transmission companies irrespective of the amount of power procured. DISCOMs must focus on tariff rationalization after analysing how much of their revenue comes from fixed charges and energy charges. Efficient tariff rationalization would ensure a stable stream of revenue.

10.6.3   Restructuring of state-level public enterprises (SLPEs)

Over time, SLPEs' financial performance has continued to decline, which has adversely affected the payouts to the state governments in the form of dividends. In fact, most SLPEs are now running at a loss and are dependent upon huge government grants and loans to keep them afloat. Improvement in the performance of SLPEs would not only help in mobilizing government revenues in the form of dividends but also reduce the financial burden of the state governments through reduction of grants and subsidies.

There are many SLPEs operating in sectors where there is a substantial presence of the private sector. The present economic scenario warrants a fresh assessment as to whether the government presence is required in these sectors. SLPEs are mainly classified as strategic sector SLPEs and non-strategic sector SLPEs. Loss-making and commercially non-viable SLPEs in the non-strategic sector could be considered for disinvestment or privatization on priority. In the case of other SLPEs in the core areas, roping in a private entity as a strategic investor would greatly improve their performance. The partnership between the public sector and private investor would make these SLPEs more competitive as it can leverage the domain knowledge and expertise of both of them.

Most of the SLPEs are overstaffed: lack of proper workforce planning is one of the main reasons for non-profitability of SLPEs. This issue has been flagged by CAG multiple times in its performance audit report. For instance, as per the CAG's performance audit report for the government of UP for 2014, 'the actual available workforce of superintending, executive and assistant engineers was much in excess of the sanctioned strength. No assessment was made for workforce requirement considering the increase in units/zones and also the subcontracting of majority of the works'(CAG, 2014). Right sizing of workforce of SLPEs and enabling efficient resource utilization will reduce operational cost and thus provide impetus to revenue.

State governments have provided continuous monetary support to SLPEs across sectors (especially in the power sector) causing serious dent in state finances. Frequent bailouts by state governments have resulted in perverse incentives, that is, enterprises have no incentive to perform well as they know the government will bail them out when they are in financial distress. Thus, states have to look for ways to improve the profitability of SLPEs.

10.6.4 Curtailing pension expenditure

Pension is a major component of state revenue expenditure. As this expenditure is committed in nature, states have no flexibility to rationalize such expenditure.

Pension expenditure accounted for about 2 per cent of Revenue Receipts (RR) of the states in 1980–81 but gradually increased to 13 per cent of RR by 2020–21 (RE). In 2020–21, pension expenditure amounted to ₹3.68 lakh crores for all states combined. To curtail the growing expenditure on pensions, in 2004–05 there was a shift from the old pension scheme (OPS) to the new pension scheme (NPS). This was based on the recommendation of a Group that studied pension liabilities of state governments (2003)which found that the old pension scheme (OPS) was unsustainable for state finances. The major difference between the old and new pension scheme is that under the OPS, the retired employee gets a monthly payment equal to 50 per cent of his/her last drawn salary. This is also popularly known as the defined benefit scheme. The entire burden of pension is borne by the government. In the case of the NPS, employees make contributions during their career and a fixed part is contributed by the government as its share. Such contributions are invested in market securities such as equities. This is also widely known as the defined contribution scheme. Thus, in the case of NPS, returns are linked to market and are not assured, which contrasts with the OPS. Income from the OPS is non-taxable whereas in the case of the NPS a portion (40 per cent) of the pension amount is taxable.

A comparison of interstate spending on pension and retirement benefits shows that there is significant variation among states. Some states expend much higher on pension as reflected in a higher share of pension

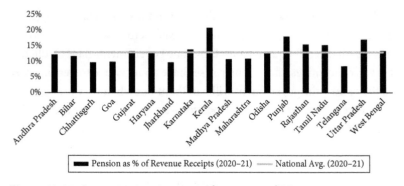

Figure 10.17 State-wise pension expenditure as % of RR
Source: author's calculation based on RBI ([state finances] various years).

expenditure as a percentage of RR. States such as Kerala, UP, Punjab, Rajasthan, Tamil Nadu spend much more on pensions and other retirement benefits as compared to other states (see Figure 10.17).

The states introduced the NPS with the objective of reducing the burden of pension on the finances. However, of late, four states—Rajasthan, Chhattisgarh, Punjab, Jharkhand, Himachal Pradesh—have withdrawn from the NPS and have reimplemented the OPS. Although by reverting to the OPS, these states will be able to reduce their expenditure in the near term because the OPS does not require contributions from government, it may be detrimental in the long run when the current crop of employees retire. As the OPS benefits the current generation, but shifts the financial burden to future generations, it breaches the principle of intergenerational equity.

However, the reasons for states not opting for the NPS or opting out of it need to be examined. There are many problems plaguing the NPS mainly due to perceived low returns on the invested pension funds and uncertain future returns. As it remains one of the major social security net for millions of government and PSU employees in the country, the political executive is tempted to revert to the OPS for political economy considerations as the NPS is not finding favour with employees. The existing drawbacks of the NPS have to be addressed and it has to be made attractive to stem this growing tendency among the states to reverse this trend.

10.6.5 Leveraging of Public Finance Management System (PFMS)

PFMS is a web-based online transaction platform which was introduced by the Government of India (GoI) in 2009–10 with the aim of providing an effective and efficient fund flow system for central government
schemes. The system tracks the disbursement of funds from the central
government to SNGs up to the last beneficiary and provides real-time information on utilization of funds under the various schemes. The system
distinguishes between release of funds and final expenditure incurred.
It is through PFMS that the funds are transferred to the Aadhaar-linked
bank accounts of the beneficiaries. This helps in removing the existing
intervening layers in the fund transfer process.

The SNGs must leverage the PFMS to the maximum possible extent
because it provides real-time granular information on advances, transfer
of funds and the utilization of funds. PFMS also helps in effective cash
management by linking future release of funds to the total float available
with a state under a scheme. This has a huge saving potential because lot
of cash sits idle in bank accounts. If cash is left idle in bank accounts, it
fetches a lower rate of interest as compared to the interest incurred by the
government in servicing its debt. Hence, the use of PFMS increases transparency and accountability thereby helping SNGs to improve fiscal and
cash management.

10.6.6 Public–private partnership (PPP) model for investment

SNGs are undergoing rapid economic development and urbanization,
which has increased the need for expanding the existing socio-economic
infrastructure facilities. These infrastructure projects require huge investments which cannot be provided solely by the government due to
limited budgetary space. Therefore, to finance large investments in the
infrastructure sector, private participation is essential. For this, PPP is an
attractive option for government financing. Under PPP projects, usually
the private sector arranges and provides financing. This reduces pressure on the public sector to finance infrastructure projects from its own

revenues or through borrowing. Also, the private sector brings in the required skill expertise and capacity which accelerates the delivery of infrastructure projects. Thus, PPP projects help in accelerating the delivery of high-quality infrastructure projects and reduce the financial burden of the government in providing the infrastructure.

10.6.7 Mobilizing revenues using green bonds

SNG borrowing by using green bonds is an innovative mechanism to finance infrastructure projects. The funds raised through green bonds are earmarked for green projects which provide environmental benefits by reducing greenhouse gas emissions, improving energy efficiency, or promoting climate resilience and/or adaptation.

In November 2022, the Indian Government introduced a framework for sovereign green bonds, aiming to issue ₹16,000 cr for green infrastructure projects. The framework outlined eligible project categories and selection procedures for the fiscal year 2022-23, prioritizing reducing the country's carbon footprint through public sector initiatives.

According to the Climate Bonds Initiative in London, twenty-four national governments collectively issued $111 billion in sovereign green, social, and sustainability bonds. In light of this, SNGs in India should consider generating revenue through green bonds, as they offer low-interest rates, minimizing the financial burden on the state while delivering environmental benefits.

10.6.8 Case studies

Before concluding the chapter, some interesting case studies of Indian states such as Odisha, Tamil Nadu, and Punjab will provide insight into the states' management of finances. These case studies are to help other state governments learn from their experiences. Odisha and Tamil Nadu have reversed their poor fiscal position by taking some key reforms whereas Punjab's fiscal condition has deteriorated continuously. For example, Odisha is one of the few states which reduced its debt-to-GSDP ratio from 62 per cent in the early 2000s to as low as 16 per cent in 2016–17 without compromising on development despite imposition of fiscal targets as per the FRBM Act (2003). Similarly, Tamil Nadu completely reversed its fiscal deterioration of 1999–2000 through implementation of a fiscal reform programme in 2001. However, Punjab's fiscal situation has deteriorated. Its debt-to-GSDP ratio stood at 53.3 per cent in 2021–22 (RE) which was the highest in the country. At this juncture, it is very important that other states learn from the experiences of these states' case studies, otherwise states which are fiscally stressed may fall into a debt trap which will not only be bad for them as a unit, but it will also adversely affect the macro-economic stability of the Indian economy.

Case study 1— Odisha - Increasing capital outlay while maintaining fiscal discipline

Studies have shown that while fiscal rules have reduced the levels of debt and deficit, they have also limited the level of DEVEX and capital expenditure which are beneficial for the economy. The states in India had introduced the FRBM Acts in different years. By 2006–07, twenty-two of the twenty-eight states had passed the Fiscal Responsibility Legislation (FRL).

Odisha has been an interesting case of a state with very poor fiscal indicators but then moved to years of fiscal surplus. However, even with such improvement, the state has not sacrificed its capital expenditure (see Figures 10.18 and 10.19).

The outstanding liability as a percentage of GSDP of Odisha was as high as 62 per cent in 2002–03. This was reduced to a low of 16.2 per cent by 2016–17 (see Figure 10.18). Similarly, throughout the same time period, the fiscal deficit as a proportion of GSDP declined from a high of 9 per cent to a low of 1 per cent (see Figure 10.19). The fiscal imbalance which the state witnessed in 2002–03 led to the initiation of broad-based fiscal reforms through a memorandum of understanding in 1999 with Ministry of Finance (MoF), GoI, to accomplish fiscal reform measures and strengthen state finances.

This was achieved through measures to contain non-plan revenue expenditure and augment RR which included: restrictions on filling base-level vacancies without the approval of the finance department

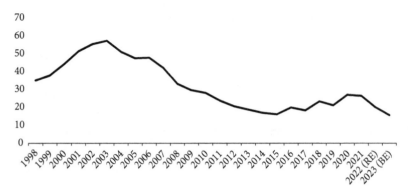

Figure 10.18 Outstanding liabilities to GSDP ratio - Odisha
Source: RBI ([state finances] various years).

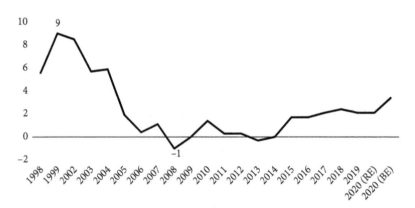

Figure 10.19 Fiscal deficit to GSDP ratio - Odisha
Source: RBI ([state finances] various years).

implementation of Voluntary Retirement Scheme in the state PSUs, elimination of 50 per cent of the base-level vacancies in personnel (as at 1 July 1999), gradual reduction of workforce by 10 per cent within three years (from 1st July 1999).

To enhance the state's revenues, the measures taken included:

- Sales tax incentives which were extended to industries were withdrawn.
- Introduction of uniform floor rates of sales tax on all agreed-upon goods.

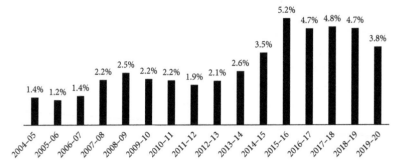

Figure 10.20 Capital outlay to GSDP ratio - Odisha
Source: RBI ([state finances] various years).

- A four-rate scheme for sales tax rates was implemented on 1 April 2000.
- A broad-based entry tax was introduced instead of Octroi which came into effect on 1 December 1999.
- Profession tax imposed from 1 November 2000.
- Wholesale trade in liquor was taken over by the state government.
- Other measures were rationalization of registration fees, stamp duty, irrigation water rates, cess on land revenue, and levy of tax and registration fees, etc. under the MV Act and rules.

However, even with drastic improvement in fiscal targets, the CO-to-GSDP ratio witnessed an appreciable increase from 1.4 per cent to around 5 per cent during the period (see Figure 10.20).

Case study 2—Tamil Nadu: Reversing the fiscal deterioration: Lessons from the fiscal reform programme of 2001

During the late 1990s, Tamil Nadu experienced significant deterioration in its finances. State fiscal deficit reached a peak of 7.2 per cent of GSDP in 2001–02 after rising quickly from 2.2 per cent of GSDP in 1997–98 to 6.7 per cent in 1999–2000. The debt as a share of GSDP of the state rose from 16.3 per cent of GSDP in 1997–98 to a whopping 25 per cent in 2001–02. This excluded the off-budget liabilities of the state government. The state had also given a huge number of guarantees to its loss-making state-owned enterprises. If those guarantees are also added to the GSDP, then the aggregate outstanding liabilities of the state stood at 30 per cent of GSDP in 2001–02. The interest-to-revenue expenditure of the state rose to 20 per cent in 2002–03 and 2003–04 which accounted for the so called debt stressed condition of the state (see Figure 10.21).

Due to this, the borrowing was largely being used to finance revenue expenditure. The state was hardly left with any fiscal space to spend on infrastructure projects. The capital expenditure of the state reduced to 1.6 per cent of GSDP significantly less than other comparable states which had CO-to-GSDP ratio in the range of 2 to 3 per cent.

There were multiple reasons behind this fiscal deterioration in the 1990s. The fundamental cause was the sharp rise in salary and pension expenditure following the implementation of the award from the Sixth State Pay Commission. The average growth in salary and pension spending increased from 14.5 to 26.75 per cent between 1990–91 and 1997–98.

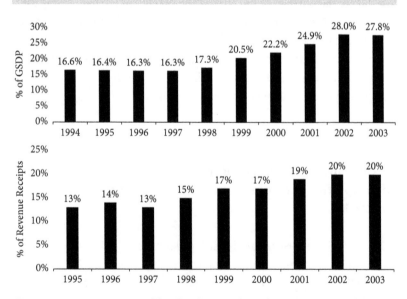

Figure 10.21 Worsening of fiscal indicators for Tamil Nadu-Debt to GSDP ratio & IP-RR ratio

Source: RBI ([state finances] various years).

Simultaneously, there was a decline in transfers from the central government based on the recommendations of the Central Finance Commissions (CFCs). Tamil Nadu's share of the central taxes was reduced from 8.05 per cent by the 7th FC to 6.64 per cent by the 10th FC and then to 5.39 per cent by the 11th FC.

How did the state government reverse the stressed condition of its state finances?

To reverse the precarious condition of the state finances, the Tamil Nadu government embarked on the path of fiscal consolidation through a fiscal reform programme, the primary objectives of which were:

- reducing the growth of revenue expenditure;
- improving tax efficiency;
- improving fiscal transparency;
- restructuring of SPSEs.

On the revenue side the state took multiple steps: sales tax constituted about 69 per cent of the SOTR. The state embarked upon to increase the effectiveness of its sales tax system, which was plagued by several tax layers, a complicated rate structure, cascading, frequent and ad hoc modifications, and many exemptions. The state also made changes to its stamp duty system. The government lowered the tax rate on property transactions and improved its administration to reduce tax evasion. On the non-tax side, the government made some progress in increasing cost recovery.

On the expenditure side, the state controlled expenditure on salaries and pensions, reduced major subsidy programmes and improved their targeting. The off-budget borrowing of the state was included in its debt-to GSDP ratio which increased the transparency of its borrowing in 2002–03. The incremental cash budgeting was replaced with a thorough and reliable projection of accrued pension liabilities and forecasted cash flow requirements based on the workforce's age-profile. Given the considerable financial obligations of power utilities, the accounts of the state power utility were finally combined with the fiscal account.

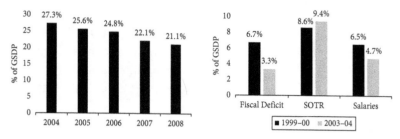

Figure 10.22 Improvement in debt-GSDP ratio and other fiscal indicators in Tamil Nadu

Source: author's calculation based on RBI ([state finances] various years).

As a result of these measures, arrears to the tune of 2 per cent of GSDP were processed in 2002–03. The fiscal deficit (including off-budget borrowing) was reduced from 6.7 per cent in 1999–2000 to 3.3 per cent in 2003–04. This was possible due to a significant increase in SOTR to GSDP from 8.6 per cent in 1999–2000 to 9.4 per cent in 2003–04 (see Figure 10.22).

Case study 3—Punjab: A case of a vicious cycle of debt

Punjab's debt situation is precarious. Punjab became a revenue deficit state in 1985. By 1990–91, the state registered the highest deficit in any state in India. Its fiscal situation has been under stress ever since. The GFD-to-GSDP ratio of Punjab was 5.07 in 1996–97, significantly higher compared to the all states average of 2.9 in 1996–97. Punjab's fiscal deficit was the third highest among GCS at 4.6 per cent of GSDP in 2021–22.

The debt to GSDP ratio of the state has grown continuously over the years from 33.06 per cent in 2010–11 to 49.1 per cent in 2020–21 (see Figure 10.23) which is highest among all states by a huge margin. Debt-servicing and interest payment on outstanding debt accounted for 82 per cent and 48 per cent respectively of SORs in 2019–20. As per the CAG report of 2020–21, around 53 per cent of its debt has to be re-paid by the state in the next seven years. In 2020–21, the state utilized about 77 per cent of its borrowing to finance its revenue deficit.

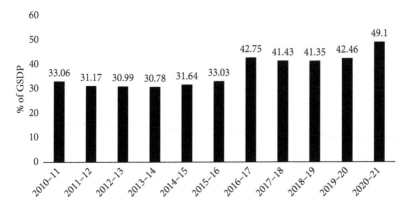

Figure 10.23 Rising debt-to-GSDP ratio of Punjab
Source: RBI ([state finances] various years).

Persistent rise in debt poses serious challenge to the economy of Punjab. The key reasons for spiralling debt are:

• High committed expenditure

Committed expenditure of states includes salaries and wages, pensions, subsidies and interest payments. Punjab's committed expenditure is very high. Consistent increases in subsidies and interest payments has further aggravated the fiscal position which is already under stress with total committed expenditure forming about 81 per cent of revenue expenditure and 97 per cent of RR, respectively. In 2021–22, Punjab has the highest interest payment-to-revenue receipt ratio among GCS at 21.3 per cent.

• High subsidy bill

Concessions and subsidies were taken to extraordinary lengths in Punjab. The subsidy bill was increased by 39 per cent from ₹8,795 crore in 2018–19 to ₹12,246 crore in 2020–21. The farm power subsidy bill increased by many times between 1997–98 and 2019–20 from ₹693 crores to ₹6,060 crores. Power subsidy accounts for the major share of state's subsidy bill. Between 2011–12 and 2015–16, power subsidies represented an average of 1.4 per cent of GSDP and 97 per cent of the overall subsidy. However, the poor fiscal situation did not put a brake on populist policy on power subsidy. Recently, in 2022, the state government has introduced free electricity of 300 units monthly which has increased the subsidy bill threefold.

- Low tax buoyancy

The growth in the state's own tax revenue has been inadequate. OTR's growth rate has not kept in pace with the growth in GSDP. The buoyancy of the state's own taxes has decreased, from 0.90 in 2014–15 to 0.42 in 2019–20. High capital expenditure is essential to facilitate asset creation and higher growth which leads to increased tax revenue. Capital expenditure in Punjab remained lower than average expenditure by GCS. In 2014–15, an average of capital expenditure to aggregate expenditure for GCS was 14.02 per cent while in the case of Punjab it was 6.24 per cent. This ratio increased to 14.28 per cent in 2018–19 for GCS but declined for Punjab to 3.05 per cent.

- Rising contingent liabilities

Contingent liabilities of state government have been increasing in recent times. Off- budget borrowing, PSU loans and government guarantees have exceeded 4.5 per cent of GSDP in 2022. However, in the case of Punjab it is more than 5 per cent of GSDP (see Figure 10.24).

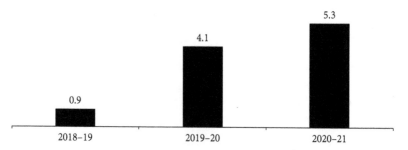

Figure 10.24 Rising guarantees issued by state government
Source: RBI ([state finances] various years).

The states' continuous deterioration of its finances shows that unlike states like Odisha and Tamil Nadu, the state government has not taken adequate steps to control its spiralling debt. Now, the debt has reached to a level where new debt is being created to finance the old debt. The state government needs to take measures to avoid a possible debt crisis.

10.7   Conclusion

With the emerging risks to debt sustainability of SNGs, it is necessary for SNGs to take corrective steps before it is too late. There are several ways in which SNGs can avoid a debt crisis by taking measures on both the revenue and expenditure fronts. The states can improve collections from GST through better compliance and expanding GST coverage in future by including commodities which are presently out of the GST net. Increasing collections from state excise, stamp duty and registration fees, and motor vehicle taxes are other options which may be explored by SNGs. Apart from tax revenues, the other measures which SNGs can undertake includes augmenting non-tax revenues, strengthening municipal finances, curtailing inefficient subsidies, reducing DISCOM losses and restructuring of SLPEs.

11

Strengthening Finances of Local Bodies

Drivers of Growth

11.1 Context

Sound debt management includes both direct and indirect measures. While direct measures include those which impact the consolidated fund of the state, indirect measures are those which promote economic growth resulting in increased economic activity and greater revenue for the SNGs. In the context of India, enabling local bodies to augment their finances through greater administrative and financial autonomy is one very important indirect measure impacting the consolidated fund of the states. The increase in revenue collection of local bodies helps them to provide basic services to the citizens in effective and efficient manner and in turn help in developing an environment conducive to economic growth and development. The resultant rise in economic growth helps in increasing revenue collection for state governments. In the Indian context, it is well established that economic growth leads to debt sustainability.[1]

India can learn lessons from China on how it used its resources to its advantage and leveraged local bodies to propel economic growth at the ground level.

11.1.1 How do local bodies contribute to economic growth and development?

Local bodies, particularly urban local bodies (ULBs), play a crucial role in the process of economic growth for several reasons. ULBs must create

---

[1] https://www.indiabudget.gov.in/budget2021-22/economicsurvey/doc/vol1chapter/echap 02_vol1.pdf

Debt Sustainability of Subnational Governments in India. Hari Krishna Dwivedi, Oxford University Press.
© Hari Krishna Dwivedi 2024. DOI: 10.1093/oso/9780198903116.003.0011

a safe and reliable environment for businesses to thrive. Roads, water supplies, waste management and other physical infrastructure that are basic requirements for economic activity are under their purview. The need of their citizens for public health, education, housing, local transportation, cultural and recreational amenities, child care and other public goods and services are also, more or less, addressed by local bodies. These needs are crucial for fostering the development of a healthy, competent, and dependable workforce.

ULBs are the best placed to bring together all of the participants in the local economy since they are the public institutions closest to the people. It is essential that ULBs are financially stable to undertake activities that enable and promote economic activity at the local level.

Large-scale infrastructure projects like electricity grids, roadways, trains and communication networks call for national and subnational development plans and regulations. International trade agreements must be negotiated and fiscal and monetary policies must be managed by national and supranational governments. These policies, however, are complemented by ULBs, which engage local stakeholders to drive bottom-up action. Local bodies can hugely complement efforts of the national and sub-national government in economic growth.

Case study 1—Role of urbanization in China's economic development

The rate of urbanization in China in the last few decades has been unprecedented in world history. The proportion of the people living in urban areas increased from around 18 per cent to more than 50 per cent in just thirty-three years (1978–2011). Japan's urban proportion increased from 18 per cent in 1920 to 58 per cent in 1955, to nearly 80 per cent in 2000, and then to more than 90 per cent in 2010. But, compared to China, it has a significantly lower population (127 million). Between 1996 and 2019, 460 million rural Chinese moved to the metropolis—nearly four times the population of Japan (Rapoza, 2017). No other country managed to make the switch from a predominately rural to an urban population in such a short time or on such a vast scale.

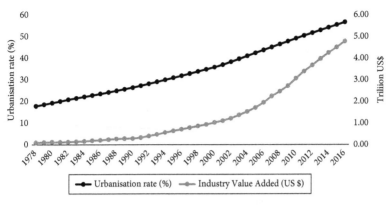

Figure 11.1 Urbanization and industrialization in China (1978–2016)
Source: World Bank (2022a); World Bank (2022b)

China's economy expanded at an average annual rate of more than 10 per cent as a result of rapid urbanization, and between 1978 and 2017, the percentage of urban GDP in the country's overall GDP quadrupled. As seen in Figure 11.1, urbanization and industrial value added have grown in tandem at a very high rate. One of the consequences of this symbiotic growth relation has been that one-third of the 300 largest metropolitan economies in the world today are found in China, and some of them have GDPs that are equivalent to those of other nations (Bouchet et al., 2018). Beijing, for instance, had the same GDP as the Philippines in 2017 (Trujillo & Parilla, 2016).

The fast growth of urban areas increased employment opportunities, the productivity of those occupations and the wages of urban workers in China. The rate of wage growth has been so rapid that the average salary in several Chinese cities now exceeds that of some European nations (Rapoza, 2017).

The increase in economic growth is likely to increase revenue collection for subnational governments (SNGs) which will reduce the pace of rising debt to a large extent. In this chapter, we will look at measures to strengthen the financial position of ULBs and rural local bodies (RLBs). However, due to a paucity of the latest data available on finances of local bodies, financial data of local bodies up to 2017–18 forms the basis of our discussion.

11.2 Rural Local Bodies (RLBs)

The Panchayati Raj Institutions under the 73rd Amendment Act of 1992 were given wide-ranging authority and social and development. However, without well-defined sources of revenue, Panchayati Raj Institutions cannot develop into effective institutions of local self-governance. Fiscal decentralization to RLBs calls for more delegation with regard to funds, functions, and officials.

RLBs' revenues originate from (1) central FC grants and funds from the Union government, (2) state FC grants and funds from the state government, and (3) their own income including tax revenue as well as non-tax revenue.

Out of these sources of revenues, transfers from higher levels are often tied funds and come with conditionalities. This reduces local governments' flexibility to spend as per their needs and priorities. Therefore, it becomes important for RLBs to mobilize their own sources of revenues so that they can spend as per the needs of the population. Since local governments play a crucial role in economic growth, they should ideally play a significant part in pursuing local development strategies to boost growth. However, RLBs continue to struggle due to limited administrative and financial capabilities despite significant decentralization initiatives in recent decades. Strengthening local government administration and finances is necessary to accelerate and spur economic growth at the local level as greater revenue realization will allow the RLBs to spend more on development needs at the local level. This will in turn ease the pressure on subnational governments and eventually have a positive impact on debt management of SNGs.

Taxes assigned to panchayats mostly include profession tax, house or property tax, animal tax, water tax, drainage tax, tax on public utility works, market fees, fee on registration of animals/cattle, pilgrim tax, tax on commercial crops, and ferry service tax. However, most of these are not being levied. Out of these, the most important source of revenue for RLBs is profession tax and house or property tax.

Also, among the three tiers of RLBs in India, namely, the lowest Gram panchayats, the middle-tier panchayat samitis at the block level, and zilla parishads at the district level, it is only the Gram panchayat that is mainly vested with the powers to raise revenue through tax and non-tax. The other two tiers are largely dependent upon FC grants and intergovernmental transfers (IGTs) with very few revenue sources of their .

11.2.1 Measures to augment RLB revenues

On analysing the own revenues and total expenditure (TE) of the RLBs for General Category States (GCS), it is observed that the own source of revenues of RLBs is very limited (see Figure 11.2). Except for Punjab, no state in the general category was able to finance even one-quarter of their total expenditure (TE) from its own sources of funds. On average, almost 90 per cent of RLBs' expenditure was financed from IGTs.

In order to increase own revenues, the collection of user fees for services like irrigation water and betterment levies should receive emphasis in addition to improvement in property tax and profession tax collection.

Revising profession tax threshold

Most states impose profession tax, which is levied on all individuals engaged in any type of employment or profession. In some states, this tax is levied and collected by the state and later devolved to the local bodies and in others it is the local bodies which are entrusted with this power. Under the Constitution, the upper ceiling of profession has been kept at ₹2,500 per person, per annum. This ceiling was fixed in 1988 and has not been revised since then. If the ceiling value was indexed to inflation,

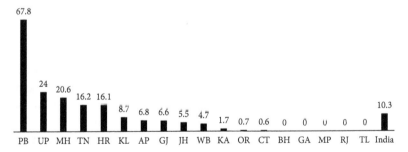

Figure 11.2 Share (%) of own revenue in TE (average of 2012—13 to 2017—18)

Source: Alok (2021).

then it would come to around ₹18,000 at 2019–20 prices. States have been asking for an upward revision of this ceiling. Several FCs have also advocated raising this cap. Raising the cap on profession tax would increase resources available to the local bodies.

Rationalization of property or house tax in rural areas

According to the Economic Survey 2017–18, the average rural collection of property taxes from houses across a chosen group of five states—AP, Karnataka, Kerala, Tamil Nadu, and UP—is roughly 20 per cent. For households with two living rooms, the survey made the assumption that taxes would be 0.1 per cent of the property value, 0.2 per cent for families with three to five rooms, and 0.3 per cent for those with six or more.

The 15th FC attempted to estimate the house tax potential for rural and urban areas separately for all states using unit level data from the National Sample Survey Office (NSSO) Seventy-Sixth Round on Drinking water, Sanitation, Hygiene, and Housing (DWSHH) conditions conducted in July–December 2018, partially adopting the methodology outlined in the Economic Survey (MoSPI, 2018). In the study conducted by the FC for rural areas, it was determined that the potential home tax receipts at 2019 prices could reach ₹42,160 crores. The RLBs at present are collecting only a very insignificant fraction of this. There is a huge potential for the local bodies to increase their revenues through scientific valuation and efficient collection mechanism. This requires increasing the panchayats' ability to manage tax collection, giving incentives to panchayats for proper enforcement and collection of property tax. Political economy largely influence property tax rates and its collection.

Tourism Levies/Eco-Development Fees

Tourism, with its vast economic reach, has prompted many local governments to collect tourism related levies or taxes. These are not merely revenue-generating tools, but also strategies to manage the influx of tourists, fund local infrastructural projects, and support environmental conservation.

Cities like Venice and Barcelona, facing the brunt of overtourism, have employed levies to both regulate tourist numbers and generate funds for local upkeep and conservation. Local government of India can improve their finances through tourism related levies.

11.3 Urban Local Bodies (ULBs)

Over the past few decades, India has witnessed rapid urbanization with around four hundred million people living at present in the urban areas. Going forward, the urban population is expected to grow from the present four hundred million to over eight hundred million by 2050, which will be more than half of the population of the country. However, to meet the needs of such a large population, urban infrastructure and services need to grow at a fast pace. To do so, the ULBs must be financially autonomous and strong to invest in better infrastructure and provision of civic services. Weak urban finances will not only hinder the growth of the country but also put strain on the already stressed finances of the state as they will have to depend more and more on IGT for resources.

Unfortunately, in terms of fiscal independence and their ability to provide civic infrastructure and services to meet the needs of expanding urbanization and rapid economic expansion, urban local governments in India are among the least capable in the world.

In 2018, municipal revenue was lower than 1 per cent of GDP while the corresponding figures were much higher for comparable countries: 6 per cent of GDP in South Africa and 7.4 per cent in Brazil (see Figure 11.3).

ULB revenues are low because of the untapped potential of property tax, low user charges and lower transfers from the state governments. Due to lower level of own revenue collection, they are able to cover only

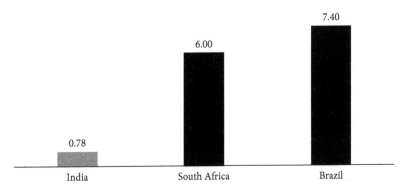

Figure 11.3 Share of municipal revenues in GDP of select countries
Source: Ahluwalia et al. (2019)

about 55 per cent of their municipal expenditure. The total expenditure of the ULBs' which is met from their own revenues has declined over the years, from 64 per cent in 2012–13 to only 55 per cent in 2017–18.

Due to the gradual takeover by the state, many of local taxes other than property taxes in the majority of states, ULBs' own revenue has decreased over time (Ahluwalia et al., 2019). Also, with the introduction of GST in 2017, several local taxes, including the octroi, entry tax and advertisement tax have been subsumed into GST. In pre-GST, many of these taxes were either collected directly by the ULBs or were collected by the SNGs and devolved to the ULBs. The urban local governments are at present left with property tax as the only major tax, and are heavily dependent on transfers from states and centre as many of their 'own' taxes have been taken over or abolished over the years (Ahluwalia et al., 2019).

11.3.1   Measures to augment ULB revenues

The ULBs have to overhaul the system, and mode of collection of property tax to make it more effective and achieve buoyancy in its collection. Apart from reforms in property tax, the ULBs in India will also have to streamline the system of collection of various user charges and make it more transparent and efficient. They will also have to explore alternative funding routes for important infrastructure projects in the areas of drinking water, sanitation, solid waste management, city transportation, health, etc. by resorting to innovative methods of issuing municipal bonds and encouraging public–private partnership ventures.

11.3.1.1   Property tax reforms

Property tax accounts for about 60 per cent of the total municipal tax revenue in India. However, the property tax collections of all ULBs of the country taken together is only 0.15 per cent of GDP of the country (see Figure 11.4). This stands below par when compared to peer nations and far less than the funds required by the ULBs for development of infrastructure. The 15th FC estimated the house tax potential of the ULBs for all the states. The commission found that the overall tax potential for all states stands at ₹23,184 cr. for urban areas at 2019 prices. The present collection of property taxes by ULBs is much lower than their potential.

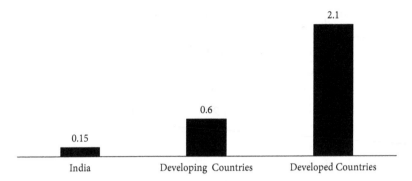

Figure 11.4 International comparison—property tax as % of GDP
Source: NFSSM Alliance (2020).

Some of the reasons for low property tax collections are manual input and updating of records in physical registers. Manual maintenance of records is not only prone to errors, but it also leads to human intervention in determination of property tax. The following measures can be undertaken by municipal bodies to enhance collections from property tax.

Adoption of a geographic information system (GIS)-based digital property register: to counter the challenges of error-prone manual maintenance of records, a GIS-based digital property register should be properly adopted and implemented. This should be backed by intensive field surveys to check the veracity of GIS maps and adequate capacity should be simultaneously built in ULBs to maintain the digital register. While GIS-based property mapping has been adopted by various cities, there is still no coherent plan for regular enumeration and updating of property records leading to ad hoc updating of property registers and incomplete records. There should be laws to mandate regular enumeration and updation of property database. Moreover, a single digital property database should be used by all municipal entities.

Implementing a capital value (CV) method: In India, there are three methods currently employed by states. First, the annual rental value (ARV) method which is the most widely used among the states of country. However, the criteria used for calculating ARV is not prescribed, but assigned on an ad hoc basis. Second, the unit area value (UAV) which is followed by nine states. The UAV is determined without clear linkages to underlying locational factors of the property. Due to the absence of the linkage, the system becomes non-buoyant and non-equitable leaving huge scope for discretion. The third method is the circle value (CV) method in which the property tax is directly linked to the circle rates determined by governments. This is the most scientific method of determining property tax as it is linked to circle rates. The circle rates are periodically revised to reflect appreciation in the value of the properties in urban centres. In view of the said drawbacks in the ARV and UAV methods, all cities should implement the CV method to ensure buoyancy in the collection of property tax. In addition, the State Acts shall provide for periodical property tax adjustments in line with increases in guidance value which is the circle rate.

Implementation of online billing and collection mechanism: the purpose of a billing and collection system is to ensure that all properties assessed are billed and taxed in a timely manner. The introduction of an online billing and collection will make the tax system transparent. An online system would make sure that all invoices are issued to property owners electronically and short message service (SMS) notifications are provided automatically on a regular basis. The collection process could be completely changed by technological intervention such as digital payments and the hiring of a dedicated team of collectors for all taxes, user fees, and other charges. This would need to be supported by effective laws that give municipal administrators more power.

Management information system (MIS)-based reporting of collections: it is essential that such MIS based reporting be institutionalized with quarterly or half-yearly review of property tax MIS at ward/city/revenue official level. Ranking revenue officers based on MIS data would also encourage healthy competition, reward revenue officials and promote best practice.

11.3.1.2 Effective levy of user charges

Other than property tax, the ULBs also need to work on efficiently levying and collecting user charges for basic services. Revenue from user charges would make it possible to allocate sufficient resources to meet public demand for basic services as well as guarantee their sustainability. While cost recovery for services such as water supply has made some progress in practice, it has lagged for sanitary and solid waste management services. Cost recovery can be increased even for the water supply services, as many Indian cities only manage to recover 50–75 per cent of their operating expenses.

Better cost recovery for ULBs could be achieved by ensuring metered water connections, frequently updating water tariffs, and promoting efficient water management using technology to identify and reduce leakages.

It has been observed that for municipal corporations, on average, the cost recovery is about one-quarter of the expenditure. Hence, there is much scope for improvement in levying local user charges (Mohanty et al., 2019).

11.3.1.3 Mobilizing investment through municipal bonds

To meet the investment requirements, the ULB should explore alternative financing mechanisms such as raising capital by issuing municipal bonds. Municipal bonds are a type of debt instrument where investors purchase the bond issued by the ULB. ULB in turn is obliged to pay annual interest and principal payment at maturity.

China and United States' (US) municipal bond markets, which are valued around US$3–4 trillion, demonstrate the enormous potential of resource mobilization using this technique. In the past few years, eleven cities in India namely, Ahmedabad, Amaravati, Bhopal, Ghaziabad, Hyderabad, Indore, Lucknow, Pune, Surat, Vadodara, and Vishakhapatnam have also leveraged the municipal bond route to raise funds. These bonds were issued with proper credit ratings and performed well in terms of resources raised by these ULBs. This reflects the potential of municipal bonds as a tool to raise capital for development and growth in urban centres in India.

11.3.1.4 Value Capture Financing (VCF)

Value Capture Financing (VCF) is a financial model wherein public infrastructure projects is funded capitalising on by the increased property value such projects often bring about. As infrastructure develops and regions become more accessible or desirable, property values naturally rise. VCF allows governments to reclaim some of this increased value—typically through taxes or levies—to reinvest in further public works or to service debts incurred from previous projects.

In 2017, Ministry of Housing and Urban Affairs (MoHUA), Government of India rolled out guidelines on adopting VCF as a strategy to finance urban infrastructure. The policy framework provided methodologies, including land value increment, betterment levies, and development charges, amongst others, to harness the increased value due to public investments (MoHUA, 2017).

For instance, Mumbai, India's financial capital, has been at the forefront of adopting innovative financing mechanisms for its infrastructure projects. The Mumbai Metro Rail Corporation (MMRC) considered using the VCF model for its metro lines, given the project's potential to elevate property values along the metro corridors (MMRCL, 2017).

In one of the proposed strategies, the Maharashtra government mulled over levying an additional 1% stamp duty on property transactions within the Influence Zone of the metro lines, potentially generating significant revenue. For the ambitious Mumbai Metro Line 3 (Colaba-Bandra-SEEPZ), it was estimated that VCF could contribute anywhere from INR 2,600 crores to INR 3,000 crores to the project's finances (MMRCL, 2017).

Additionally, Transfer of Development Rights (TDR), another VCF tool, was explored in Mumbai. TDR usually allows property owners to sell the development rights of their property to developers, enabling the latter to build additional square footage elsewhere. By tying TDRs to areas near metro lines, the government aimed to capture a fraction of the increased land value resulting from the metro project.

On the other hand, Bangalore, one of India's sprawling metropolises, offers an illustrative example of VCF's potential. As the city recently underwent rapid urbanization and infrastructural development, especially with the expansion of its metro rail system, surrounding property values soared. Recognizing the potential to harness this appreciation, the local authorities are exploring VCF mechanisms. This will not only help the city offset some of the massive costs associated with constructing the metro but also established a sustainable model for future infrastructural projects.

In essence, Value Capture Financing, as evidenced by Mumbai and Bangalore's approach, establishes a virtuous cycle. Infrastructure boosts property values, and a portion of that increased value is channelled back into further development, ensuring that urban growth is both sustainable and self-supporting.

11.3.1.5 Congestion Pricing

Congestion pricing, often termed as congestion charges or tolls, aims to alleviate heavy traffic in urban centers by charging drivers a fee to access specific city areas, especially during high traffic timings. Beyond just reducing traffic congestion, the system seeks to diminish air pollution and promote alternative modes of transportation, such as public transport: buses & metro rails or cycling.

London introduced its congestion charging scheme in February 2003, marking one of the earliest significant endeavours to address the city's escalating traffic and environmental challenges. Though the fee and hours have been modified over time, the primary goal has remained consistent.

Economically, the revenue accrued from these charges found its way back into the city's coffers, primarily supporting public transportation, infrastructure upgrades, and various transportation projects.

Another noteworthy example is Stockholm's congestion pricing system. Since 2007, this initiative charges vehicles based on their driving patterns within the city, leading to a marked decrease in traffic congestion and carbon emissions while bolstering city coffers. Beyond traffic mitigation, the system has been a robust revenue source for Stockholm. The funds accrued are often directed towards enhancing city infrastructure and public transport (Börjesson, M., & Eliasson, J., 2019).

11.4 Augmentation of IGTs to Local Bodies

In addition to own source of revenues, local bodies receive substantial funds through IGTs which include transfers from the state government based on the recommendations of state FCs (SFCs), transfers from the central government through central FC (CFC) recommendations, and other grants from various ministries for implementing Centrally Sponsored Schemes (CSS).

ULBs in India are heavily reliant on IGTs by the central and state governments since their own sources of revenues are insufficient to meet their expenditure requirements. A study shows that the fiscal transfers to ULBs in India, as a share of GDP, is only about 0.45 per cent (Ahluwalia et al., 2019), whereas, in developing countries like Indonesia, Mexico, and Brazil, it is between 1.6 and 5.1 per cent (OECD, 2016) (see Figure 11.5).

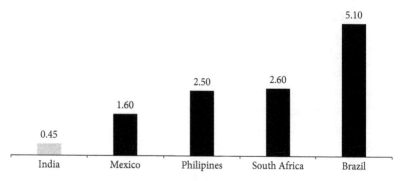

Figure 11.5 Comparison of intergovernmental transfers (as % of GDP) in select countries

Source: NFSSM Alliance (2020).

Besides, the low levels of IGTs, there is a lack of predictability of these transfers that incapacitates the ULBs to plan for any medium- or long-term projects to upgrade urban services.

It is also necessary to keep in mind that grants from state governments account for two-thirds of all IGTs given to ULBs. However, it is observed that the transfers to local bodies from SFCs are ineffective and less significant. According to the constitutional provision, states must set up SFCs which should give recommendations regarding devolution of taxes and other transfers to local bodies. However, in many states, SFCs are not properly developed and not even constituted at regular intervals (Gupta & Chakraborty, 2019). Only fifteen states had formed the 5th or 6th SFC as of 2020, according to the report of the 15th FC. Some states have only constituted a 2nd or 3rd SFC.

It is observed that although the quantum of transfers to local bodies from CFCs has increased, the conditionalities have also increased due to which the actual release of grants as against the amount recommended by CFCs has declined. As per the RBI report on municipal finances (RBI, 2022a), the actual release of grants to local bodies (RBLs and ULBs) is 15 per cent lower than the amount recommended by the FCs, due to their failure to meet various different conditions. This aspect was also highlighted by the 15th FC.

Various studies have shown that conditional grants adversely influence the efficiency of the local government. In the context of RLBs, it has been established that the RLBs' autonomy to distribute resources in accordance with their own priorities has decreased as a result of their reliance on fiscal transfers, especially conditional and purpose-specific ones. Thus, it is important to enable and empower local governments to enhance their fiscal capacity. In order to make this happen, a mechanism of untied transfer of funds to local governments is essential for enhancing their fiscal capacity and functional autonomy (Alok, 2021).

Actual release of conditional grants to local bodies vis-à-vis recommendations

As mentioned earlier, the proportion of conditional grants recommended by CFCs has been increasing. Thus, it is critical to analyse the impact of such conditionalities on the actual release of funds to local bodies as against the recommended amount. The 12th FC recognized that the imposition of conditionalities for release of funds to local bodies ultimately crippled their finances. It recommended that no more conditionalities be imposed in addition to those suggested by them, namely the submission of utilization certificates (UCs) for grant expenditure. Despite such a liberal approach, RLBs were unable to draw around 6 per cent of total allocated grants.

Component-wise breakup (basic and performance grants) of actual withdrawal of grants by states has also been recorded and analysed for RLBs under 13th and 14th F C. Table 11.1 indicates that only 79 per cent of the allocation of performance grants to states were drawn during the period of the 13th FC which further reduced to 55 per cent (2015–16 to 2017–18)[2] during the period of the 14th FC. Even though the 14th FC prescribed relatively simpler conditionalities, namely, submission of audited accounts and increase in own source revenue (OSR) for the preceding year, for the performance grants, significant amount could not be drawn. A state-wide comparison of grants received as a percentage of amount recommended by CFCs shows that there are interstate variations. During the 13th FC, only ten states were close to completely drawing their allocated share of performance grants; all the other states performed poorly in this regard. In 2016–17, the first year of the 14th FC, nearly 89 per cent of the performance grant allocation was released to the states. However, the situation was made worse by the introduction of additional conditionalities by the Ministry of Finance (MoF) and

---

[2] Data on performance grants available up to 2017–18 for 14th FC.

Table 11.1   Grants recommended vs released for RLBs (in ₹ Crores)

Period	Basic			Performance		
	Allocation	Released	% Released	Allocation	Release	% Released
10th FC	4,381	3,576	81	0	0	0
11th FC	8,000	6,602	82	0	0	0
12th FC	20,000	18,927	94	0	0	0
13th FC	41,771	39,732	9	22,031	17,472	79
14th FC (2015–16 to 2017–18)*	86,164	79,181	92	8,372	4,606	55

* Data available up to 2017–18.

Sources: Government of India. (2020) *Fifteenth Finance Commission (2021–2026)*. Ministry of Finance, New Delhi & Government of India. (2020): Devolution of union FC grants to panchayats. Fifteenth Finance Commission (2021–2026) , October 2020, Ministry of Finance, New Delhi

Ministry of Panchayati Raj (MoPR), over and above those suggested by the 14th FC. The released performance grant was only 25 per cent of the allocated figure in 2017–18 with seventeen states receiving no performance grant at all as a result of these conditionalities.[3] This has been the case in spite of the centre accepting the recommendations of the 14th FC, including that no more conditionalities ought to be imposed other than those suggested by the Commission.

Since the data on basic and performance grants are not available separately for ULBs, we have presented the total figures in Table 11.2.

The shortfall for RLBs ranged from 5 per cent to 18 per cent and for urban bodies from 10 per cent to 18 per cent. The failure of local governments to comply with the performance grant conditions set forth by the Commissions was a major factor for the shortages that were largest for RLBs under the 10th FC and for ULBs under the 13th FC (15th FC, 2020).

The following case study on one of the states, West Bengal (WB), elucidates the shortfall in grants recommended by FCs and the actual receipt of funds by ULBs.

[3] States that received no performance grant in 2017–18 include Telangana, Himachal Pradesh, Assam, Madhya Pradesh, Punjab, Uttarakhand, Jharkhand, Tamil Nadu, Odisha, Maharashtra, Kerala, Arunachal Pradesh, Goa, Uttar Pradesh, Jammu and Kashmir, West Bengal, Bihar.

Table 11.2 Grants recommended vs released for ULBs (in ₹ Crores)

ULBs				
Grants	Recommended	Released	% released	% shortfall
10th FC	1,000	834	83.4	16.6
11th FC	2,000	1,752	87.6	12.4
12th FC	5,000	4,470	89.4	10.6
13th FC	23,111	18,980	82.1	17.9
14th FC	87,144	74,259	85.2	14.8

Source: Government of India. (2020) *Fifteenth Finance Commission (2021–2026)*. Ministry of Finance, New Delhi

Case study 2—ULB grants received vs recommended: WB

The state of WB is considered for comparing the actual release of local body grants as against that recommended during the 14th CFC period (2015–20). Analysis shows that WB has received only 50 per cent of the performance grants allocated for each of the years 2016–17 and 2017–18 as can be seen in Table 11.3. This 50 percent withdrawal was due to partial fulfilment of the performance conditions imposed, that is submission of audited accounts and an increase in OSR in the preceding year.

Table 11.3 Performance grants allocated vs released under 14th FC to ULBs of WB (in ₹ Crores)

Period	Basic			Performance		
	Allocated	Received	% Received	Allocated	Received	% Received
2015–16	11,95.4	558.1	46.6	—	—	—
2016–17	17,64.6	882.3	50.0	520.8	260.4	50.0
2017–18	20,38.9	1,019.4	49.9	589.3	294.6	49.9
2018–19	23,58.6	11,79.3	50.0	0.0	0.0	0.0
2019–20	29,70.3	13,76.7	46.3	0.0	0.0	0.0

Source: Finance Department, Government of WB.

11.5 Conclusion

Local bodies are one of the key drivers of growth of SNGs in India. Despite their recognition by the 73rd and 74th Amendment Act of the Constitution as the third tier of governance with well-defined powers and responsibility, fiscal autonomy seems to be long way off. The own sources of revenues of the local bodies are very low and not sufficient to cover their expenditure. With abysmally low own revenues, these local bodies are virtually dependent upon IGTs from the central and state governments. Strengthening the finances of local bodies is expected to boost growth and development which in turn will contribute to reducing the debt-to-GSDP ratio of SNGs. The local bodies have to be granted fiscal autonomy with greater devolution of powers to levy and collect tax. The local bodies also have to reform the structure and system of collection of property tax and user charges for the services rendered by them. With regard to IGTs from the state, states have to constitute SFCs religiously after every five years and increase the share of transfer to these local bodies. Although transfers from the centre to local bodies based on the recommendations of CFCs has increased, the number of associated conditionalities has also increased. This is more so in the case of the 15th FC. Going by the past performance of local bodies, there is every likelihood that they may not be able to draw the entire grants due to their failure to meet all the conditionalities. Well-designed conditional transfers can improve the capacity of local governments and improve the sustainability of revenues and thereby improve the fiscal health of local bodies. However, a right balance needs to be struck, and very stringent entry-level conditions which result in serious fund shortages for local bodies prevent them from discharging their constitutional responsibilities .

12

Conclusion

With the recent surge in the number of countries finding it difficult to service their debt, the concept of debt sustainability has again taken centre stage in policy debates. Leading institutions such as the IMF and the World Bank have raised serious concerns about the debt position of the developing economies across the world. In 2022, the World Bank and the IMF warned that almost 60 per cent of low-income countries were in debt distress or at a high risk of it. Right after these warnings, Sri Lanka defaulted on its debt for the first time in its history in May 2022. Soon after, Pakistan was on the brink of default on its debt until it secured emergency loans. The debt crises in these countries has pushed thousands of people into poverty and hunger .

This book discusses the reasons behind the debt crises in Sri Lanka and Pakistan and earlier crises in Greece, Portugal, and Latin American countries. Given the various instances of debt crises across the world, the book first attempts to answer the question of whether public debt good is good or bad, by considering various schools of thought. Since most contemporary schools of thought view debt as an instrument that has great potential for bringing positive change when used appropriately, the ever-so-important question of how much debt is too much debt arises.

Further, the different ways are explored in which borrowing is kept within limits especially in the case of subnational government (SNG) borrowing where there are moral hazards at play. An analysis of the controls on SNG borrowing across the world show that most countries are moving towards the use of rule-based and administrative controls as the dominant form of regulation. The FRBM regime, which is a rule-based control, has been performing reasonably well in the context of SNG borrowing. However, there are challenges and issues with the FRBM regime, such as the weak link between policy-making and budget implementation, inadequate accountability mechanism for missed targets,

Debt Sustainability of Subnational Governments in India. Hari Krishna Dwivedi, Oxford University Press.
© Hari Krishna Dwivedi 2024. DOI: 10.1093/oso/9780198903116.003.0012

lack of independent fiscal institution to monitor compliance and lack of flexibility.

Trends in the debt position of India's SNGs reveal that it has improved following the implementation of the FRBM Act (2003). However, since 2014–15, the debt of SNGs in India has slowly begun to raise concerns. This is on account of the slowdown in the Indian economy from 2014-15 onwards, the introduction of the UDAY scheme and the Covid pandemic. The debt-to-GSDP ratio of the states in 2020–21 reached the same levels as that of 2004–05. Evaluating the sustainability of SNG debt thus becomes very critical. Most of the studies using the existing approaches to evaluating SNG debt sustainability agree that their cumulative debt is sustainable. An alternative approach to assessing debt sustainability, which shifts the focus from total revenue receipts to state's own revenue, was considered in Chapter 8, together with all the interdependencies of the related variables. The analysis found that although the SNG debts are sustainable at the moment, there are significant risks, given that the average debt-to-GSDP ratio of SNGs crossed 31 per cent in 2020-21.

12.1 Challenges to State Debt Sustainability

States face many new challenges which will put significant pressure on SNGs' finances, both on the revenue and expenditure front. On the revenue side, SNG revenues are likely to take a serious hit due to the discontinuation of GST compensation and declining actual tax devolution to the states from the divisible pool. On the expenditure side, SNGs have exposed themselves to significant risks, namely rising outstanding guarantees, huge losses of DISCOMs, rising subsidies, poor performance of SLPEs and increasing debt-servicing cost from rising interest rates.

The GST compensation arrangement ended in June 2022 despite many of the states raising requests to extend it. Many of the states are heavily dependent on the GST compensation, as much as 48 per cent in the case of Punjab. Barring five, all other GCS states have GST compensation at more than 20 per cent of total GST revenues. When looking at the overall tax devolution by the centre to the states, there has been a decline in the actual devolution with respect to the recommended devolution. The increasing reliance on cesses and surcharges by the central government deprives the states of revenue that otherwise would have formed part of the divisible pool.

Guarantees issued by the state fall under its contingent liabilities. This poses significant risks to the state finances as their enforcement can result in huge expenditure for them. The total quantum of guarantees outstanding as a percentage of GDP for all the states combined climbed from about 2 per cent in 2017 to about 3 per cent in 2020. Out of the total guarantees given by state governments, about 60 per cent were given to the power sector, while the transport sector received an allocation of less than 5 per cent. State-level enterprises continue to show poor performance, especially the power distribution companies (DISCOMs). Many of the DISCOMs have continued to incur losses and are at risk of requiring rescue packages from the state. Another issue is rising expenditure of SNGs on subsidies. Although subsidies play an important role in certain cases to correct market imperfections and to provide social security, a tendency to overspend on subsidies poses a risk to state finances. The share of subsidy in revenue expenditure for the states have grown from 7.8 per cent in 2019–20 to 8.2 per cent in 2020–21. Further, the interest rates on debt instruments are expected to go up as the monetary authority revises the policy rate upwards to combat the high level of inflation. This is a cause of worry for states, as the debt-servicing costs will go up.

12.2 Policy Lessons: Strategies and Actions to Ensure Debt Sustainability

The states need to have a holistic strategy to ensure debt sustainability. The roadmap for better fiscal management of states involves both reducing debt and increasing GSDP. This may appear contradictory, but, with the right strategy, both these objectives can be achieved. These two objectives require a strategy that augments the revenues and curtails inefficient expenditure. Although GST has subsumed about 50 per cent of the state's indirect taxes, the states can increase collections from GST through better compliance and thereby improve the efficiency of GST collection. Further, once the GST revenues to states stabilize at least at the levels of the taxes it replaced, states may explore bringing some of the excluded items for GST such as petroleum and electricity under its purview. Although this would temporarily result in a shortfall in revenue collection in the short term, the benefits to the businesses in terms of using input tax credits on these items and a uniform tax structure would result in improving the ease of doing business. This would spur economic growth in the medium to long term which ultimately would reflect as growth in revenue collection. Increasing collections from state excise, stamp duty and registration fees, and motor vehicle taxes are other options. Collection from stamp duty and registration may be achieved through streamlining of the methodology of valuation of immovable properties, digitization of their market value database property records, transaction records and utilizing the digitized cadastral maps for effective revenue collection by the department. Green taxes on motor vehicles is another policy action that could augment the state's tax revenues. Apart from tax revenues, states can take steps to augment non-tax revenues as they are currently untapped in most states. However, political economy consideration prevent states from increasing non-tax revenues. As augmentation of local governments' own revenue can reduce the fiscal burden on the state government, it would be prudent to improve the efficiency of revenue collection at local level. As the country urbanizes, land and property revenue for the local governments becomes a very viable revenue source that should be tapped into adequately to improve local governments' own revenues. The tendency to evade taxes and user charges diminishes when the beneficiary of government programmes and the revenue collection agency are sensitive to the needs of the people and taxpayers. Further, addressing expenditure on inefficient subsidies and rationalization of schemes is imperative to contain debt. Discontinuing free unmetered electricity for farmers will greatly reduce subsidy expenditure and prevent widespread ecological damage due to reckless use of free water.

The strategies outlined should be exercised in such a way that is not detrimental to the well-being of the people (as discussed in Chapter 5). The state should take utmost care in ensuring that the development expenditure of the state is maintained at an optimal level. This requires a customized approach for each state. A uniform approach, with the same fiscal target for all states that does not take into account variations in social and economic development across the state, runs the risk of significant reduction in its development expenditure. However, if flexible approach to fiscal targets is used, special care needs to be taken to deal with issues of moral hazards. A holistic and customized approach is essential for long-term fiscal management and consolidation of SNGs so that debt sustainability is ensured.

Appendix

Table A.1 Sales tax/VAT on petrol and diesel (as at 17 October 2022)

State/UT	Petrol	Diesel
		Sales tax/VAT
Andaman & Nicobar Islands	1%	1%
AP	31% VAT + ₹4/litre VAT+₹1/litre road development cess and VAT thereon	22.25% VAT + ₹4/litre VAT+₹1/litre road development cess and Vat thereon
Arunachal Pradesh	14.50%	7.00%
Assam	20.67% or ₹15.50/litre whichever is higher	16.69% OR ₹10.25/litre whichever is higher rebate of ₹1.92/litre subject to minimum tax of ₹10.25/litre
Bihar	23.58% or ₹16.65/litre whichever is higher (30% surcharge on VAT as irrecoverable tax)	16.37% or ₹12.33/litre whichever is higher (30% surcharge on VAT as irrecoverable tax)
Chandigarh	₹10/KL cess +15.24% or ₹12.42/litre whichever is higher	₹10/KL cess + 6.66% or ₹5.07/litre whichever is higher
Chhattisgarh	24% VAT + ₹2/litre VAT	23% VAT + ₹1/litre VAT
Dadra and Nagar Haveli and Daman and Diu	12.75% VAT	13.50% VAT
Delhi	19.40% VAT	₹250/KL air ambience charges + 16.75% VAT
Goa	20% VAT + 0.5% green cess	17% VAT + 0.5% green cess
Gujarat	13.7% VAT+ 4% cess on town rate & VAT	14.9% VAT + 4 % cess on town rate & VAT

State/UT	Petrol	Diesel
	Sales tax/VAT	
Haryana	18.20% or ₹14.50/litre whichever is higher as VAT+5% additional tax on VAT	16.00% VAT or ₹11.86/litre whichever is higher as VAT+5% additional tax on VAT
Himachal Pradesh	17.5% or ₹13.50/litre whichever is higher	6% or ₹4.40/litre whichever is higher
Jammu & Kashmir	24% MST+ ₹2/litre employment cess, rebate of ₹4.50/litre	16% MST+ ₹1.00/litre employment cess, rebate of ₹6.50/litre
Jharkhand	22% on the sale price or ₹17.00/litre, whichever is higher + cess of ₹1.00 per lite	22% on the sale price or ₹12.50/litre, whichever is higher + cess of ₹1.00/litre
Karnataka	25.92% sales tax	14.34% sales tax
Kerala	30.08% sales tax+ ₹.1/litre additional sales tax + 1% cess	22.76% sales tax+ ₹.1/litre additional sales tax + 1% cess
Ladakh	15% MST+ ₹.5/litre employment cess, Reduction of ₹.2.5/litre	6% MST+ ₹.1/litre employment cess, reduction of ₹.0.50/litre
Lakshadweep	nil	nil
Madhya Pradesh	29 % VAT + ₹.2.5/litre VAT+1% cess	19% VAT+ ₹.1.5/litre VAT+1% cess
Maharashtra—Mumbai, Thane, Navi Mumbai & Aurangabad	26% VAT+ ₹.5.12/litre additional tax	24% VAT
Maharashtra (rest of state)	25% VAT+ ₹.5.12/litre additional tax	21% VAT
Manipur	25% VAT	13.5% VAT
Meghalaya	13.5% or ₹12.50/litre whichever is higher (₹.0.10/litre pollution surcharge)	5% or ₹5.50/litre whichever is higher (₹.0.10/litre pollution surcharge)
Mizoram	16.36% VAT	5.23% VAT
Nagaland	25% VAT or ₹. 16.04/litre whichever is higher +5% surcharge + ₹.2.00/litre as road maintenance cess, Rebate ₹. 5.5/litre	16.50% VAT or ₹. 10.51/litre whichever is higher +5% surcharge + ₹.2.00/litre as road maintenance cess, rebate ₹. 5.1/litre

State/UT	Petrol	Diesel
		Sales tax/VAT
Odisha	28% VAT	24% VAT
Puducherry	14.55% VAT	8.65% VAT
Punjab	₹.2050/KL (cess)+ ₹.0.10/litre (urban transport fund) + 0.25/litre (special infrastructure development fee) + 13.77% VAT plus 10% additional tax or ₹.12.50/litre whichever is higher	₹.1050/KL (cess) + ₹.0.10/litre (urban transport fund) +0.25/litre (special infrastructure development fee) + 9.92% VAT plus 10% additional tax or ₹.8.24/litre whichever is higher
Rajasthan	31.04% VAT+₹1500/KL road development cess	19.30% VAT+ ₹.1750/KL road development cess
Sikkim	20% VAT+ ₹.3000/KL cess	10% VAT + ₹.2500/KL cess
Tamil Nadu	13% + ₹.11.52/litre	11% + ₹.9.62/litre
Telangana	35.20% VAT	27% VAT
Tripura	17.50% VAT+ 3% Tripura road development cess	10.00% VAT+ 3% Tripura road development cess
Uttarakhand	16.97% or ₹13.14/litre whichever is greater	17.15% or ₹10.41/litre whichever is greater
Uttar Pradesh	19.36% or ₹14.85/litre whichever is higher	17.08% or ₹10.41/litre whichever is higher
West Bengal	25% or ₹.13.12/litre whichever is higher as sales tax+ ₹.1000/KL cess – ₹1000/KL sales tax rebate (20% additional tax on VAT as irrecoverable tax)	17% or ₹.7.70/litre whichever is higher as sales tax + ₹1000/KL cess – ₹1000/KL sales tax rebate (20% additional tax on VAT as irrecoverable tax)

Notes

(As per details provided by OMCs (Oil Marketing Companies)

For petrol and diesel, VAT/sales tax at applicable rates is also levied on dealer's commission in Arunachal Pradesh, Delhi, Gujarat, Dadra and Nagar Haveli and Daman and Diu, Punjab, Haryana, Madhya Pradesh, Rajasthan Chandigarh, Puducherry, Andaman & Nicobar, Meghalaya.

MST = Motor Spirit Tax

KL = Kiloliter

Sources: PPAC (2023b)

Table A.2 Green tax rate on old vehicles (state-wise)

Non - Transport

Vehicle Category	Andhra Pradesh	Telangana	Karnataka	Maharashtra	Uttar Pradesh
Non-transport (age criteria)	15 years (₹ p.a. basis)	15 years (₹ p.a. basis)	15 years (₹ p.a. basis)	15 years (₹ p.a. basis)	15 years (₹ p.a. basis)
Two-wheeler (motor-cycle) (5 years)	250	250	250	2000	10% of the tax paid at the time of re-registration
Other than two-wheeler (petrol) (5years)	500	500	500	3000	
Other than two-wheeler (diesel) (5years)	500	500		3500	

Transport

Vehicle Category	Andhra Pradesh	Telangana	Karnataka	Maharashtra	Uttar Pradesh
Transport (Age criteria)	7 years (₹ p.a. basis)	7 years(₹ p.a. basis)	7 years(₹ p.a. basis)	8 years(₹ p.a. basis)	-
2-Wheeler	200	200	200		-
3-Wheeler	200	200	200	750 for 5 years	-
Taxi (petrol)	200	200	200	1250 (metered)	-
Taxi (diesel)	200	200	200	2500 (tourist) for 5 years	-
Light commercial vehicle	200	200	200	2500 for 5 years	-
Medium commercial vehicle	200	200	200	10% of annual tax every year	-
Heavy commercial vehicle	200	200	200		-
Contract Carriage buses / Tourist Buses / Private Service vehicles / Other	200	200	200	2.5% of annual tax every year	-

Source: GoI (2021).

References

Accountability Initiative Staff, Centre for Policy Reseach. (2019) *Devolution of Union Finance Commission Grants to Panchayats*. Centre for Policy Research, New Delhi.

Afonso, A., & Rault, C. (2007) Should we care for structural breaks when assessing fiscal sustainability? *Economics Bulletin, 3*(63), 1–9.

Ahluwalia, I., Mohanty, P., Mathur, O., Roy, D., Khare, A., & Mangla, S. (2019) *State of municipal finances in India: A report prepared for the Fifteenth Finance Commission.* ICRIER.

Ahn, S. K. (1993) Some tests for unit roots in autoregressive–integrated–moving average models with deterministic trends. *Biometrica, 80*(4), 855–68.

Akin, C., Carrasco, B., Mundle, S., & Gupta, A. S. (2017) *Fiscal Responsibility and Budget Management Act in India: A review and recommendations for reform.* (ADB South Asia Working Paper Series No. 52).

Alesina, A., & Perotti, R. (1995) The political economy of budget deficits. *IMF Staff Papers, 42*(1), 1–31.

Alesina, A., & Tabellini, G. (1990). A positive theory of fiscal deficits and government debt. *Review of Economic Studies, 57*(3), 403–14.

Alok, V. N. (2021). *Fiscal decentralization in India.* Springer Singapore.

Amsler, C., & Lee, J. (1995) An LM test for a unit root in the presence of a structural break. *Econometric Theory, 11*, 359–68

Anantha Ramu, M. R., & Gayithri, K. (2017). Fiscal consolidation versus infrastructural obligations. *Journal of Infrastructure Development, 9*(1), 49–67.

Asif, M., & Husain, S. (2018) Public debt sustainability in India: A co-integration approach based on structural breaks with regime shift. *Journal of Internet Banking and Commerce, 23*(3). 1-21.

Auerbach, A. J., & Gorodnichenko, Y. (2011) *Fiscal multipliers in recession and expansion* (NBER Working Papers 17447).

Badaik, S. (2017) Impact of fiscal policy legislations on state finances in India. *Theoretical and Applied Economics, 24*(3(612)), 115–24.

Bahl, R., & Linn, J. (1992) *Urban public finance in developing countries.* Oxford University Press.

Bevilaqua, A. S. (2002). *State government bailouts in Brazil.* (IDB Working Paper No. 153).

Bilan, I. (2010) Models of public debt sustainability assessment and their utility. *Anale: Seria Stiinte Economice, 16*, 685-693

Bispham, J. A. (1987) Rising public sector indebtedness: Some more unpleasant arithmetic. In Michael Boskin et al. (Eds.), *Private savings and public debt.* Basil Blackwell: 40-71

Blanchard, O. (2007) Adjustment within the euro: The difficult case of Portugal. *Portuguese Economic Journal, 6*(1), 1–21.

Blanchard, O., & Portugal, P. (2017, June) Boom, slump, sudden stops, recovery, and policy options: Portugal and the euro. (Gabinete de Estratégia e Estudos (GEE), Ministério da Economia Working Paper 72).

Bohn, H. (1998) The behavior of U.S. public debt and deficits. *The Quarterly Journal of Economics*, 113(3), 949–63.

Bohn, H. (2005, April) *The sustainability of fiscal policy in the United States* (CESifo Working Paper Series 1446).

Börjesson, M., & Eliasson, N.R. (2019). Experiences from the Stockholm congestion charging trial. *Transport Policy*, 20, 82-91.

Bose, S., & Bhanumurthy, N. R. (2013) *Fiscal multipliers for India* (Working Paper No. 2013–125, National Institute of Public Finance and Policy, New Delhi, India).

Bouchet, M., Liu, S., Parilla, J., & Kabbani, N. (2018). *Global Metro Monitor 2018*. Brookings Institution. https://www.brookings.edu/research/global-metro-moni tor-2018/

Braun, M. (2006). The political economy of debt in Argentina, or why history repeats itself. In *World Bank Conference on Sovereign Debt and Development: Market Access Countries, Washington DC.* Available at: https://citeseerx.ist.psu.edu/docum ent?repid=rep1&type=pdf&doi=3148be887f4a6eae0d9794e32384763754ed54da

Breusch, T. S., & Pagan, A. R. (1980). The Lagrange multiplier test and its applications to model specification in econometrics. *The Review of Economic Studies*, 47(1), 239–53.

Buiter, W. H. (1985) A guide to public sector debt and deficits. *Economic Policy*, 1(1), 13-79.

Buiter, W. H. (1987) The current global economic situation, outlook and policy options, with special emphasis on fiscal policy issues. CEPR Discussion Paper No. 210.

Buiter, W. H., Corsetti, G., & Rubini, N. (1993) Excessive deficits: Sense and nonsense in the Treaty of Maastricht. *Economic Policy*, 8(16), 57–100

Buiter, W. H., & Patel, Urjit R. (1992) Debt, deficits, and inflation: An application to the public finances of India. *Journal of Public Economics*, 47(2), 171–205.

Burnside, C. (2005) *Fiscal sustainability in theory and practice*. World Bank. doi: 10.1596/978-0-8213-5874-0.

Cap-and-Trade Program. (2023) California Air Resources Board. https://ww2.arb. ca.gov/our-work/programs/cap-and-trade-program.

Cashin, P., & Olekalns, N. (2000) *An examination of the sustainability of Indian fiscal policy* (Working Papers Series 748, University of Melbourne).

Chabert, G., Cerisola, M., & Hakura D. (2022) Restructuring debt of poorer nations requires more efficient coordination. *IMF Blog, 7 April.* Available at: https://www. imf.org/en/Blogs/Articles/2022/04/07/restructuring-debt-of-poorer-nations-requires-more-efficient-coordination

Chakraborty, L. (2019) *Indian fiscal federalism at the crossroads: Some reflections* (Levy Economics Institute, Bard College, Working Paper 937).

Chakraborty, P., & Dash, B. B. (2013) Fiscal reforms, fiscal rule, and development spending: How Indian states have performed? *Public Budgeting & Finance*, 37(4), 111–33.

Choudhury, R. (2022) *What led to the economic crisis in Pakistan?* Indian Council of World Affairs.

Chouraqui, J., Chaude, R., Hagemann, P., & Sartor, N. (1990) *Indicators of fiscal policy: A re-examination* (OECD Working Paper, No. 78).

Chowdhury, S., & Chakraborty, S. (2016) *Employment growth in West Bengal: An assessment* (Occasional Paper No. 52, Institute of Development Studies Kolkata).

Chowdhury, S., & Dasgupta, Z. (2012) Fiscal problem in West Bengal–Towards an explanation. *Economic and Political Weekly, 47*(13), 57–64.

Cordes, T., Guerguil, M., Jaramillo, L., Moreno-Badia, M., & Ylaoutinen, S. (2014). Subnational fiscal crises. In Cottarelli, C., & Guerguil, M. (Eds.), *Designing a European Fiscal Union : Lessons from the Experience of Fiscal Federations (1st ed.).* Routledge: 198-223.

Council on Foreign Relations (2022) Greece's debt crisis. https://www.cfr.org/timel ine/greeces-debt-crisis-timeline

Das, P. (2016) *Debt dynamics: Fiscal deficit and stability in government borrowing in India: A dynamic panel analysis* (ADBI Working Paper No. 557).

Deyshappriya, N. R. (2012) Debt and fiscal sustainability in Sri Lanka. *International Journal of Scientific and Research Publications, 2*(3): 1–8.

Dilasha Seth, G. C. P. (2022) To prevent GST evasion, a new plan is on the cards, *Live Mint*, 28 June. Available at: https://www.livemint.com/politics/policy/council-wei ghs-gst-s-integration-with-npci-11656355477918.html

Dillinger, W. (1998) Brazil's state debt crisis: lessons learned. *Economica, 44*(3): 109-143.

Dillinger, W. R., & Webb, S. B. (1999). *Fiscal management in federal democracies: Argentina and Brazil* (World Bank Policy Research Working Paper No. 2121).

Ditzen, J., Karavias, Y., & Westerlund, J. (2021). Testing and Estimating Structural Breaks in Time Series and Panel Data in Stata. (Discussion Papers 21-14, Department of Economics, University of Birmingham).

Domar, D. E. (1944) The burden of the debt and the national income. *American Economic Review, 34*(4), 798–827.

Downing, P. B. (1992) The revenue potential of user charges in municipal finance. *Public Finance Quarterly, 20*(4), 512–27. doi:10.1177/109114219202000408

Dutta, P., & Dutta, M. K. (2014) Fiscal and debt sustainability in a federal structure: The case of Assam in North East India. *Romanian Journal of Fiscal Policy, 5*(1): 1-19.

Dwivedi, H. K., & Sinha, S. K. (2021). The debt sustainability of West Bengal. *Call for Papers, 56*(24), 61.

Eichengreen, B., Hausmann, R., & Panizza, U. (2007). Currency mismatches, debt intolerance, and the original sin: Why they are not the same and why it matters. In Edwards, S. (Ed.), *Capital controls and capital flows in emerging economies: Policies, practices, and consequences* (pp. 121–70). University of Chicago Press.

Eliasson, J. (2009). A cost–benefit analysis of the Stockholm congestion charging system. *Transportation Research Part A: Policy and Practice*, 43(4), 468-480.

Engle, R. F., & Granger, C. W. J. (1987) Co-integration and error correction: Representation, estimation, and testing. *Econometrica, 55*(2), 251. doi:10.2307/1913236

Estevao, M. (2022) Are we ready for the coming spate of debt crisis? *World Bank Blogs, 28 March*. Available at: https://blogs.worldbank.org/voices/are-we-ready-coming-spate-debt-crises

European Commission (DG ECFIN). (2009). Sustainability Report 2009. European Commission

EuroStat. (2022) Database. https://ec.europa.eu/eurostat/data/database, last accessed 17 November 2022.

Feldstein, M. (2004), *"Budget Deficits and National Debt", L.K. Jha Memorial Lecture,* Reserve Bank of India, Mumbai, 12 January

Ferrarini, B., Giugale, M. M., & Pradelli, J. J. (Eds.) (2022) *The sustainability of Asia's debt.* Edward Elgar.

Ferrarini, B., Jha, R., & Ramayandi, A. (2012) *Public debt sustainability in developing Asia.* Asian Development Bank/Routledge.

Finance Division, Government of Pakistan. (2021) Fiscal policy statement.

Finance Division, Government of Pakistan. (2022) The Economic Survey 2021-22

Finance Division, Government of Pakistan. (2023) The Economic Survey 2022-23.

Fisher, R. A. (1932) *Statistical methods for research workers* (4th ed.). Oliver & Boyd.

Sarafidis, V., Panagiotelis, A., & Panagiotidis, T. (2017) When Did It Go Wrong? The Case of Greek Sovereign Debt. In Floros, C., Chatziantoniou, I. (Eds.), *The Greek Debt Crisis.* Palgrave Macmillan, Cham: 1-35

FRBM Review Committee. (2017) *FRBM Review Committee Report: Responsible growth—A debt and fiscal framework for 21st century India.* Department of Economic Affairs, New Delhi.

Freire, M., & Petersen, J. E. (Eds.) (2004) *Subnational capital markets in developing countries: From theory to practice.* World Bank Publications.

Friedman, M. (1995) *Capitalism și libertate/Capitalism and freedom.* Editura Enciclopedică.

Galvao, F., Gomes, F., & Kishor, N. (2011) Testing public debt sustainability using a present-value model. http://dx.doi.org/10.2139/ssrn.1916922

Gaspar, V. (2012, 19 March) *Portugal: Gaining credibility and competitiveness.* Lecture presented at the Peterson Institute for International Economics. http://www.iie.com/events/event_detail.cfm?EventID=216

Gaspar, V., Medas, P., & Perrelli, R. (2021) Global debt reaches a record $226 trillion. *IMF Blog.* https://blogs.imf.org/2021/12/15/global-debt-reaches-a-record-226-trillion/

Giugale, M., Trillo, F.H., & Oliveira, J.C. (2000) Subnational Borrowing and Debt Management. In Giugale, M., Webb, S.B. (Eds.), *Achievements and Challenges of Fiscal Decentralization - Lessons from Mexico.* World Bank, Cham: 23-28

Goel, G. (2022) Putting the spotlight on state budgets. *Hindustan Times, 19 February.* Available at: https://www.hindustantimes.com/business/putting-the-spotlight-on-state-budgets-101645237600309.html

Government of Bhutan. (2022) *Tourism Levy Act of Bhutan.* Thimphu: Royal Government of Bhutan. Available at: https://www.tourism.gov.bt/uploads/attachment_files/tcb_eTgzI6X8_Tourism%20Levy%20Act%20of%20Bhutan%202022.pdf, last accessed 17 November 2022.

Government of India [GoI] (2000a) *Report of the Eleventh Finance Commission 2000–2005.* Ministry of Finance, New Delhi.

Government of India. (2000b) The Fiscal Responsibility and Budget Management Bill, Bill No. 220 introduced in Lok Sabha: 29 December 2000, Ministry of Finance, Government of India.

Government of India. (2005) *Report of the Twelfth Finance Commission 2005–2010.* Ministry of Finance, New Delhi.

Government of India. (2010a) *Report of the Thirteenth Finance Commission 2010–2015.* Ministry of Finance, New Delhi.

Government of India. (2010b) *West Bengal Development Report, 2010.* Planning Commission, Government of India, New Delhi: Academic Foundation.

Government of India. (2014) *Report of the Fourteenth Finance Commission (2015–2020).* Ministry of Finance, New Delhi.

Government of India. (2016) *Status paper on government debt.* Ministry of Finance, New Delhi.

Government of India. (2017) Volume IV Domain Experts FRBM Review Committee. Ministry of Finance. https://dea.gov.in/sites/default/files/Volume-4-Domain%20 Experts.pdf

Government of India. (2018a) *Economic Survey 2017–2018.* Ministry of Finance, New Delhi.

Government of India. (2018b)*Report of the Comptroller and Auditor General of India on compliance of the Fiscal Responsibility and Budget Management Act, 2003 for 2016–2017.* Department of Economic Affairs, Ministry of Finance, Report No. 20 of 2018.

Government of India (2018): Ministry of Statistics and Program Implementation (2018)

Government of India. (2019a) *Bulk Data Sharing Policy & Procedure.* Ministry of Road Transport and Highways.

Government of India. (2019b) *Economic Survey 2018–2019.* Ministry of Finance, New Delhi.

Government of India. (2020) *Report of the Fifteenth Finance Commission (2021–2026)* . Ministry of Finance, New Delhi.

Government of India. (2021) *Draft guidelines for imposition of green tax on older vehicles by State/UT Governments.* Ministry of Road Transport and Highways, New Delhi.

Government of Kerala. (2020) *State finance audit report of the Comptroller and Auditor General of India for the year ended March 2019.* Government of Kerala.

Government of Uttar Pradesh. (2014) *Audit report on public sector undertakings for the year ended 31 March 2013.* Government of Uttar Pradesh.

Government of West Bengal. (2016) *Report of the Comptroller and Auditor General (CAG) of India on state finances for the year ended March 2016.* Government of West Bengal.

Goyal, A., & Sharma, B. (2018) Government expenditure in India: Composition and multipliers. *Journal of Quantitative Economics, 16*(1), 47–85

Goyal, R., Khundrakpam, J. K., & Ray, P. (2004). Is India's public finance unsustainable? Or, are the claims exaggerated? *Journal of Policy Modeling, 26*(3), 401–20.

Granger, C. W. J. (1969) Investigating causal relations by econometric models and cross-spectral methods. *Econometrica, 37*(3), 424. doi:10.2307/1912791

Gregory, A. W., & Hansen, B. E. (1996) Residual-based tests for co-integration in models with regime shifts. *Journal of Econometrics, 70*(1), 99–126.

Gupta, M., & Chakraborty, P. (2019) *State Finance Commissions: How successful have they been in empowering local governments?* (Working Paper No. 263, NIPFP).

Gupta, S., & James, K. (2023) *An Analysis of Off-Budget Borrowings by Indian Governments and their Legal Context* (CSEP Working Paper-53).

Gurnani, S. (2016) The financial crisis in Portugal: Austerity in perspective. *The Libraries student research prize, paper, 9.*

Habib, A., Rehman, J., Zafar T., & Mahmood, H. (2016) Does sustainability hypothesis hold in developed countries? A panel co-integration analysis. *Quality & Quantity: International Journal of Methodology, 50*(1), 1–25.

Hakkio, Craig. S., & Rush, M. (1991) Is the budget deficit too large? *Economic Inquiry, 29* (3), 429–45.

Hamilton, J. D., & Flavin, M. A. (1986) On the limitations of government borrowing: A framework for empirical testing. *American Economic Review, 76* (4), 808–19.

Haque, N. U., & Montiel, P. (1992) Pakistan: Fiscal sustainability and macroeconomic policy. In W. Easterly, C. Rodriguez, & K. Schmidt-Hebbel (Eds.), *Public sector deficits and macroeconomic performance* (pp. 413–57). Oxford University Press.

Hodrick, R. J., & Prescott, E. C. (1997) Postwar U.S. business cycles: An empirical investigation. *Journal of Money, Credit and Banking, 29*(1), 1–16.

Horne, J. (1991) *Indicators of fiscal sustainability* (IMF Working Papers). https://www.imf.org/en/News/Articles/2019/03/25/sp-032519-lessons-from-portugal-recovery https://www.ppac.gov.in/content/149_1_PricesPetroleum.aspx

Hume, D. (1758) *Essays, Moral, Political and Literary* (pp. 366)

Im, K., Pesaran, M., & Shin, Y. (2003) Testing for unit roots in heterogeneous panels. *Journal of Econometrics, 115*(1), 53–74.

Indian Oil Corporation Ltd. (2022) *Price buildup of petrol & diesel in Delhi.* https://iocl.com/petrol-diesel-price.

Institute of Economic Growth [IEG] (2018) Study Report: Fiscal scenario in Punjab: Past trends, future prospects and challenges. NITI Aayog.

International Monetary Fund [IMF]. (2000) *A framework for assessing fiscal vulnerability* (IMF Working Papers 2000, 052, A001). https://doi.org/10.5089/9781451847246.001.A001

International Monetary Fund. (2014) *Public expenditure reform: Making difficult choices.* IMF Fiscal Affair Department.

International Monetary Fund. (2022a) *General government gross debt.* Available at: https://www.imf.org/external/datamapper/GGXWDG_NGDP@WEO/OEMDC/ADVEC, last accessed 17 November 2022.

International Monetary Fund. (2022b) *General government net lending/borrowing*. Available at: https://www.imf.org/external/datamapper/GGXCNL_NGDP@WEO/PAK/LKA, last accessed 17 November 2022.

International Monetary Fund (2022c) *Global Debt Monitor.* Fiscal Affairs Department.

International Monetary Fund (2022d) *World Revenue Longitudinal Data set (WoRLD).* Available at: https://data.imf.org/?sk=77413f1d-1525-450a-a23a-47aeed40fe78, last accessed 17 November 2022.

Kao, C. (1999) Spurious regression and residual-based tests for co-integration in panel data. *Journal of Econometrics, 90* (1), 1–44.

Kaur, B., & Mukherjee, A. (2012) Threshold level of debt and public debt sustainability: The Indian experience. *Reserve Bank of India Occasional Papers*, *33*(1 &2), 1–37.

Kaur, B., Mukherjee, A., & Ekka, A. P. (2017, October) *Debt sustainability of states in India: An assessment* (MPRA Paper No. 81929).

Kelkar, V. (2019) Towards India's new fiscal federalism. *Journal of Quantitative Economics*, *17*(1), 237–48.

Khasnabis, R. (2008) The economy of West Bengal. *Economic and Political Weekly*, *43*(52) 103–15.

Komanoff, C., & Gordon, M. (2015). British Columbia's Carbon Tax: By the Numbers. *Carbon Tax Center*. New York, NY.

Krugman, P. (2011) Ricardian confusions (wonkish). *New York Times*, 10 March 2011. Available online at https://archive.nytimes.com/krugman.blogs.nytimes.com/2011/03/10/ricardian-confusions-wonkish/

Kuştepeli, Y., & Onel, G. (2005) Fiscal deficit sustainability with a structural break: An application to Turkey. *Review of Social, Economic and Business Studies 5* (6), 1–20

Lahiri, A., & Yi, K. M. (2009) A tale of two states: Maharashtra and West Bengal. *Review of Economic Dynamics*, *12* (3), 523-542.

Lalvani, M. (2009) Persistence of fiscal irresponsibility: Looking deeper into provisions of the FRBM Act. *Economic and Political Weekly*, *44*(37). 57-63.

Lane, T. D. (1993). Market discipline. *IMF Staff Papers*, *40*(1), 53–88.

Lerner, A. P. (1943) Functional finance and the federal debt. *Social Research*, *10*(1), 38–51. http://www.jstor.org/stable/40981939

Levin, A., Lin, C. F., & Chu, C. S. (2002) Unit root tests in panel data: Asymptotic and finite sample properties. *Journal of Econometrics*, *108*(1), 1–24.

Lipton, D. (2019) *Lessons from Portugal's recovery*. International Monetary Fund Articles.

Lok Sabha Secretariat. (1958) *Estimates Committee twentieth report (1957–1958)*. https://eparlib.nic.in/bitstream/123456789/4890/1/ec_2_20_1958.pdf.

Lorio, F. D., & Fachin, S. (2022). Fiscal reaction functions for the advanced economies revisited. *Empirical Economics*, *62*(6), 2865-2891.

Lourtie, P. (2012) Understanding Portugal in the context of the euro crisis. In William R. Cline & Guntram Wolff (Eds.), *Resolving the European debt crisis*. Peterson Institute for International Economics: 51-94

Lusinyan, L., & Thornton, J. (2009) The sustainability of South African fiscal policy: An historical perspective. *Applied Economics*, *41* (7), 859–68.

McKinnon, R. I. (1997). Market-preserving fiscal federalism in the American monetary union. In Blejer, M., & Ter-Minassian, T. (Eds.), *Macroeconomic Dimensions of Public Finance: Essays in Honour of Vito Tanzi (1st ed.)*. Routledge: 73-93.

Maddala, G. S., & Wu, S. (1999) A comparative study of unit root tests with panel data and a new simple test. *Oxford Bulletin of Economics and Statistics*, *61*(S1), 631–52.

Marini, G., & Piergallini, A. (2007) *Indicators and tests of fiscal sustainability: An integrated approach* (Centre for Financial and Management Studies, Discussion Paper 75).

Marjit, S., Sasmal, J., Dwibedi, J., & Hati, K. (2013) *West Bengal state finances: A report prepared for Fourteenth Finance Commission*. Government of India.

Martinez-Vazquez, J., & Vulovic, V. (2016) *How well do subnational borrowing regulations work?* (ADBI Working Paper 563, Asian Development Bank Institute, Tokyo). http://www.adb.org/publications/how-well-do-subnational-borrowing-regulations-work/

Martinez-Vazquez, J., Vulovic, V., & Liu, Y. (2011) *Direct versus indirect taxation: Trends, theory, and economic significance.* In Albi, E., & Martinez-Vazquez, J. (Eds.), *The Elgar guide to tax systems.* Edward Elgar Publishing: 37-92.

Masson, P. (1985) The sustainability of fiscal deficits. *IMF Staff Papers, 32* (1985), 577–605.

Maurya, N. K. (2013) *Debt sustainability of a sub-national government: An assessment of state finances of Uttar Pradesh* (Working Paper 213, Giri Institute of Development Studies).

Maurya, N. K. (2014) Debt sustainability of state finances of Uttar Pradesh government. Available at: https://mpra.ub.uni-muenchen.de/55692/1/MPRA_paper_55692.pdf

Medas, Paulo, El Rayess, Majdeline, Perrelli, Roberto, Soto, Mauricio, & Glória, André (2019) *Strengthening the framework for subnational borrowing (Brazil).* International Monetary Fund.

Miller, M. (1983) Inflation adjusting the public sector financial deficit. In J. Kay (Ed.), *The 1982 budget.* Basil Blackwell: 48-74

Ministry of Finance, Government of India (2004) *Report of the task force on implementation of the Fiscal Responsibility and Budget Management Act, 2003.* Ministry of Finance, Government of India.

Ministry of Finance, Government of India. (2021). *National Monetisation Pipeline.* NITI Aayog.

Ministry of Finance, Government of India. (2023). *Previous Union Budgets (2017-18 to 2022-23).* Available at: https://www.indiabudget.gov.in/previous_union_budget.php, last accessed 17 November 2022.

Ministry of Housing and Urban Affairs, Government of India. (2017). *Value Capture Finance Policy Framework.* Available at: https://mohua.gov.in/upload/whatsnew/59c0bb2d8f11bVCF_Policy_Book_FINAL.pdf

Misra, S., Gupta K., & Trivedi P. (2020) *Subnational government debt sustainability in India: An empirical analysis* (Reserve Bank of India WPS (DEPR)).

Mohanty, K. R., & Panda, S. (2019) *How does public debt affect the Indian macroeconomy? A structural VAR approach.* National Institute of Public Finance and Policy.

Mondal, S. P., & Maitra, B. (2020) Assessing growth impact of public debt in Sri Lanka. *Arthaniti: Journal of Economic Theory and Practice, 20* (2), 201-226.

MOSPI. (2023) Data. Available at: https://www.mospi.gov.in/data, last accessed 3 November 2023.

Mumbai Metro Rail Corporation Limited (MMRCL). (2017). *Mumbai Metro Line 3 - Financial Strategy and Implementation.*

Nallathiga, R. (2009) User charge pricing for municipal services: Principles, fixation, process and guidelines. (CCG Working Paper).

Narayan, L. (2016) *An analysis of public debt and fiscal sustainability for Haryana* (MPRA Paper No. 70100).

Narayan, L. (2017) Public debt sustainability for India: A survey of recent literature. International Journal of Advanced Research and Development, 2(4), 177-183.

Nayak, S. K., & Rath, S. S. (2009) *A Study on debt problem of the special category states*. Study Conducted for 13th Finance Commission Government of India, Rajiv Gandhi University Itanagar Arunachal Pradesh. http://fincomindia.nic.in/writer eaddata%5Chtml_en_files%5Coldcommission_html/finco   13/discussion/report19.pdf\

NFSSM Alliance. (2020) *Municipal Strengthening for Improved Urban Services*. NFSSM Alliance. Available at: https://cwas.org.in/resources/file_manager/ White%20Paper%20Municipal%20Strengthening%20for%20Improved%20Ur ban%20Services.pdf

Niti Aayog. (2015) *Report of the sub-group of chief ministers on rationalisation of centrally sponsored schemes*. NITI Aayog.

Nworji, I. D., Okwu, A. T., Obiwuru, T. C., & Nworji, L. O. (2012) Effects of public expenditure on economic growth in Nigeria: A disaggregated time series analysis. *International Journal of Management Sciences and Business Research, 1*(7). 1-15.

Oates, W. (1968) The theory of public finance in a federal system. *The Canadian Journal of Economics, 1*(1), 37–54. org/10.1177/0976747920917478

OECD. (2022) , *Revenue Statistics in Asia and the Pacific 2022: Strengthening Tax Revenues in Developing Asia*. OECD Publishing, Paris, https://doi.org/10.1787/ db29f89a-en.

Ogbeifun, L., & Shobande, O. (2020) Debt sustainability and the fiscal reaction function: Evidence from MIST countries. *Future Business Journal, 6*(1), 1-8. https://doi. org/10.1186/s43093-020-00037-6

Organisation for Economic Co-operation and Development [OECD] (2013) *Government at a glance 2013*. OECD Publishing, Paris, https://doi.org/10.1787/ gov_glance-2013-en.

Organisation for Economic Co-operation and Development (2016) Mexico profile. Available at: https://www.oecd.org/regional/regional-policy/profile-Mexico.pdf

Oshikoya, T. W., & Tarawalie, A. B. (2010) Sustainability of fiscal policy: The West African monetary zone (WAMZ) experience. *Journal of Monetary and Economic Integration, 9*(2): 1–29.

Pattnaik, R. K., Prakash, A., & Mishra, B. S. (2005) *Sustainability of public debt in India: An assessment in the context of the fiscal rules* (pp. 679–736). RBI.

Pedroni, P. (1996) *Fully modified OLS for heterogeneous cointegrated panels and the case of purchasing power parity* (Working paper No. 96–020, Department of Economics, Indiana University).

Pedroni, P. (1999) Critical values for cointegrating tests in heterogeneous panels with multiple regressors. *Oxford Bulletin of Economics and Statistics, 61*(1), 653–70.

Pedroni, P. (2004) Panel cointegration: Asymptotic and finite sample properties of pooled time series tests with an application to the PPP hypothesis. *Econometric Theory, 20*(3), 597–625.

Petroleum Planning & Analysis Cell. (2023a) *Contribution of Petroleum Sector to Exchequer*. Available at: https://ppac.gov.in/prices/contribution-to-central-and-state-exchequer, last accessed 2 November 2023

Petroleum Planning & Analysis Cell. (2023b) *Statement Showing The Actual Rates of State Taxes/GST*. Available at: https://ppac.gov.in/prices/vat-sales-tax-gst-rates, last accessed 2 November 2023

Policy Development and Review Department (2002) *Assessing Sustainability.* International Monetary Fund

Portrafke, N., & Reischmann, M. (2015) *Fiscal transfers and fiscal sustainability.* https://doi.org/10.1111/jmcb.12231

Power Finance Corporation [PFC]. (2022) *Report on performance of power utilities 2020–2021.* Power Finance Corporation Ltd.

Pradhan, K. (2014) Is India's public debt sustainable? *South Asian Journal of Macroeconomics and Public Finance,* 3(2), 241–66.

Pradhan, P. (2015) *Fiscal sustainability: Concept and application* (Symbiosis School of Economics, Annual Working Paper Series, WP/SSE/2015/004).

PRS. (2019) Overview of power sector. Available at: https://prsindia.org/policy/ana lytical-reports/overview-power-sector, last accessed 17 November 2022.

PRS Legislative Research. (2017) *Report Summary FRBM Review Committee .* PRS Legislative Research.

PRS Legislative Research. (2021) *State of state finances.* PRS Legislative Research.

PTI. (2021) PIA pays USD 7 million to Irish company after plane seized in Malaysia over lease dispute, 23 January. *The New Indian Express.* Available at: https://in dianexpress.com/article/world/pakistan-international-airlines-lease-dispute-7159012/

PublicFinance.lk. (2021) *Non-Compliance with the Fiscal Management Responsibility Act Has Been a Demonstration of Irresponsibility.* Available at: https://www.public finance.lk/en/topics/non-compliance-with-the-fiscal-management-responsibil ity-act-has-been-a-demonstration-of-irresponsibility-1624966502

Purohit, M. C., & Purohit, V. K. (2009) Mobilising non-tax revenue: An empirical analysis of trends in states. *Economic and Political Weekly,* 44(5), 54–62.

Rajaraman, I., Bhide, S., & Pattnaik, R.K. (2005) *A study of debt sustainability at state level in India.* Reserve Bank of India. (RBI) Mumbai.

Rajaraman, I., Bohra, O. P., & Renganathan, V. S. (1996) Augmentation of panchayat resources. *Economic and Political Weekly,* 31(18), 1071-1083.

Rajiv Kumar R., Pankaj Vashisht P. (2009) *The global economic crisis: Impact on India and policy responses* (ADBI Working Paper Series).

Rajmal . (2006) *State finances and effectiveness of policy measures: An analysis of Indian states* (RBI Occasional Papers, 27, Nos. 1 and 2).

Raju, S. (2009) Analyzing the fiscal stance of state governments in India: Evidence from fourteen major states. (University of Mumbai, Working Paper UDE 29/1/ 2009)

Ramirez, M. D. (2006) *A panel unit root and panel co-integration test of the comple mentarity hypothesis in the Mexican case, 1960–2001* (Economic Growth Center Yale University Discussion Paper No. 942).

Ramu, A. M. R., & Gayithri, K. (2017) Fiscal consolidation versus infrastructural ob ligations. *Journal of Infrastructure Development,* 9(1), 49–67.

Rangarajan, C. (2003) *Fifty years of fiscal federalism: Finance Commissions of India.* 12th Finance Commission.

Rangarajan, C., & Prasad, A. (2013). Managing state debt and ensuring solvency: The Indian. In Canuto, O., & Liu, L. (Eds.), *Until Debt Do Us Part: Subnational Debt, Insolvency, and Markets. The World Bank:* 109-144.

Rangarajan, C., & Srivastava, D. K. (2005) Fiscal deficit and government debt: Implications for growth and stabilisation. *Economic and Political Weekly*, 40(27), 2919+2921-2934.

Rangarajan, C., & Subbarao, D. (2007) *The importance of being earnest about fiscal responsibility* (Madras School of Economics, Monograph 3/2007).

Rao, M. G. (2000) Fiscal decentralization in Indian federalism. Institute for Social and Economic Change.

Rao, M. G. (2002) State finances in India: Issues and challenges. *Economic and Political Weekly*, 37(31), 3261–71.

Rao, M. G. (2019) Redesigning the fiscal transfer system in India. *Economic and Political Weekly*, 54(31)., 52–60.

Rao, M. G., & Vasanth, U. A. (2008) Expanding the resource base of Panchayats: Augmenting own revenues. Economic and Political Weekly, 43(04)., 54–61.

Rapoza, K. (2017, 16 August) China wage levels equal to or surpass parts of Europe. *Forbes.* https://www.forbes.com/sites/kenrapoza/2017/08/16/china-wage-levels-equal-to-or-surpass-parts-of-europe/#2b462a553e7f

Rath, S. S. (2005) Fiscal development in Orissa: Problems and prospects. NIPFP

Ravishankar, V. J., Zahir, F., & Kaul, N. (2008) Indian states' fiscal correction: An unfinished agenda. *Economic and Political Weekly*, 43(38), 57–62.

Razdan, N. (2022) *Pakistan's economic crisis: In dire need of $36 billion.* NDTV.

Reddy, G. R. (2019) *Unique features of Indian fiscal federalism.* Panel on "Indian Fiscal Federalism", at the book launch by Y. V. Reddy and G. R. Reddy, India International Centre, New Delhi, 28 March.

Reddy, G. R. (2021) Fifteenth Finance Commission's recommendations on local bodies: Far too many concerns. Economic and Political Weekly, 56(51), 17–20.

Reddy, Y. (2018) *Fiscal federalism in India: Emerging issues.* 10.1007/978-981-10-6217-9_1.

Reddy, Y. V., & Reddy, G. R. (2019) *Indian fiscal federalism.* Oxford University Press.

Reddy, Y.V., Valluri, N., & Ray, P. (2014) Financial and fiscal policies: Crisis and new realities. Oxford University Press.

Reserve Bank of India [RBI]. (various years) Handbook of statistics on Indian states.

Reserve Bank of India. (various years) National Summary Data Page (NSDP)

Reserve Bank of India. (various years) State finances: A study of state budgets.

Reserve Bank of India. (1982) *Report of the Committee to Review the Working of the Monetary System.* https://rbidocs.rbi.org.in/rdocs/PublicationReport/Pdfs/050385_1985606EE0A77CF1477797856D41802779D5.PDF

Reserve Bank of India. (2002) *Report of the Group to Assess the Fiscal Risk of State Government Guarantees.*

Reserve Bank of India. (2003) *Report of the Group to Study the Pension Liabilities of the State Government*

Reserve Bank of India. (2012, March) *State finances: A study of budgets of 2011–2012* (Reserve Bank of India).

Reserve Bank of India. (2013) *Sub-national debt sustainability: An assessment of the state governments.*

Reserve Bank of India. (2014) *Debt sustainability at the state Level in India.*

Reserve Bank of India. (2020) *Monetary policy and financial markets: Twist and tango*. https://www.rbi.org.in/Scripts/BS_ViewBulletin.aspx?Id=19719.

Reserve Bank of India. (2022a) *Report on municipal finance*.

Reserve Bank of India. (2022b) *State finances: A risk analysis*.

Rodden, J. (2002) *Bailouts and perverse incentives in the Brazilian states*. World Bank

Rodden, J. A., Eskeland, S. G., & Litvack, J. (2003) Fiscal decentralization and the challenge of hard budget constraints, MIT Press, England.

Sardoni, C. (2008) The sustainability of fiscal policy: An old answer to an old question? (International Economic Policy Institute, Working Paper 2009-03)

Sawhney, U. (2005) *Fiscal reforms at the sub-national level: The case of Punjab*. NIPFP

Sawhney, U. (2018) An analysis of fiscal policy in an emerging economy: Innovative and sustainable fiscal rules in India. *Millennial Asia*, 9(3), 295–317.

Schmidt, P., & Phillips, P. C. B. (1992) LM test for a unit root in the presence of deterministic trends. *Oxford Bulletin of Economics and Statistics*, 54(3), 257–87.

Sengupta, A., Sharma, A., & Sharma, R. (2014) *Research report on queries raised by the Fourteenth Finance Commission*. Finance Commission

Simone A., & Tapalova, P. (2009) *India's Experience with fiscal rules: An evaluation and the way forward*. International Monetary Fund

Sims, J., & Romero, J. (2013) *Latin American debt crisis of the 1980s*. Federal Reserve History.

Singh, C., Prasad, D., Sharma, K., & Reddy, S. (2017) *A review of the FRBM Act*. IIMB

Singh, N. K. (2019) Indian Fiscal Federalism. Panel on "Indian Fiscal Federalism", at the book launch by Y. V. Reddy and G. R. Reddy, India International Centre, New Delhi, 28 March.

Smith, A. ([1776] 1937). *The wealth of nations (1937)*. Oxford, England, 753)

Spaventa, L. (1987) The growth of public debt—Sustainability, fiscal rules and monetary rules. *IMF Staff Papers 34* (2), 374–99.

Srivastava, D. K. (2022) The future of fiscal consolidation in India. *Economic & Political Weekly*, 57(13), 29-35.

Stojkoski, V., & Popova, K. (2016) *Financial development and growth: Panel cointegration evidence from South-Eastern and Central Europe* (MPRA Paper 69029, University Library of Munich, Germany).

Subbarao, D. (2022). Fiscal dominance of monetary policy: Global and Indian experience. In Hashim, S.R., Mukherji, R., & Mishra, B. (Eds.), *Perspectives on inclusive policies for development in India: In honour of Prof. R. Radhakrishna* (pp. 31–50). Springer Nature.

Subramanian, A., Anand, A., & Sharma, N. (2022) *Power, a reality check*. The Indian Express, 18 August. Available at: https://indianexpress.com/article/opinion/colu mns/power-a-reality-check-analysis-of-state-government-finances-8094214/

Sucharita, S., & Sethi, N. (2011) Fiscal discipline in India. *Romanian Journal of Fiscal Policy 2*(1), 1–23.

TERI. (2010). *Review of current practices in determining user charges and incorporation of economic principles of pricing of urban water supply*. (TERI Project Report No. 2009IA02)

Ter-Minassian, T. (2007). Fiscal rules for subnational governments: Can they promote fiscal discipline? *OECD Journal on Budgeting*, 6(3), 1–11.

Ter-Minassian, T., & Craig, J. (1997). Control of Subnational Government Borrowing. In Ter-Minassian, T (Ed.), *Fiscal Federalism in Theory and Practice. International Monetary Fund:* 156-172.

Tiwari, A. K. (2012) Debt sustainability in India: Empirical evidence estimating time varying parameters. *Economic Bulletin, 32*(2), 1133-1141.

Tourism Council of Bhutan. (2019) *Bhutan Tourism Monitor 2019.* Available at: https://www.tourism.gov.bt/uploads/attachment_files/tcb_K11a_BTM%202019.pdf.

Transport for London. (2006) Central London congestion charging: Impacts monitoring Fourth Annual Report, June 2006. https://content.tfl.gov.uk/fourth-annual-report-overview.pdf

Transport for London. (2023) Transport for London. https://tfl.gov.uk/

Trehan, B., & Walsh, C. (1988) Common trends, the government budget constraint, and revenue smoothing. *Journal of Economics Dynamics and Control, 12*(2-3), 425-444.

Trehan, B., & Walsh, C. E. (1991) Testing intertemporal budget constraints: Theory and applications to US Federal budget and current account deficits. Journal of Money, Credit and Banking, 23(2), 206–23.

Trillo, H., & Cayeros A., & González R. (2002) Determinants and consequences of bailing out states in Mexico. *Eastern Economic Journal, 28*(3), 365–80.

Trivedi, P., & Rajmal (2011) Growth effects of fiscal policy of Indian states. *Millennial Asia, 2*(2)), 141-162.

Truger, A. (2016) *The golden rule of public investment—A necessary and sufficient reform of the EU fiscal framework?* (IMK Working Paper 168–2016, IMK at the Hans Boeckler Foundation, Macroeconomic Policy Institute).

Trujillo, J. L., & Parilla, J. (2016). *Redefining global cities: The seven types of global metro economies.* Brookings Institution.

Turan, T., & Iyidogan, P. (2022) Estimating fiscal reaction functions for developing and developed countries: A dynamic panel threshold analysis. *Ekonomický časopis, 70,* 393–410. 10.31577/ekoncas.2022.05.01

Vulovic, V. (2011). Sub-national borrowing, is it really a danger? (Dissertation, Georgia State University). Available at: https://doi.org/10.57709/2398513

Westerlund, J., & Breitung, J. (2009) *Myths and facts about panel unit root tests* (Working Papers in Economics 380, University of Gothenburg, Department of Economics).

Westerlund, J., & Edgerton, D.L. (2008) A simple test for cointegration in dependent panels with structural breaks. *Oxford Bulletin of Economics and Statistics, 70*(5). doi: 10.1111/j.1468-0084.2008.00513.x

Wilcox, D. (1989) The sustainability of government deficits: Implications of the present-value borrowing constraint. *Journal of Money, Credit and Banking, 21*(3), 291–306.

World Bank. (2005) *State fiscal reforms in India: Progress and prospects.* Macmillan.

World Bank. (2018) *Approach Paper: Public Finance for Development Evaluation.*

World Bank. (2022a) DataBank | World Development Indicators. https://databank.worldbank.org/reports.aspx?source=world-development-indicators#, last accessed 16 November 2022.

World Bank. (2022b) Industry (including construction), value added (constant 2015 US$) - China. https://data.worldbank.org/indicator/NV.IND.TOTL.KD?locations=CN, last accessed 16 November 2022.

World Bank. (2022c) GDP (current US$)—Portugal. https://data.worldbank.org/indicator/NY.GDP.MKTP.CD?end=2021&locations=PT&start=1961, last accessed 16 November 2022.

Zee, H. H. (1988) *The sustainability and optimality of government debt* (IMF Staff Papers), 658–85.j

About the Author

Dr. Hari Krishna Dwivedi is a distinguished Indian civil servant of the Indian Administrative Service who retired as Chief Secretary of the Government of West Bengal. He has previously served in many key positions including State Finance Secretary and Head of Taxation in the state. He is a recipient of Joint –Japan World Bank Scholarship in 2004-05 under which he did M.Sc in Development Management from the London School of Economics (LSE). He also holds a Ph.D in Development Studies from Calcutta University. He is a prolific writer and his publications primarily cover topics ranging from community participation, women empowerment, rural development, debt sustainability, local body finances, state finances, fiscal consolidation and fiscal federalism. As the State Finance Secretary, he has been instrumental in introducing wide ranging reforms in financial restructuring and fiscal management of the state finances. He is presently the Chief Advisor (Finance) to the Chief Minister of the Indian state of West Bengal.

Index

For the benefit of digital users, indexed terms that span two pages (e.g., 52–53) may, on occasion, appear on only one of those pages.

Boxes indicated by *b* following the page number

Printed in the USA
CPSIA information can be obtained
at www.ICGtesting.com
CBHW071808061224
18616CB00003B/25